OUT OF OUR SKINS

20th Anniversary Edition
with new introduction and epilogue

LIAM HAYES

First Published (Gill and Macmillan) 1992
Republished (Blackwater Press) 2010

Design & Layout/Cover
Jessica Maile

Front Cover Photograph
Peter Doyle

Inside Photographs
Inpho Sports Agency Ltd

ISBN 978-0-9563541-5-0

Produced in Ireland by
BWP Ltd.,
1-5 North Frederick Street,
Dublin 1
Email: jloconnor@eircom.net

200.931   €17.00

CONTENTS

INTRODUCTION

"I remembered again my father's words to me as a boy: 'You can have a serious life or a nonserious life, Teddy. I'll still love you whichever choice you make. But if you decide to have a nonserious life, I won't have much time for you. You make up your own mind. There are too many children here who are doing things that are interesting for me to do much with you.'"

- Edward Kennedy: *True Compass* (2009)

"My father yells everything twice, sometimes three times, sometimes ten. 'Harder' he says, 'Harder'. But, what's the use? No matter how hard I hit a ball, no matter how early, the ball comes back, every ball I send across the net joins the thousands that already cover the court. Not hundreds. Thousands. They roll towards me in perpetual waves. I have no room, to turn, to step, to pivot. I can't move without stepping on a ball - and yet I can't step on a ball, because my father won't bear it. Step on one of my father's tennis balls, and he'll howl as if you stepped on his eyeball."

- Andre Agassi: *Open* (2009)

The green and gold jersey was like a second skin.

I was 29 years-old, and had spent 16 of those years as a Meath footballer, when I began writing an autobiographical account of my life. Naturally, so much more than anything else, it was the story of a Gaelic footballer. And it was the first time a Gaelic footballer, who was still plying his trade on a GAA field, had decided to publish his story. I had worn my first Meath jersey when I was 13 years-old, and by representing Meath under-14 teams, Meath under-18 teams, Meath under-21 teams, and finally the Meath senior football team, I had never taken that jersey off my back.

I'm now 48 years-old.

These days, Gaelic football and hurling fans have a choice of purchasing three or four worthy autobiographies at the end of every year. There is a soft, but constant flow of autobiographies usually from managers and, occasionally, from the bigger named footballers and hurlers in the country. Those football and hurling fans, who are under 30 years of age, have probably never heard of my autobiographical account of my football life, which was titled *Out of Our Skins*.

The book was first published in April of 1992 by Gill and Macmillan, and it sold more than we ever imagined it would, and it was reprinted that same year and sold some more, and everyone seemed very happy that it had fulfilled its potential. I was for sure. I received a couple of thousand pounds (the book had retailed in shops at £7.50) and spent the money, very quickly, as a young married man with two little kids, is prone to do.

And when all of the money was spent the Taxman asked me about his share? And I spent the next 18 months paying him his due in small, painful monthly instalments. That done, I was happy to forget about *Out of Our Skins* entirely. One copy of the book existed in my home. There was also one copy in the homes of each member of my family. I can honestly say that, over the next 18 years, I never once picked up the book.

• • • •

In the second half of the 1980s and in the very early 1990s, the Meath team won two All-Ireland titles and lost two All-Ireland titles, and through good times and bad the team which had been built by one of the most honest and decent-minded men I have ever known, Sean Boylan, earned a thoroughly deserved reputation for being hard as nails, uncivil and, usually, unapologetic.

At the end of a game, the Meath team might spit on your grave! The true character of the manager and his team was one of the staggering dichotomies in the modern history of Gaelic football.

The Meath team was also made up of some outstanding footballers (who will also be revealed in the book which follows). While writing the book, and still a fully paid-up member of the Meath team, I was defensive and truculent in equal measures on lots of occasions. At the time I was 'going to war' every second Sunday alongside the men to the left and right of me on that Meath team. We believed we were winning games the way we had to win games. We won our All-Irelands, and we won two National League titles and five Leinster titles, and in four of those five

Leinster finals we defeated the greatest of all our enemies, Dublin.

In 1991, *Out of Our Skins* arrived at a fitting climax with Meath and Dublin meeting four times in the first round of the Leinster Championship. The book actually opens and closes with that historic encounter which lasted for almost six hours before it was finally ended by a goal which was, only recently, voted the greatest goal ever scored in the long and bountiful history of the game.

Writing *Out of Our Skins*, and having it published and read by my team-mates and opponents, does indeed seem a lifetime ago!

Someone else's lifetime.

I disconnected from the book entirely. Over the years, I received phone calls from friends and emails from perfect strangers, enquiring about the book for one reason or another, and usually wondering where one more copy of *Out of Our Skins* might be purchased?

I am not saying that I have been swamped by these enquiries. Mostly, there were one or two per month, every month, but even after 18 years, the enquiries still come, and just last week a young woman from Wexford emailed me, hoping that she might be able to make a present of *Out of Our Skins* for her fiance? When I meet GAA people, I am asked quite regularly about *Out of Our Skins*, and these people sometimes remind me of something or other which I had written in the book and, genuinely, there are occasions when I have no recollection of what they are talking about, nor any memory whatsoever of writing any such thing!

A long time ago, there was indeed a total disconnect between my present life and my former life as a Gaelic footballer. *Out of Our Skins*, therefore, was written by someone else and belongs to someone else. I am not too sure, anymore, who that person was? Or what he was thinking half of the time?

Having now read the book, again, for the first time in almost two decades, I was left surprised by parts, but mostly I am disappointed to learn of the agonizing self-doubts I had as a footballer and my almost complete inability to enjoy my football career. There is an absence of laughter. By the end of the book, there's no real sense of fun and daily enjoyment and, instead, there's dollops and dollops of whining and moaning about playing the game.

When all it was, after all, was just a game! Why did I let it rule and govern my life, and why did I let it beat me down?

Mostly, after reading *Out of Our Skins*, I felt it was, if not important, then certainly worthwhile bringing anyone who might be interested on an honest, fast-paced and hopefully revealing journey from 1991, when the book concludes, to the cusp of 2011. I had talked so much, in the latter half of *Out of Our Skins*, about leaving the Meath dressing-room, about finally taking off that jersey and walking out the door eagerly enough, and leaving the people in that room behind me for good.

When that door closed behind me, I left my affection and genuine care for the Meath football team behind me as well, and that was surprising. I've attended Leinster finals and not been too bothered whether Meath won or lost. And that was shocking! The present Meath team I can take or leave any Sunday, no problem. The old Meath team?

My Meath team?

I've never phoned any of my team-mates or looked to meet up with them. If we bump into one another at a funeral or a GAA function, that's it! I've only attended one of the annual golf outings which my former team-mates have organized over the last 19 years.

In the epilogue of this revisited edition of *Out of Our Skins* I'll try to explain my journey or long walk from that room I once loved. And I hope other footballers and hurlers will understand, and perhaps privately admit, to having the same thoughts and experiences themselves when they ended their careers and restarted their lives, and suddenly felt very much alone. Who knows?

••••

On first publication, *Out of Our Skins* was generously received by GAA people. Some people loved it. Some people did not. The esteemed GAA Correspondent of *The Irish Times*, Sean Moran, who was writing in *The Sunday Tribune* at the time, and who is one of the most respected writers on Gaelic football and hurling, considered the book to be a bit of a disappointment and thought a great many of the characters in the book to be portrayed in 'two-dimensional form'. That was a blow to my solar plexus that Sunday morning.

The following Sunday, the late John B Keane wrote in *The Sunday Independent* that *Out of Our Skins* was a book he loved reading. Naturally, my chest expanded for several days after reading the thoughts of the great Kerry playwright.

I wanted to republish the book in its entirety, and allow future readers to make up their own minds on its worth? However, in wishing to write this introduction and also a fairly lengthy epilogue, constraints in terms of the length of the book had to be considered. I have chosen to delete from the original publication my memories of my childhood and my family, and my experiences of growing up in the parish of Skryne. I have also deleted five short individual chapters (titled The Full-Back, The Midfielder, The Right Half-Forward, The Right Corner-Forward, and The Substitute) which were my personal reflections on five of my former team-mates, Mick Lyons, Gerry McEntee, David Beggy, Colm O'Rourke, and Mattie McCabe.

I have retained in this edition the chapter in which I explained and reflected on the death by suicide of my only brother, Gerard.

My Dad and I never spoke to one another about Gerard's death. Never. Not once. My beloved, huge-hearted mother, who privately counsels families bereaved by suicide, and who possesses a small book in which there are over 100, possibly 200 names, I am told, will bring Gerard up in conversation with me perhaps once per year, and when she does so she knows that I will keep the conversation extremely short.

When my mother talks to me about Gerard, I am overcome by an immediate, fanatical need to stop or escape the conversation, and most often I do within a minute or two. I always feel a small sense of guilt at being so useless and completely unhelpful at these times.

I know my mother would love to talk to me about my brother, but being the most generous person I have ever known, in addition to being unselfish beyond the belief of everyone who has ever met her, she will hardly ever restart the conversation with me.

I have never come to understand why I can behave like that towards such a deserving person. Neither do I have any idea why the emotion I feel at these times is, somehow, almost physical, in a strange sort of way. It is as though there is some place I am not prepared to go to! It does not make sense to me. I don't want to talk to my mother about my own brother who died 27 years ago, but I am prepared, and able, to write about my brother in this book.

To the best of my knowledge my 'refusal' to talk with my mother is not a fear of returning to the day of Gerard's awful, violent act against himself, or the days and weeks which followed and which built themselves into months from which there seemed no end.

The horror, for all of us who loved my brother, ruled our whole existence through those months, and still grips our family, tightly for some of us, more lightly for me and others. For me, night-time was the worst of it, but, eventually, it was night-time which also brought me to a more peaceful place with my brother.

After his death, I continued to sleep in the room I had shared with my brother all of my life, but always with the lights on and with the radio playing, and I waited for sleep to come. And when sleep finally came, I would commence my search for Gerard, again, and again.

In my dreams I would always find him alive. We would talk. We would physically struggle on the ground. We would struggle over his knife. I would always win. The dreams continue still, but any hint of violence has left them. In them now, Gerard and I talk in the bedroom we shared in our family home, and we talk about everything and anything - why he went away, and why he has come back? Everything and anything, apart from his death.

Now, in 2010, all those years after Gerard left our warm, family home on a windy January night and walked down the back garden and cut down the cord on my mother's clothes line with his Stanley knife, and ran across the field adjoining our family property to our local football field, and took his own life, I am still at a complete loss. I have no understanding of the final act of his life.

All I know is that happy and sad people, and people with fantastic futures and people who think their futures look hopeless, are each equally susceptible to ending their own lives. That is all I know for certain.

Families who have lost loved ones to suicide always ask, why? All families do. Forever, they ask why? My family did, and still does. The hundreds of families whom my mother has helped all carry the same question.

We have all attempted to piece together the acts and conversations, and every little interaction, which took place before the death of our mother, father, brother or sister, and we don't just content ourselves with the weeks and days before their suicide. We look back over the years and search through all sorts of happenings in our loved one's life. Families search blindly, and families are doomed to end their search back where they began, knowing nothing for sure, and finding nothing of any help. Whether a loved one left notes, or a good-bye letter, as Gerard did in his pocket, we are left knowing so very little.

There are absolutely no clues.

••••

Ireland became a changed place between the time when *Out of Our Skins* was first written and more recent years, though, strangely enough, as the book is now republished this country has well and truly buried the daft notion that it ever was a 'Celtic Tiger' and is now experiencing the same sort of hard times, and fearful economic backdrop, which was also in place in the late 1980s and early 1990s.

There is much mention made in the book of the Irish Press Group and, in particular, *The Sunday Press*, and some younger people picking up this book will have to go and Google to see what these were? The Press Group was founded by Eamonn de Valera and *The Sunday Press* was my employer until 1995 when the company floundered and disappeared from sight with the loss of many hundreds of jobs. I was the newspaper's Chief Sportswriter when it closed, and one hour before the shutters came down on the company premises for the last time, I was still at work at my desk on a Saturday afternoon.

At the end of *Out of Our Skins*, four years before the Press Group closed, I expressed the fear that I would one day end up working for the most prolific entrepreneur on the Meath football team, my clubmate and my closest friend for most of my football career, Colm O'Rourke. Thankfully, that did not happen, and after the Press Group was no more I began a publishing career of my own, and have had the fantastic and fortunate experience of launching several national and regional newspapers, one of which died quickly and without mercy, but most of which have endured and thrived.

••••

I had decided, midway through my football career, to retire from the Meath team at 30 years of age. And I did. I announced my retirement and, a few weeks later, I had my left arm mangled and broken into seven or eight different little pieces, in an accidental collision in a football game with my club. The arm remains locked, to this day, at a 30 degree angle, and there was never going to be a place on the Meath football team for a midfielder choosing to make a 'comeback' with one long right arm.

I was still playing on the Meath team, and my retirement was a few months into the future, when this book was first published. I was not enjoying myself. I was not training as hard as I should have been, as one of the older lads in the dressing-room - though, I had 'won' myself some time by taking larger football shorts from the County Secretary for the year ahead and, wearing a size 38 instead of a size 36, I fooled one of the team selectors into telling me, 'The weight is falling off you lad, with all the training you're doing!'

The truth was that I was preparing for the end.

My relationship with Sean Boylan, between manager and footballer, was also about to ground to a finish, within weeks of *Out of Our Skins* hitting the book shelves.

The book shelves in my home remain heavily weighed down with the autobiographies of great sportsmen and women, and with the memoirs of politicians from all over the world. In the last 12 months I have hugely enjoyed two of the greatest autobiographies I have ever had the pleasure of taking into my hands and slowly, ever so slowly reading. A great book is a book which you do not want to end, and the life stories of Andre Agassi in *Open* and Ted Kennedy in *True Compass* are two books which offer so many lessons in life - lessons learned by the authors, and lessons offered to the reader to take into their lives also.

Agassi writes so movingly and honestly about a career at the very top of the toughest sport in the world, and a career which he 'suffered' more than anything else for over two decades, but midway through his autobiography there is warmth and passion and great happiness to be found alongside the chunks of constant pressure and great weariness of chasing an elusive ending point for his career as a tennis professional.

Kennedy's story, of course, is immense in every single facet of his private life and public life, and the great man tucked the experiences of three or four 'lives' within his 77 years.

In so many ways, I guess, *Out of Our Skins* appeared so incomplete when I picked it up and read it for the first time in almost two decades. It was a snapshot, only, of a footballer in a place and time where he felt fulfilled, but where he also felt trapped and was growing increasingly curious and fearful about when that football career might end.

The months which immediately followed the ending of that career, and all of the years which have passed since, form the story of a former Gaelic footballer who has a whole different view of life, on and off the field of play.

Naturally, there are some people who will feel that a book, written in a place and time, should remain untouched. Undoubtedly, there is great substance to that belief. There is the possibility that I will regret ever having taken *Out of Our Skins* off the book shelf, after 18 years, and reading it for a second time.

However, I hope you will understand, by the end of this revisited and enlarged book, why I chose to have *Out of Our Skins* republished in the autumn of 2010.

Liam Hayes
April, 2010

OUT OF OUR SKINS

PROLOGUE

I have spent the greatest part of the last ten years of my life in this room. It's dull, and it's always dusty and cold. Even in summertime the room is sombre and cooling. It is also, usually, crowded and noisy. And the staleness of the passing years and the steam rising from bodies oiled with perspiration make it a place where I feel very much at home. It's not just my home. A great many footballers live here. Some of them have lived here longer than I have. Some have come and gone. A few have just arrived.

The Meath Gaelic football team lives in this room, a room without windows. Walls of naked cement blocks, long wooden benches polished a darker shade by thousands of muddied arses, a single table in the centre of the floor, looking apologetic, the ceiling, high and wooden and uncaring, and that old familiar smell. That perfect smell.

It's a great room. It's also, perhaps, my favourite room. Though some day I know I must leave it. I've been entering it for ten years and some day, as I leave, I will have to shut the door behind me for good. I'm sorry if that sounds dramatic. It's not meant to be, I assure you. The moment when it arrives is unlikely to be accompanied by background music (though, if I had a choice I would select the theme music from *Raging Bull*). There are some friendships I will want to take from this room, but most of the relationships will be sealed and buried as soon as the door bangs closed. I know that, and I think I'll be quite happy to leave them there.

This book was born in this room, and it has been written in this room. I know it will also be read by others sitting on the wooden benches around me, and I can't expect everybody to approve of it, or even like it. My only hope and wish is that they recognise this room in all its magnificence.

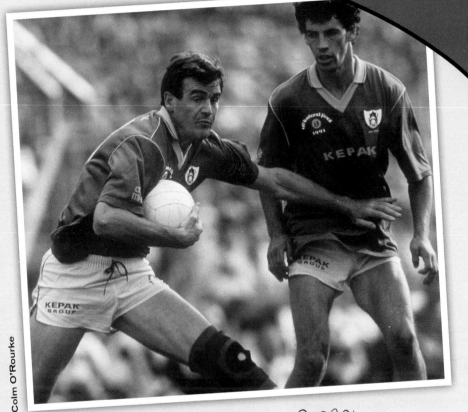

Colm O'Rourke

LIFE **AFTER** DUBLIN

6 July, 1991

I had to thank the troops.

I made my way along one side of the dressing-room, slowly, slapping and laughing and hugging, until I arrived at Mick Lyons sitting in his usual corner. Mick can sometimes have the greatest of smiles. We went to shake hands, and grabbed each other's forearms instead.

'We fucking did it Hayes.'

Liam Harnan was also sitting down and I took his head in my right arm and held it against my chest. He wrapped both arms around my waist. Gerry McEntee and myself looked at each other and Gerry Mc turned his head at an angle, as he does when he's so happy or so angry, and grinned. Gerry Mc can sometimes have the greatest of grins. We hugged, and talked into each other's ears.

'You're the greatest Mc. The greatest!'

Colm O'Rourke held Brian Stafford in an embrace, and as they released each other Rourkey turned to me. We gripped each other's shoulders and there was no need to say anything.

Soon, I slumped down onto the wooden bench, between Harnan and Finian Murtagh, dropped my gumshield into the bag beneath me, and cupped my head in my hands. I was the happiest footballer in Ireland but I knew that feeling wasn't going to last for very long. I had captained Meath to our greatest victory over Dublin, and I had played possibly one of the worst games of my life. Minutes earlier, we had scored the greatest goal which has ever been witnessed in Croke Park. I really think it was.

It began on the endline underneath the Canal End. Martin O'Connell grabbed a stray pass, and as he did so his left boot crossed over the endline. It was a long way to the Dublin goal. Marty passed to Mick Lyons. Mick tapped the ball to Mattie McCabe who managed to gain possession and get away his pass, by inches, before a Dublin forward crashed into him. Harnan hit a long, straight ball down the field to Rourkey. As he went to collect it he was shoved in the back. Rourkey took a quick, wild free-kick to Jinksy on his left.

He managed to take the ball before it went over the sideline. Jinksy didn't seem to know what to do with it at first and soloed it twice. He passed it off to Kevin Foley who was standing still. Foley passed to PJ Gillic. PJ passed to Tommy Dowd. Tommy passed to Rourkey. Rourkey passed to Tommy. Tommy passed to Foley, who was now four yards in front of the Dublin goals. He scored the goal.

Mattie got the ball from John O'Leary's kick-out. He punched the ball to me beneath the Hogan Stand. I raced thirty yards, slipped inside Mick Deegan, looked up and decided to go for a point. For some unknown reason I lobbed the ball crossfield to PJ. He tapped it over a defender's head to Jinksy. He scored the point.

We scored one goal and one point in the last sixty seconds of the game, and beat Dublin by one point in the first round of the Leinster Football Championship. However, the game lasted a total of five hours and forty minutes, as we had to play four times before unveiling the result.

Meath have now beaten Dublin in five out of the last six Leinster Championships. Yet, this was the ultimate victory. We had played poorly, and the more the games mounted up the more we struggled to climb over

Dublin. This was, undoubtedly, our poorest performance of the four. We led 0-4 to 0-2 after sixteen minutes. We trailed 0-5 to 0-7 at half-time, and 0-6 to 0-12 after fifty minutes. But there are good reasons why we managed to cling to Dublin and finally beat them this afternoon. We had our share of good luck (though we also had a few unlucky breaks). We remained calm all through. We knew what it was like to beat Dublin. We hate losing to them. We hate them. We believe they dislike us too and we honestly believe that they're not good enough to beat us.

That's why we won in the end.

None of those reasons had ever existed in earlier days when Meath and Dublin shared the same football field. Meath teams had lost to Dublin teams almost dutifully, as if we were born to lose to them. Our football lives may just as easily have been contained in a stately home in an earlier century. We knew our place in that home, and that place was generally below ground level; making some noise, but seldom seen. That same order, that subservience, has now been erased, I think. Although we may still need to pray that it has gone forever.

This afternoon, in our dressing-room we shook hands and hugged (and Joe Cassells walked in and landed a smacking kiss on my forehead) as we have never done before, though in recent years the men and boys on the Meath team have often removed the chains of their masculinity and fallen into each other's arms. It's happened each time we beat Dublin in a Leinster final, and twice when we beat Cork in All-Ireland finals.

Grasping Colm O'Rourke on this occasion was the most personal moment for me. We're both Skrynemen, and we have been friends for fourteen years, since I followed him into manhood and onto the football field. Yet, one month ago, our friendship was clearly broken in two. This tiresome duel with Dublin had commenced long before the teams first met last month. For weeks we had been thinking about them, and seven days before we first played them in Croke Park Colm and myself had an almighty row in the dressing-room. I told him he didn't give a damn about the team, and that he should get the fuck out of the dressing-room, and stay out. He was less irate, but he still traded words and insisted on having the final say.

We drew with Dublin on June 2, and I had one half of the best game of my life in the middle of the field. Colm played well at centre-forward. It was the first good game he had in months. In fact, it was the first time in the same number of months that he seemed to have any desire to have a good game.

Colm had remained good during those four games with Dublin, and in two of those games he was very good. In the same five weeks my performance had come apart. In the second and third games Dave Foran managed to distract me easily and still play quite well himself. This afternoon Foran was injured and couldn't play, and Paul Bealin found me in a shrivelled condition with barely an ounce of confidence left in my body. I felt drained like a long, slim, empty bottle of someone's favourite drink. This evening, at the end of it all, Colm and myself smiled into each other's faces and we didn't need to say anything.

I quietly said 'Thanks'.

After the game I had to rush back to *The Sunday Press* office to write about it. The top half of the front page had been held over to take my feelings about 'the event'. Because that's what this football game has become - the event of the summer. For one month it came perilously close to rivalling last year's World Cup finals in Italy for the amount of newspaper space it consumed. And I was in the middle of it, writing about it, and captaining the Meath team.

This evening, the Lord Mayor of Dublin, Michael Donnelly, held a reception for both teams in the city's Mansion House. I had to speak to his several hundred guests on behalf of the Meath team. Myself and the Dublin captain, Tommy Carr were presented with magnificent Tipperary crystal vases. Carr looked like death, and yet he spoke with great conviction. My speech was shorter, and dignified, as it has to be in a moment of victory. I probably looked very happy. Inside I felt gripped by self-doubt. And the intense satisfaction of beating Dublin was almost equalled by the disgust at my own defeat in the middle of the field. That was another reason why I didn't want to stand on the stage for too long.

Tomorrow morning, I know, I will feel an even greater sense of personal failure. And our journey to the All-Ireland final will only be beginning.

CHAPTER 2

Sean Boylan

AWAKENING

21 September, 1982

Within thirty minutes of sitting down each of us were steeped in guilt. Sean Boylan was meeting the Meath team for the first time, and that may not have been his intention. Certainly, it surprised us. We knew Boylan. He was someone who had been seen darting around the edges of the county team, doing the little things which need to be done before a team rushes out onto the field. Skryne had invited him into their dressing-room one afternoon to help out - he handled a twisted ankle and a bloodied nose - and it was considered, briefly, asking him to manage the senior team, until the idea was crumpled up and tossed onto the committee room floor.

On this night, Sean was standing in front of us on a tiny platform. He kept his white raincoat buttoned, as if he wasn't going to stay too long. The room underneath the stand in Pairc Tailteann in Navan contained about twenty players, who were listening to him, but mainly looking. He had been speaking only a couple of minutes when his eyes filled up.

It was a little embarrassing initially. I had been on the team two years, and already my dream had been shelled and left cruelly exposed. Boylan's dream was suspended in the air, like a child's balloon filled with helium. Four months earlier Longford had beaten Meath by one point in the first round of the Leinster Championship, and during successive summers my career as a Countyman had evaporated. I was now employed as a general reporter by the Meath Chronicle and that summer the paper carried a drawing of a coffin on its front page with 'Meath Football Team' printed on the lid.

It wasn't funny, wasn't sad.

Boylan continued speaking with an incredible depth of feeling. He knew that nobody else particularly wanted to coach or manage the team. We were aware of that too. The names on the County Board list had been ticked off, one by one. A player was approached, but Gerry McEntee also placed the idea to one side. It came to pass, out of desperation, that the offer was finally left on Sean Boylan's doorstep in Dunboyne.

We left the room, and the dampness in the night air hurried me back to my senses. We had witnessed one man's faith, but the Meath team wasn't populated by innocents. There were very few believers. I felt sorry for Boylan that night. He looked a lonely, imploring figure.

In the following years that same man would divide himself up into many different parts, manager, coach, herbalist, child, Christian, and friend. That winter and spring, Meath won promotion to Division One of the National Football League - not because Boylan was a good manager. He wasn't at that time. He was in charge, and he talked to the players, and he could promise us the sun, moon and stars, but the only thing he could deliver was a single opinion. The Meath team was chosen by a Chairman, a Secretary, four selectors and Boylan, and that's the way it remained for two years.

Sean Boylan was an only son in a flock of sisters. And it was he who remained at home after his father died, at first taking the family herbal business into his own hands and later personally nursing his mother who knew poor health for the last ten years of her life.

He is a short, muscular, iron figure of a man, who has always prided himself in saying 'Fellas, I'll never ask you to do something which I can't do myself'. Although Sean had never been a very good footballer, he played the game well, but alas, he had a fascination for hurling and played on the Meath senior hurling team for twenty years. Which, considering the slovenly and ragged nature of Meath hurling, was ultimately a tragic love affair. Not that Sean would ever agree.

Sean's training methods will never be found in any coaching manual. Almost everything is instinctive, highly imaginative, and a little crazy.

Every year, almost every month, he has turned to me at some stage during a training session, and laughed 'Gerry Mc thinks I'm making this up as I go along, y'know". All I can do is smile, and agree 'Really, Sean'. Most of the lads agree with Gerry Mc. In particular, Bob O'Malley, who is convinced that most of our training sessions should be conducted behind large stone walls and supervised by men in white coats. Each week, at some idle point on the field, Bob will walk by me, insisting 'He's mad, y'know! Off his head!'

Sean also has a passion for fast cars, though he always arrives late wherever he goes. His life is a jungle of herbs and patients, friends and acquaintances who double as friends, and strangers whom he treats like the best of friends. And us, his football team.

He is normally one of the last to arrive at our training sessions. One week in every second month he dramatically gets his life in order and makes a huge effort to be first into the dressing-room. And he waits there for us, fidgety and tense (probably thinking of all the things he could be doing if he wasn't in the empty dressing-room) and half-seriously he gives most of us a hard time about our time-keeping.

Sean Boylan is also a religious man. He is perfectly at home amongst Priests, Brothers and Sisters. In 1989, he had the opportunity to take a Christian Brother onto his squad. From the evening Sean Kelly first entered our dressing-room Boylan had a very public desire to see him make it on the team. That's the way it seemed to me and to most of the lads.

Sean Kelly is a good footballer, and he's very athletic and determined. One evening, Boylan had a team training session on the Royal Canal. He had borrowed four-man skiffs from a friend in the Dalkey Rowing Club, and he was hugely optimistic about the benefits to be gained from two weeks of rowing up and down the canal. The first evening, as he waited for the entire squad to arrive, Boylan became eager for us to warm up. One of the locals looking on had a bike, and Boylan borrowed it and advised Sean Kelly to go for a quick spin and get a sweat up.

Sean Kelly was gone a long time. I didn't know how far he went, but the entire squad was waiting with Boylan for him to return. We were all staring down the road, waiting for the bike to appear. It did eventually. And as Sean Kelly was sprinting towards us in the distance, Boylan inopportunely remarked 'He's some man, isn't he?'

He shouldn't have said that. Sean Kelly was cycling furiously towards us, on the road running parallel to the canal. Nobody said anything. Boylan's words hung in the air. The silence was too much. Everybody was thinking why the hell had Boylan got the poor sod to do that? Still nobody said anything. Then Joe Cassells asked, with the straightest, most concerned face:

'Jesus, Sean, you mean he can't cycle on water?'

Everybody, finally, broke up laughing. Boylan just smiled back at Joe. Then he congratulated Sean Kelly.

The standard joke in the dressing-room was that we would make a manager out of Boylan, if he stayed around long enough. It always produced a few smiles, and released some tension. Boylan would laugh too, because normally the joke was carried around in a glass case and opened only in Boylan's presence. That presence was apologetic, his touch light. Boylan was prepared to get down on his knees in the cause of Meath football, and it was becoming increasingly difficult to avoid joining him.

At the end of spring 1983, Sean Boylan led his team into Croke Park for the first time, for a National Football League semi-final against Armagh. An Armagh team which had been to an All-Ireland final, and was slipping back down the ladder.

It snowed that afternoon, and midway through the first half I thought I heard the gods openly snigger at our huge efforts.

For the opening eighteen minutes of the game we had raced and harried, and kicked seven wides. We led 0-4 to 0-0 and we had played most of our cards, and Armagh watched us. Their move! We didn't intend letting them make that move, but we were waiting for them to try, to score! They had to score sometime. And whenever that happened we knew we would have to respond – immediately. In the meantime, we were still looking over our shoulder.

At the end of the game in our dressing-room Boylan spoke with pride. We had been beaten, 2-8 to 1-7, but his speech immediately unveiled a certain amount of happiness and satisfaction at a defeat well borne. We didn't realize it at the time but our respect for Armagh had been far too great. Sean Boylan had received his first thorough lesson as a manager.

Sean Boylan is a man who believes in respecting people. Two months after losing to Armagh, at a team meeting on the eve of playing Dublin in the first round of the Leinster Championship, he laboured on about an injury Barney Rock had picked up, and left a little bouquet at the feet of the Dublin corner-forward. As he did so a shriek of annoyance escaped Joe Cassells' lips. But Sean always believes in respecting things, and that always includes opponents and places.

. . . .

Over the Christmas of 1982 Joe Cassells saw more than a finger of light. His eight-year-old career had degenerated to a point where, the previous summer, he had been holding onto the Meath team by his fingertips. He had been selected at left half-forward for the Championship opener against Longford, and was only granted a move to his normal place of residence in the middle of the field because of a late injury. In the opening years of his career Joe had reigned supreme over Brian Mullins in the provincial undergrowth, even though across the countryside and in All-Ireland finals the blond Dubliner was mistakenly considered a vastly superior breed of footballer. That was during 1976 and 1977. Four years later, Cassells had hardly any ambition left, and his football career had visibly greyed. In January of 1982 he was handed the No. 6 shirt by Boylan. Cassells had never played centre half-back in his life – his former life, as it would turn out. For the next four years he was positioned in the doorway of the Meath defence.

Joe had always been a big kid, and naturally he took to Sean Boylan's kindergarten faster than anybody else. He enjoyed life, and had continued busily to feast on the funny side of it during the days when the Meath team was living on its substantial belly. Joe was Joe, the most graceful athlete I'd ever seen up close and a great clown.

In the pre-Boylan years the former personality had dominated and while Joe was still the most influential player on the team, sorrow and dejection had never threatened to pull his career apart at the seams. Even after Boylan arrived, that strange sense of humour, which Joe had been carrying around under his arm (since his fourth or fifth birthday) was never fully erased.

I don't mind admitting (well, not too much!) that Joe Cassells had always been my hero, and is still occupying that role. He was so graceful and, at the same time, he was as hard as nails. And his hands were huge. I suppose I may as well admit that I often imagined I was Joe Cassells. When I sat in the lower deck of the Hogan Stand in the mid-Seventies and watched Meath losing Leinster finals to Dublin I was Joe Cassells. Even now, as I share the same field with him, there are times in games – usually when I'm playing badly – that I try to become Joe Cassells. I try to be him, and I hope that he will have a calming influence on me. If that seems strange, I'm sorry, but I've always felt that we all, at some time or another, need to be somebody other than ourselves – in life, and especially on the football field.

Joe is the calmest man I've ever known. Nothing distracts him or unnerves him, and one of the very few times I saw him angry and verging on the uncontrolled (rather than angry and defiantly composed) was in a Championship match between Skryne and Navan O'Mahonys. The game had started off on a sour note, with a Skryne defender partially decapitating a Navan forward.

Early on, Joe and myself contested a high ball and ended up in a tangle on the ground. Our arms and legs were wrapped up, and in our rush to get to our feet a fist was thrown, a light punch. I honestly can't remember who started it. But, by the time I got to my feet, Joe was still on the ground and I nudged him in the back with my boot. Play continued, and I chased after the ball. Joe chased after me, and I looked around and one of his huge fists was descending in an arc. I moved and he missed. Mickey Downes went to throw a punch at me, and as he did our centre-back Padraig Finnerty kicked him in the arse. A lightweight melee continued. We won the game.

The next evening I felt I needed to face Joe. I rang the front doorbell of his house and Louise answered. Louise Cassells, amazingly, seems just as serene as her husband. Joe was sitting at the kitchen table. The kids were in their playroom. Joe looked up at me, and his eyes seemed cold, distant. He spoke, 'You're an awful dirty bollocks Hayes. Are you having a cup of tea?'

Joe Cassells has five children. He's an electrician, and he works with the same face with which he plays football. Very few men do! But then Joe has been the greatest footballer who has ever played for Meath. In Sean Boylan's presence, Joe was older and less athletic, but he was also wiser, and yeah, beautifully calming. If Sean Boylan hadn't appeared in front of him, Joe would almost certainly have quit his life as a Countyman, a pauper!

••••

When Sean Boylan moved his training camp from the home of Meath football in Pairc Tailteann to the home of the Columban Fathers in Dalgan Park, five miles outside the town, team customs changed too. Training sessions on Saturday and Sunday mornings were immediately interrupted when the Angelus sounded. Two days before a Leinster final, on a dull, showery evening, he spotted Jack Fitzgerald, one of the grandfather figures of Meath football, standing outside the wire. Jack Fitzgerald was getting over a recent illness. The session was stopped once he had been noticed. The players were lined up, and introduced to Jack one by one. It was a nice gesture. It was also respect getting in the way of a training session.

It was a crazy, forced respect, but was Sean teaching the team to respect itself too? I think so!

We didn't realise, not for a long time, the methodical way in which Boylan was scraping away at the years of inhibition and acceptance which had built up around the Meath team. A team which hadn't won an All-Ireland since 1967, and hadn't beaten Dublin in a Leinster final since 1964.

A large part of the winter and spring of 1983 was spent on the beach at Bettystown, and in the sea, in the water up to our knees, 'jogging through' and up to our thighs, 'stretching out.' Until someone got tripped or thrown under, and surfaced in an inflated tracksuit. First one person, then a second, and quickly the squad began to tumble like dominoes until one last, dry soul remained, and was plunged underneath the giant octopus. It sounds childish. It was childish. The same as weeks spent on the Hill of Tara would be murder; evenings rowing up and down the Royal Canal ridiculously eccentric; Saturday and Sunday mornings racing across the football field on our bellies, madness! Each year, Boylan excitedly presented something different. That was his very idea, to have grown men behaving like children, thinking like them, and issuing fresh, childish squeals of laughter at the beginning of each year, trying on their innocence for size once again, sharing the threats they had last issued in short trousers, and turning imbecilic without having to apologize to anybody.

What was it Richard Dreyfus punched on his word processor at the very end of the buddy movie *Stand By Me*? 'You'll never have friends like you had when you were twelve years old.' Something like that! It's true, but Sean thought we should try.

CHAPTER 3

Gerard Hayes

GERARD

23 January, 1983

The journey home was short, and yet the monotony remained undiluted. There were five of us in the chuckling diesel mini-bus, and I was the second last to be dropped off. We talked, mostly about the game, randomly picking at different bits and pieces like tiny particles of meat which had lodged between our teeth. We continued talking for a while, about anything and nothing in particular until only the quarrelsome voice of the engine remained. The last twenty or thirty minutes were the longest. They always are.

Twenty or thirty minutes, and then another ten or twenty minutes or more while, one by one, we said goodnight. The usual villages, crossroads, sharp corners, homely dark stretches, 'see you Tuesday', twisting, stopping and starting, an old familiar turn, a little more conversation, past the church and the school, down the hill, left at Swan's pub, and left again, and I reached for my bag, and eventually slid the door shut behind me.

Another Sunday!

We had played Down, in Newry, a somber, grey football ground, lonely and destitute, on a windy and quite chilling afternoon. No different than any other ground, anywhere else that day I'm sure. Maybe there were a dozen curious souls present, who somehow wanted to watch two adult teams clumsily trying to find their feet at the beginning of a new year. It was a challenge match, and we could have won or lost. I couldn't have cared.

It must have been 8 pm Everybody seemed to be at home. Dad's car was around the back, and my mother's brother Brian was down for the day. I was glad he was still there: he'd want to know about the game and I didn't mind talking about it. I could hear the bus turning at the crossroads. It was really dark, and a light drizzle was beginning to fall but if anything the wind was strengthening. The family room was warm and cosy, and everybody looked tired. Happy and full and tired, and descending into lethargy, as they expected to be on a Sunday evening, though most of them had questions for me. Mum immediately wanted to know had I eaten? Dad and Brian wanted to hear about the game, and I told them as much as I could in one great take. Then Brian started asking me about individual players. Mum still wanted to know was I hungry? Gerard wasn't in the room, but there was nothing terribly strange about that.

At some point later in the evening somebody asked, 'Where's Gerard?' It was a perfectly normal question, but I remember it distinctly. He had left the house about an hour earlier passing through the living room on his way next door. I remember also, clearly, him saying 'goodbye', and I presumed he was looking at Brian. I hadn't looked up from the newspaper I was reading.

Another one of my uncles, Denis, lives beside us. He and Brenda were going out, and Gerard was due to mind their boys, Russell and John, for a little while, until my youngest sister Eileen was ready. Gerard was twenty-four years old. He liked to spend time alone. That afternoon he had played a league match for Skryne against a neighbouring parish, Seneschalstown, in the football field, only 400 yards down the road, or a short run from the bottom of our garden, over a ditch and across one large field. It wasn't surprising that nobody could find him, not at first. Gerard liked to read, in different rooms, especially a room where he would not be disturbed. He had remained at home after graduating from St Patrick's College in Maynooth almost two years earlier and refused to take his H. Dip.

When Gerard couldn't be found, the laziness in the room was immediately replaced by anxiety, as if one of us had loudly clicked our fingers. Minutes later, only minutes later, everybody seemed frightened. It happened that fast. I think each of us had been worried about Gerard for a long time, and that fear quickly rose to the surface of our consciousness. I don't know why that fear for Gerard had been there, untouched, buried within each of our lives. But, obviously it was. And when Gerard suddenly went missing from our lives, from this house, everybody knew that only something bad could have happened to him.

I was already beginning to think that Gerard was dead. I didn't say it. But we all thought it. He was gone. And less than an hour earlier he had been with us, alive and healthy, and strangely content, I thought. Thinking that Gerard was gone was scaring and numbing, but that fear was also enclosed within an eerie calmness.

Gerard was my closest friend, and we'd shared the same bedroom all our lives. He was quiet and shy and kind, and God was he stubborn! That is one of the many things we had in common. Most of our lives we also played football together, and argued and fought. He was four years older than me, but I started most of the fights. Close to the end of the game we were playing I'd get thick and try to land a kick on him, and run.

He seldom hurt me. One of our last great fights was on a wet Sunday night, in the garage, where we were playing soccer with a tennis ball. He was shoving me around with his hips, and inevitably, I kicked him and raced to the door, and I just had it opened when he pushed me. I landed, arse down, in one of the rubbish bins which had been a goalpost and I couldn't get out. Gerard stood there laughing, and walked out the door.

He had a great deep laugh.

Gerard had no car, he didn't drink and he had gathered few friends.

He should have been somewhere around the house. We had been in Denis' and the Parish Priest's house which is also next door, and he wasn't there. There were few other places to look. In his room, our room, there were pages from used notebooks lying open on his shelves, waiting to be read it seemed, by someone, by me? I glanced through them, I didn't need to read them. I went running downstairs and outside and searched underneath the rows of fir trees surrounding the garden (I don't know why. I felt confused and angry and frightened, and for some awful, morbid reason I kept picturing the summer's morning I found our old family cat under one of the trees, her body stiff and rotting, when I was twelve years old).

I expected to find Gerard, I think, barely alive. Or dead. Or alive and about to do something. By now, my Dad and each of my uncles, Brian, Denis and Sean, were out looking. It was so awfully dark. I was running up from the bottom of the garden and Dad was walking through the gate, and I knew he could see me in the distance, and I was afraid he might think I was Gerard.

'It's me, it's me,' I shouted.

'Gerard. GERARD,' he replied.

'It's me, LIAM!'

We stared at each other. We were both angry. It was long after midnight. Dad and Sean went off in one car. I went with Brian. We looked around the school and the church, any place which might have been familiar. For a moment I was sure he would be at our grandfather's grave, or behind the headstone. Where?

Brian and I had searched through the Priest's barns and sheds. He wasn't there. Mum was in tears. There was nothing left to do, nothing.

The squad car stopped at the gates of the football field although they had already been opened. Pat Tierney, who played football with Skryne, with Gerard and myself, was driving. I was in the front with my hand directing the searchlight on the roof. Brian was in the back. Pat wanted to go inside, even though Brian had told him Sean and my Dad had already been in there. We drove in, over the crunching stones, shining the light on the trees and the smashed windows of the dressing-rooms. We were passing behind one of the goals when Brian told me to shine the light on the field, towards the goals – on the goals, he demanded.

Pat suddenly stopped the car and jumped out. Brian went with him. I sat there, I just sat there. Everything after that, driving home, walking into the house, hugging each other, it all seemed like one of those pictures which are blurred around the edges.

Gerard was dead.

I ran onto the field to play with Skryne two weeks later. It was unnerving, and disturbing. The field was also a little repulsive, but not fully so. Colm O'Rourke came into the house and asked me to come down. It didn't seem an unnatural place to be. This field had always offered warmth, reassurance, happiness, and it's where I had drifted all my life.

A month later, Meath were playing Tyrone in a vital Division Two promotion game in Pomeroy. In the days after Gerard's death I had told people I never wanted to play football again. I would never go back to the field again. But I did. Sean Boylan kept me at midfield for our next League game, the first after Christmas. Boylan told me he wanted to start me, and see.

I was booked after ten minutes for a foul on Eugene McKenna. The referee gave me a warning and told me the next time I'd be off. At half-time Sean told me he was taking me off. I didn't mind. I would have been happy to continue if he wanted me to. I wasn't playing well, and yet I didn't think I was playing badly. I didn't know. I wanted to care, but I suppose I felt far too noticeable on the field. I felt there was me, and then there was the game. Maybe I was relieved to be taken off. I honestly don't know. Meath won by one point.

After that, I'm not sure what happened or how long it took before one day I ran onto the field for a game, or a training session, and felt something. I know I remained angry for a long time, with Gerard, with myself for not seeing him and what was happening with him. For two, three months I couldn't sleep. I was terrified of lying there, alone in the dark, thinking. And then, one night I suppose I started sleeping again. The same as I played football again, one day.

Dad and myself, we dealt with Gerard in the same way, I think. I didn't want to think about him, didn't especially want to talk about him. My mother, and my sisters, they were different. Especially my mother. She couldn't move. She needed to have Gerard in front of her, to ask him why, and why, and why, and she needed to ask us. I answered her but I seldom listened to her. To minutely observe the act of his death was the very same as entertaining a perfect stranger who had attempted to destroy each of our lives. I wouldn't. I didn't want anybody else to do so either. I've seldom examined the final days of Gerard's life with my family. I've wanted to, occasionally, but a great weight seems to be sitting on my memory of him. Unintentionally (intentionally?) my brother was being pushed further and further into the darkest corner of my mind. The room we shared I had obliterated.

His bed was removed, mine changed direction. His hundreds of books and his belongings were stored away in cardboard boxes, elsewhere in the house. The walls and shelves and doors were painted orange, brown and green. One side of the room was wallpapered with photographs of Marilyn Monroe. Until only my mind remained to be emptied, and that too was hurriedly being swept clean.

More and more Gerard was being pushed back, away, hidden. At some point he ceased to exist, for me. His grave had, sometimes, seemed important. The words ('I die happy with the knowledge that one day a better way of life will be brought about for everyone') from the note found in his pocket, and inscribed on his headstone, had seemed precious. The grave too disappeared out of sight. This morning, as I wrote, I couldn't remember those last words, and I had to phone my sister Mary for them.

My football career easily survived. I didn't think of Gerard on the mornings or evenings of All-Ireland finals. And I didn't think of him on the night and morning our children David and Sarah were born. Not an ounce of guilt breathes within those admissions. Yet, now, I am telling myself that one day I will attempt to discover Gerard again, search for the happy times we had together. Funny, it's difficult to picture the two of us together. I try. I close my eyes. Finally, I can just see him, alone.

••••

Fifteen months before Gerard died, Skryne had reached the Meath County final for the first time in ten years. I was playing centre-forward. The match programme had Gerry Hayes at right corner-forward. But Gerard never played in the game. The fifteen had been picked and announced in the usual way but was hastily rearranged in the middle of the week. At the end of the training session before the final I told the players I wanted to talk to them.

They had gathered around me in a corner on the field. I spoke about what happened, and told them that Gerard and myself would not complain. I also told them that what happened was wrong. Gerard was amongst those listening, at the back of the group, quiet, his arms folded, chewing on his lower lip. He didn't say anything about his own treatment, and didn't talk much about it at home either. He didn't seem very disappointed. Long before, Gaelic football had stopped being a matter of life and death to him.

You could see it on the field when he took the ball in his hands. It was something beautiful in his hands, not the same worn piece of leather, its whiteness daubed by weeks-old sheep shit. He treated the moment as something wonderful. Tension, agony, exhilaration, they no longer seemed to pierce his consciousness when he held the ball to his chest. It was like he was out on the back lawn kicking the ball about on his own. Obviously, the furious waves of activity during matches frequently swept him up, and left him stranded elsewhere without the ball.

He had stopped competing. He had also stopped being my big brother. When I spoke up for him and myself at that final training session Gerard had looked like a small, distracted boy in the distance. Not the brother who would tease me about playing 'Cowboys and Indians' (I never did play cowboys and indians!) on the sideline when I was supposed to be a substitute, and when he was out on the field winning under-fourteen and under-sixteen championships with Skryne. At some stage, we had swapped roles. He was uncaring about that, and I felt it happening, and we never talked about it. The week before he died, we were on the back lawn together, kicking a ball about. Kicking. Doing what we had been doing there, and in the field, since when? Since he was Arsenal and I was Chelsea, and long before.

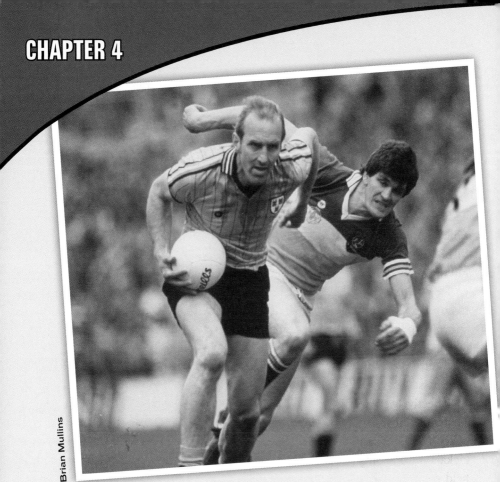

CHAPTER 4

Brian Mullins

NEIGHBOURS

22 July, 1984
Dublin 2-10, Meath 1-9, Leinster final

The game started, exploded and ended, and all through we were busily picking up the pieces. Myself and Gerry McEntee were supposed to be playing Brian Mullins and Jim Ronayne: that's the way the team lists promised it would be. Instead there were blue and green jerseys everywhere and in the confusion, noise and heat, McEntee's final words before we left our dressing-room had already been suffocated.

'We can't lose this. We can't. WE CAN'T,' he had shouted, before turning and running out the door.

A year earlier, at the beginning of July, Meath had been beaten by Dublin in a replayed first round game in the Leinster Championship.

The 1984 Leinster final was minutes old and the game I knew was no longer recognisable. We shot four wides in the first nine minutes, including a penalty kick which corner-back Padraig Lyons had raced the length of the field to take. He scooted past us back to his corner twice as quickly. We weren't particularly devastated, everything was happening too fast to be absorbed at once.

They scored two goals from Barney Rock and Ciaran Duff, and we had missed our penalty. John Caffrey was sent off ten minutes before half-time. But we were playing like men who were holding their breath, and rushing around Croke Park in a highly agitated state, especially Gerry. He was chasing after every ball, and was getting every second ball.

I was playing okay in difficult circumstances, because Gerry was trying to cover so much ground. We, Mullins and Ronayne and me, didn't see that much of him in the middle of the field. It was better before Caffrey was sent off though, because eventually Dublin would fall back into defence. They virtually conceded the centre of the field, and launched long passes into wide open spaces in our defence.

Effectively they divided the game in two. Their half of the field was a cluster of activity. Ours was an open field. And, damn it, my legs were still heavy. My boots and socks had felt full of cement since the pre-match kickabout, and they remained like that until Joe Cassells raced up the field with the ball, set me up on his right, and I popped the ball over the bar. Running back to the middle of the field was easy. I felt light, as if a liquid solution had been emptied into my legs, and instantly dissolved their great weight. A minute earlier Ben Tansey had scored our goal: 2-3 to 1-4. Half-time. We drank our sugared tea, and calmed ourselves. We were missing Mick Lyons in the full-back line. He had broken his thumb three weeks earlier, and had it taken out of plaster four days before the game. It was immediately wrapped up again! Mick's absence had been costly, but we weren't ruined, and we could have been ahead.

They led, 2-9 to 1-9 ten minutes from the end. Four minutes from the end Colm O'Rourke took a twenty-one yards free, took it quickly to a team mate and in blind panic chipped the ball into the stomach of a Dublin defender. The ball was played the length of the field through Joe McNally towards Anton O'Toole who lofted a magnificent point. The sea of blue on the hill overflowed, and trickled onto the field, bathing O'Toole and two or three other Dublin players. It was hot, over eighty degrees in the middle of the field, with 56,051 people breathing down upon us. Sixty-eight minutes, sixty-nine. It was all over.

I taped the highlights of the match from *The Sunday Game*. The same tape also contained bits and pieces of the Los Angeles Olympics, and it was played repeatedly during the remaining days of that summer as I examined every inch of John Treacy's etched face and marveled at his composure on the streets leading into the LA Coliseum, as he bravely stretched out his tightening limbs to touch his silver medal. It was truly magnificent, but I could never force myself to fully rewind the tape and inspect the remains of what was to have been the greatest day of my football career.

After the match, in the Dublin dressing-room, Mullins would point to bruising on his body in reply to a nervous question from an enquiring reporter. He had been hit several times before being taken off the field fifteen minutes before the finish. For Dublin's second goal he had carried the ball deep into our defence. I was after him and knocked him to the ground on the twenty-one yards line. As he fell he stretched out and tipped the ball to Duff, but as he did, O'Malley hit him full on, wide open. There was further punishment in store for him too.

It was nothing personal. It was just that Mullins' name usually popped up in conversation amongst Meath players more often than any other. He and Rock and Duff symbolised Dublin's inner confidence, and we knew that had to be removed. Nobody had to tell us. Similarly, there were certain Meath players who had been observed, and marked down as points of strength and weakness. McEntee and O'Rourke, and later Flynn, Stafford and Beggy. I too, would seem to be favoured by some Dublin players. They saw me, I presume, as someone to be put down, who would stay down. And that suited me fine, because given a choice between groping my way into a match and being introduced with a thump, I actually would have chosen the latter (not every Sunday, but in Leinster finals and when the stakes were clearly visible).

••••

I have never held a grudge against somebody who has tried to hurt me. It's accepted as part of the game. And only once, have I ever regretted punishing an opponent myself. It was earlier in 1984, in a Centenary Cup quarter-final against Galway. The previous month Galway had beaten Meath in a replayed semi-final in the National League, and their midfielder Brian Talty had made a high and dangerous tackle on Colm O'Rourke. When the two teams met again in the Centenary Cup some of the lads asked quietly in the dressing-room, was I going to see to it that Talty got what he had asked for by flooring Rourkey. I said I would. I was asked again. I promised I would, and I tried! A couple of years later, after joining *The Sunday Press*, I would get to know Brian Talty and discover a most competitive and refreshingly honest individual. Even though we never subsequently talked about that Centenary Cup game, when I repeatedly tackled him late, thumped him in the back of the head when we both jumped for any high ball and how I spent the first twenty minutes of the match generally sizing up opportunities to hit him. It was a subject I never wished to bring up with him, and he seemed to have forgotten about it. Or, maybe he had considered my efforts quite pathetic. I don't know, and I never wanted to find out.

In Meath, the same unhealthy relationship which exists between ourselves and Dublin also breathes. In every county, there are relationships between parishes which leave a great deal to be desired. In Meath, Summerhill and Walterstown and Skryne have had little appetite for each other's company over the last decade. Interestingly, it was a decade which has been dominated by Navan O'Mahonys. They too, occasionally, have been seen fighting it out with their neighbours in the village square, though whenever they brought shame upon themselves it has usually been in self-defence.

Good and bad blood has always flowed through the veins of the GAA, usually a few hours after Sunday Mass. It's accepted. It simply has to be. We are a violent, tribal race and the GAA is the place where the pages of our bloodied history continue to be turned. The GAA field is a place of honour, a place of truth. Unquestionably, a place which can look foolish, unnecessary and violent. Sometimes a pathetic place, a place which would fill your nostrils with disgust, if you weren't suitably initiated.

I was born and immediately deposited into the arms of the GAA. Seventeen years later, the first time I played on the Skryne senior team, I felt nauseous. I was shocked. I had frozen over. It was a warm summer's evening, and we were playing Summerhill in a tournament game in Dunshaughlin, and one of their players had just spat on my right leg. I'd been standing, slightly in front of him, and I asked myself if he had meant that? He hadn't said anything.

The ball was down the opposite end of the field, and we'd been standing there. A couple of seconds later something struck my leg again. I didn't wipe it off this time, I didn't know exactly what to do. Was I scared? That night, I told Gerard I wasn't, that I felt cold with disgust and he insisted that I should have walked calmly off the field, and explained why in the local newspapers the following week.

'Imagine!' he exclaimed.

Gerard was angry and excited. I told him I should have hit the bastard. I said something to the centre-back at the time – ridiculous, limp words which served as a hopeless counter-punch. If I struck him I knew all hell would break loose and I had never fought my way out of hell before. I should have thumped him though, because five minutes later Colm O'Rourke was in the centre of a free-for-all on the Summerhill endline. I ran towards him, conscious of who was behind me. I grabbed someone, one of their defenders, and attempted to pull him away. I felt a coward. I told myself I wasn't, although I realized the game no longer interested me.

It's unnerving now to recount that evening. A moment ago I deliberated, stalled, and quietly agonized before writing 'I felt a coward.' Because nobody I know has ever formed those words or courageously worn that badge. Even the biggest cowards in the parish of Skryne have served their time in the local football club and skilfully avoided baring their stomachs. I was never a coward, but often I felt like one.

Bare-knuckle fist-fighting has never intrigued me or appealed to me even in the remotest form. I find it distasteful, frightening (another word which GAA doctrine frowns upon). It leaves me frigid.

Yet, I've entered the imaginary ring, stood there, and invited others to join me. Twelve months after keeping my fists somewhere in the vicinity of my knees, during my first game for the Skryne senior team, I was prepared to sound the opening bell for a fight myself. I had thrown the first punch in a Feis Cup game against Syddan on a miserably wet evening in Navan. One of their defenders had struck me, awkwardly with a knee in the back as I stooped to collect a ball. He was well-known, a troublemaker! I turned, and threw. It didn't matter, I later explained to myself. Syddan always came for a fight whenever they played Skryne, and it would have commenced anyhow, at any second. The tension was raised. I was booked by the referee.

Forty minutes later I stood in the middle of a melee, in the teeming rain, issuing threats to two opponents. Colm O'Rourke was on the ground, writhing in agony, after taking two flying boots in the chest thirty seconds earlier. A couple of his ribs had been cracked. I had to race over to the sideline and collect a stretcher, and help him onto it.

Martin Coyne was standing with his hands on his hips talking to one of the Dublin players. He was still in his damp jersey and shorts, and his face, forearms and thighs were covered in a layer of sweat. It was like he was shining, Gerard said. He didn't look angry or dejected or anything like that. If anything he looked stronger than he did on the field. Martin Coyne was the Meath captain. They hadn't stripped him of his pride. That meant something to us, to Gerard and myself, as we lay on our beds talking about the game over and over into the early hours of the morning. Several times I asked him to sketch the same picture of Coyne for me.

Meath would beat Dublin next year, we promised. In the 1977 Leinster final Dublin beat Meath by four points, 1-9 to 0-8, on another warm, humid, blue day. It had happened again, and I couldn't understand why.

Joe Cassells had once again matched everything Mullins did, and by the end had left him a frustrated bundle in the centre of the field. The Meath defence had remained firm and superbly disciplined, refusing to bend at the knees after one brilliant Dublin movement early in the second half which concluded with Anton O'Toole flicking the ball over his head into the net. We missed a great many chances, but it was more than that. That wasn't why Dublin had won, and why they always seemed to pull away from Meath anytime the game was left on a knife edge. To them it seemed a matter of life and death. To Meath, death didn't really enter into it, because we knew what it was like to lose, we knew we could accept it and that life would continue. There would be a Monday morning, a dull and painful Monday morning, but daylight nevertheless. There always was.

History will undoubtedly leave that Dublin team trailing behind Kerry, when it attempts to evaluate the greatest football teams of all time. And the managers will be buried with their teams. Mick O'Dwyer won eight All-Ireland titles. Heffernan won three, and his team gathered a fourth without him in 1977, and yet, when balanced in either hand his achievement seems that bit heavier. The history books are unlikely to take the space to describe how Heffernan breathed life into his team (whereas O'Dwyer was present at the birth), and made it a likeness of himself. Heffernan was a quiet, brooding figure, behind a face etched with determination. He also looked unforgiving, and seemed naturally suspicious. Scary and calm, purged of emotion, and brilliantly intimidating, he unnerved me and almost everybody else.

••••

In February of 1986, the week I started working in *The Sunday Press*, I decided to dive in at the deep end and interview him. Heffernan's obvious disregard for most sports reporters fuelled my unease. Tuesday morning was my first day at the desk. On Wednesday morning, at 8 am, I was due to breakfast in the Burlington Hotel with the former Dublin manager. We had never met before. I was fourteen minutes late. We spoke for half an hour over coffee and he seemed relaxed, and I almost succeeded in joining him. He had been appointed manager of the Irish team which would tour Australia later in the year and he knew I was interested in making his squad. In the carpark he joked that it might be advisable for me to take up karate if I wanted to survive on tour. I think I smiled, and I was seated in my car before I realised he had told me something. I interviewed him over the phone a few times after that. I was also on his initial Irish squad and we often spoke on the training field.

However, the five Meath players chosen didn't participate seriously in that many Irish training sessions because of our involvement in the All-Ireland Championship. One Saturday afternoon Heffernan was short one player to stand in goals during a practice match. We looked at him, Padraig and Mick Lyons, Colm O'Rourke, Joe Cassells and myself. Nobody said anything, and finally I stepped forward and broke the ice. The other four remained sitting and standing in the carpark. FOOL! I had to be back in the office by 4.30 pm Each Saturday afternoon training session was a rush for me, but I never missed any of his sessions. My role on the training field was also an awkward one. I didn't want to seem to be pushing myself and, at the same time, it was my professional duty to seek his opinions from time to time. In August, three months down the uncomfortable road, he cut his squad to forty players. I was left out. Heffernan never explained why, he never even whispered to me, and we never again spoke after that. I always avoided calling him, telling whoever asked me 'Oh, Heffo and myself don't talk'.

I thought he had behaved badly. He should have called me to explain why I was being dropped. He still had a responsibility to speak up. Two years later, before a Leinster final against Dublin, we met one Saturday evening. He approached me and I was surprised. He said he didn't want to talk about football. He said he had heard I got married and he asked about life in general. We chatted for several minutes and then he left me, more bewildered than ever, and wondering what lay behind that worn and remarkable face.

In 1983, in one of the most bizarre and brutal All-Ireland finals, twelve Dubliners performed one of Heffernan's greatest works by refusing to fold themselves in two despite being outnumbered by fourteen Galwaymen. Afterwards, Mick Holden would ask reporters 'Had we three men sent off? If I'd known that I might have got worried'. Duff, Mullins and Hazeley had been dismissed, and Rock scored the winning goal while Heffernan himself was running across the middle of the field. Subsequently, the incredible achievement was trampled underfoot as newspaper reporters and photographers and the public gorged themselves on the game's consequences - investigations, accusations, suspensions, and generally any tatty little detail which poked its head up in the air. The magnificence of the performance was shelved, Heffernan's genius deposited in a cardboard box. In 1984 and 1985, his Dublin team would again be beaten by the same trusted Kerry team.

In the summer of 1985 Meath had been thrown out of the Leinster Championship by Laois. We lost the Leinster semi-final by ten points. While Heffernan's young Dublin team was losing All-Ireland finals, Sean Boylan was not in a position to take advantage of their troubles. We weren't even in their company anymore. Boylan's team had been intact for three years, and he had embraced his players and trusted them, and made them feel good about themselves. And it wasn't working!

It wasn't enough. He needed to change, and he needed to change his team. One Sunday night, in a noisy public house, he had some advice thrown at him by Padraig Lyons, who told him it was time to take off his apologetic cap and stuff it in his back pocket for good.

'Do you mind me saying something to you?'

Whenever Padraig Lyons says that you know he's about to whack you over the head with the most brutally honest remark. Boylan repeated Padraig's suggestion at subsequent team meetings, and ironically, when he finally acted upon it Padraig Lyons was one of the players who was swatted by the same cap. Padraig had been born strong, and with a mind capable of reading any game in minutes. Unfortunately, he was also born with shorter legs than his older brother, Mick and his younger brother, Terry. Boylan and his co-selectors, Tony Brennan and Pat Reynolds, convinced themselves that Padraig just wasn't fast enough to turn and chase a ball which was played over his head into the corner of the Meath defence.

Boylan was uncertain how Mick would take the news. On the evening of the announcement of the deed, he travelled to Summerhill where Paddy

Lyons had reared his sons to be hard and proud, and later he arrived at training in Dalgan Park with Mick in the passenger's seat beside him. Padraig didn't appear that week, but in time he too took the decision on the point of his square jaw. Despite spending some of the best years of his life largely condemned to a selection of dugouts, Padraig's humour, and his attitude to his predicament, served as an example to everybody else. It could happen to anybody, and it did, though Padraig Lyons was one of the last to be fingered by Boylan. He remained in the left corner of the defence until 1987. Others were extracted before him, as Boylan spent the winter of 1985 and the spring of 1986 experimenting madly. He seemed to choose randomly, as if his eyes were closed. In truth, he had at least one open, because a vastly inexperienced Meath team kept its head above water all winter. By March we had scrambled into the quarter-finals of the National League. There we played Dublin in Croke Park.

Dublin were still scoring goals against us. After only four minutes our defence was wrong-footed. Padraig Lyons was the last man, and he was forced to commit himself and lunge at Charlie Redmond. The ball was tipped over his head to Barney Rock. He was fifteen metres out to the right of the posts. 1-0 to 0-0. Fifteen minutes: 2-1 to 0-2. Joe McNally had played a long ball through the middle of our defence, and Tommy Carr side-footed it past Mickey McQuillan.

In the second half Brian Stafford was moved to centre-forward and for the next twenty minutes he performed as a ringmaster, holding the ball, moving it left and right. O'Leary made a brilliant save after Staff flicked the ball on within a crowded square. Bernie Flynn was brought down by Pat Canavan one minute later. I decided to hit the penalty kick hard and low to the bottom right corner. I mis-hit it, and the ball bounced softly between the goalkeeper and the right-hand post. O'Leary had made a movement in the opposite direction. He tried to twist back and the ball rolled underneath his body. We kicked three further wides. And, there it ended. Dublin composed themselves. Rock struck two points. We held onto them: 2-8 to 1-10. We lost, but it felt good.

It was a different Meath team which had lost, beginning with Stan Gibney who thought there was something funny to his being on the team. Before the game, as we left our dressing-room, Stan had turned to me, and asked 'You do know they've picked me as centre-forward?' Stan played centre-forward, and played well.

Boylan had also taken John McEnroe back after several years in exile. Johnny Mc had been as fiercely competitive and indisciplined as his namesake on the tennis court, and he had been left to his own devices in the north Meath village of Oldcastle. He marked McNally that afternoon, and was majestically controlled all through. There was an entirely new half-back line. Des Lane, a quietly promising minor from 1983; Liam Harnan who had a cigarette dangling from his lower lip when I shared a dressing-room with him in the minor days in 1979, and then he didn't seem to have any great desire to serve his county for a lifetime; and Terry Ferguson who had been labelled mediocre in the shadow of his father's magnificence. In the forwards Boylan had Stan and Brian Stafford, and later David Beggy ('Jinksy'). That afternoon, they all did okay.

Harnan, Ferguson, Stafford and Beggy would all remain on the team, with Staff winning the Texaco Footballer of the Year trophy in 1987.

•••

Springtime! The evening beach and cooling water, and laughter, and bloody hard running through the softening sand from Bettystown to Mornington and back. Three, four miles in all. The Leinster Championship waited, but in the distance. It was a good time to be alive and training hard, and looking up. It was a particularly exciting time for me. I had joined *The Sunday Press* in February, and I felt just as excited, and nervous behind my desk as I did on the playing field. More so.

In June, the day after Meath beat Carlow in the first round of the Leinster Championship, I flew to Las Vegas for an eight-day stay, and for that ill-fated Monday evening in Caesar's Palace when Barry McGuigan lost his World Featherweight title to a boy from Texas, called Stevie Cruz. Boylan had asked me to train while I was there. I told him I would, and had tucked some gear into my suitcase. But I didn't train. I was too excited. I was a sports journalist crossing the casino floors, not a Gaelic footballer.

The Sunday Press was also spending a couple of thousand pounds to have me write one article from the desert. One article, and a tailpiece - 2,000 words, at £1 a word! They trusted me, and as my Friday morning deadline approached I became increasingly uptight. The Leinster Championship? I locked myself away in my room on Thursday afternoon, and gave myself twenty-four hours to come to terms calmly with what was expected of me, to give *The Sunday Press* value for their money.

At 11.30 pm, still Thursday night, Martin Breheny popped in to say goodnight. He was covering the fight for the *Evening Press* and *Irish Press*. He asked how I was doing. I told him not too well, that I was going to start rewriting through the night. At 7.30 am Martin knocked on my door again. I had been staring at Caesar's Palace, a blue neon cathedral in the distance, and as daylight broke, the colour slowly began to fade. By the time Martin looked out the window with me the Palace was a large grey cathedral again. I told him I was in trouble. I couldn't send what I had written. He left, and returned with a jug of fresh orange juice. I hadn't eaten in almost twenty-four hours, and he told me to sleep for a couple of hours, then re-read what I had written.

I didn't sleep, and at 3 pm, finally, I sent my words home. I felt awful for twenty-four to forty-eight hours. I felt an impostor who was waiting to take his ringside seat. McGuigan lost. Nine months later, I received the Benson and Hedges Sports Journalist of the Year award for describing McGuigan's last wretched days as World Champion.

I was transported from Las Vegas almost directly to my second Leinster final. We spent more time talking than training as the game approached. We'd spend an hour on the field, get into the dressing-rooms, shower and chat, eat in a local restaurant and have a bit of a laugh, before getting our chairs into a circle. There we'd talk and talk, trampling the same ground over and over; though we talked about Dublin more than ourselves. We looked at them, and had looked for three, four weeks and it was all getting very tiring, but now we could see them. Mullins was no longer in the middle of the field. He was on the sideline, and Heffernan was nowhere in sight.

The morning of the game was cold and dark. We ate our chicken salads in Ashbourne at 1 pm, and kicked around the footballs for twenty minutes in the carpark. Everybody was serious, more composed, less fidgety than ever before. It was cold. The sky was a faint grey, and the breeze was strengthening. I didn't like it. Leinster finals were supposed to be savagely hot. The team should have been bubbling over in the dressing-room. Instead, there was quietness, peacefulness, as though everyone was aware of the courage Boylan was displaying in switching Joe Cassells from midfield back to right corner-back, a position he had never played in his life. The plan was this: their full-forward Tommy Carr was sure to wander out towards centre-field, and try to take Mick Lyons with him. So Cassells would follow Carr into more familiar territory for him, and Lyons would stay in a very vacant full-forward line keeping Joe McNally company. Lucky Joe!

An almighty downpour commenced twenty-five minutes into the game, and amazingly, it didn't begin to abate until midway through the second half. But my adrenalin was flowing nicely. As a kid I had once caddied for Denis, my uncle, in a pro-am and we were with Simon Owen, a New Zealander who had finished runner-up in the British Open the previous day. He told us that on the 17th he had taken a seven iron, and mistakenly hit the ball thirty yards further than he had ever hit a seven iron in his life. Owen's ten-year-old words surfaced in my mind after I had taken a free-kick, fifty-five yards from the Dublin goal, which sailed over the bar and deep into the Canal End. Unbelievably, two minutes earlier I had jumped for our kick-out, and caught it over the heads of Gerry McEntee and Jim Ronayne. Yards over their heads, it felt. My kick screwed into the Hogan Stand, but something weird and wonderful was racing through my body.

The game began with Beggy - whose only previous visit to Croke Park had been for a U2 concert a couple of years before - getting the ball, running forty yards, racing between Canavan and McCaffrey, falling on his backside, immediately regaining his feet, and kicking the ball over the bar. Beggy had only been introduced to us three months before. We didn't know him, and I didn't trust him greatly on the field.

Anything was possible after that! At half-time they led by two points. 0-6 to 0-4. Ten minutes before the interval Harnan had collided with Rock, and Barney fell to his knees on the soft turf, one hand clutching his left shoulder, begging for help. The referee ignored him, and turned his back to keep play going. Rock was in agony. He stayed on his knees, attempted to get to his feet at one stage, and fell back down again. His collar-bone had cracked. He was a pathetic sight, and at half-time the picture of his face stayed with us in our dressing-room. It was a comforting and most encouraging picture to have.

It turned out that Dublin scored only one point, from a free-kick, in the entire second half. They had lots of chances. Ciaran Duff was short with two free-kicks, and afterwards in the losers' dressing-room he stared back at enquiring reporters and honestly asked them 'How can you take a free-kick with your boots full of water?' McNally missed a good chance. Canavan came forward and screwed the ball wide from in front of the posts. Harnan dived full length and blocked a Tommy Conroy shot from twenty-five yards. With two minutes left there was still only one point in it for us. Mick Kennedy collected a ball deep in his own half and badly mis-kicked it, and I punched it from Ronayne's hands. I had only played reasonably, but that punch was also the longest punch I had every made in my life. Very strange indeed!

O'Rourke collected the ball and left a great chasm between the teams with the last point of the game. We were Leinster Champions. And next we had Brian Mullins served up to us, standing in the middle of our dressing-room floor, acting like a damn good loser.

Icing on our massive wet cake!

CHAPTER 6

Jack O'Shea

THE GREATEST

24 August, 1986
Kerry 2-13, Meath 0-12, All-Ireland semi-final

A second enormous thumb, also called tradition, had been slowly descending upon the new Leinster Champions once Dublin's great weight had been lifted clear. We continued to train enthusiastically, sometimes fitting ourselves into the roles of giddy explorers. I told anybody who asked me that we could beat Kerry in the All-Ireland semi-final. I overheard and read other Meath players saying the same thing. We also told each other that we could beat the greatest team of all time. And still, the thumb descended. We became increasingly aware of it, even though we continued to ignore it once we were together on the field.

Tradition. What the hell is it? One wise gentleman bottled it, and labelled it several years ago for me.

The old gent was the late Cus d'Amato, who spent a lifetime on the street-corner of boxing rings throughout the United States. A bald, wrinkled archangel, who held the hand of Mike Tyson amongst others. That included a former light-heavyweight champion of the world, called Jose ('Chequi') Torres, who gained as much fame for his intriguing biography of Muhammad Ali as he did for the movement of his own leathered fists inside the ropes. In his book, *Sting Like A Bee* Torres quoted d'Amato ringside at one of Ali's fights in the mid-Seventies. 'In professional boxing when you step into the ring you come to understand that you are to participate in a contest of wills, not of abilities (assuming the abilities are roughly equal of course).'

Kerry were the greatest. That was indisputable. But that, in itself, didn't entitle them to seven All-Ireland titles in eleven years. Too many teams, good wholesome teams, actually lacked the will or the resolve to challenge them for some of those titles. In the summer of 1986 Mick O'Dwyer was focusing on eight All-Irelands in twelve years. Meanwhile, the entire Meath team, its manager and selectors, were focusing in on O'Dwyer's team. It left us at an immediate disadvantage, in their slip-stream days before the game even began.

On the Thursday evening before the semi-final we met on the field in Dalgan Park as usual. Loosened up, chatted, pushed ourselves towards laughter as we ate our usual steak and chips, and started talking seriously, same as ever, about the game, about Kerry, and largely about how we should play in their presence, conduct ourselves in their presence! It was almost midnight, and we left it at that. We had talked in ever-decreasing circles, and there was nothing more to say.

Outside, in the semi-darkness of the carpark, I found Martin O'Connell at my side, asking 'What'll I do?' He looked distraught.

• • • •

Martin O'Connell, by coincidence, happened to be the greatest footballer on the Meath team. That had still to be proven to others, and to Martin himself. His career had been sprawled on the dressing-room floor for almost two years, but even at his lowest point the ball remained a plaything in his hands or at his feet. Martin had been at his lowest about twelve months earlier. He felt that Pat Reynolds, who also happened to be an exceptional left half-back for Meath in his day, didn't rate him, and didn't want him on the team. Martin also had trouble understanding why Sean Boylan seemed to have lost trust in him (and, in truth, I had a great deal of trouble understanding it too). At one point in 1986 Martin quit the panel. He felt he was being nudged off it anyway.

In 1984, in the first round of the Leinster Championship against Westmeath in Mullingar, Martin had broken a bone in his hand. Boylan felt his confidence remained bruised long after the injury had healed. For those two years he was on his back, and we all watched, but I never felt there was anybody standing over him, waiting to give him a hand up. Certainly there was nobody in sight, and into 1986 Martin O'Connell still felt he was being shadowed by the question marks of others. He had been introduced as a substitute in the 1986 Leinster final. In a challenge match against Cavan seven days later he was accurate and sharp as a full-forward (and scored seven points). That's when he was chosen to play against Kerry.

At the team meeting on 21 August, Martin's role against Kerry full-back, Seanie Walsh turned out to be the centre of attention. There's always one position, one topic which comes under the searchlight and remains there longer than any other! Sean Boylan told Martin what he wanted him to do. Cassells, McEntee and O'Rourke also served up their views. I, too, had my ideas about Martin moving away from the square, making room for O'Rourke.

One or two others added their tuppenny's worth. At the end of the night Boylan knew exactly what he wanted of Martin, the majority of those in the room knew it. Unfortunately, Martin O'Connell wasn't one of them. He now looked like a man who had been dragged through the team meeting. He asked several people what they thought he should do during the game.

With Martin, football was normally instinctive. He didn't have to think about what to do. He was an artist, and the green canvas was spread out at his feet, though like all artists there was a part of him which was misunderstood, and throughout his career Martin O'Connell was seen to be one of the most errant passers of a ball on the Meath team.

Also, those who had to build obstacles in a defence alongside him didn't always appreciate his free spirit. They complained that he was a loose marker - and rightly. Martin was the most complete and articulate footballer on the team, but that didn't make him perfect. To begin with he didn't want to cope with a whole catalogue of instructions. From A to Z, they clashed with his instinctive abilities and tied them up in knots in his head. Martin didn't know what to do with himself in the All-Ireland semi-final, as it quickly approached him.

We raced out onto the field, and headed straight for the bench in front of the Hogan Stand as the stewards had instructed. We then started kicking the ball in and out at the Canal End. Twice I looked over at the tunnel, expecting to see them appear, imagining that I had heard the slightest lift in the voice of the crowd. I began to imagine how Monaghan must have felt twelve months earlier. Waiting, waiting for an audience, waiting for the hour of judgment to commence. I didn't want to look in that direction a third time. There was a brief struggle to prevent myself from snatching another glance. We hadn't met them on our way into the ground. The Bomber, Jacko, Spillane! Their door was still firmly shut as we hurried down the corridor towards the field. And now, we were still alone. I wanted to know they were there, to see them at the other end of the field.

0-4 to 0-2.

We were playing out of our skins. There were sixteen minutes gone and we were winning. Gerry Mc and myself were getting our hands to all the balls in the centre of the field. Gerry was marking Jack O'Shea. I was taking Ambrose O'Donovan. Gerry was shouting to me that we had them. He wanted them to hear. He always wanted the opposition to know what he was thinking. Staff had roamed back into our defence. He picked up a clearance, soloed the ball, floated around Liston, hopped the ball, but Liston had managed to get a hand in, a giant paw. The ball was broken loose. Ogie Moran picked it up, and thumped it towards our goalmouth. Our defence was ever, ever so slightly relaxed. Then it panicked. McQuillan, at half-time, said he had called for the ball (adding his voice to 45,405 others, unfortunately). He came racing out. Cassells and Mick Lyons were racing back. The three of them spilled to the ground. Cassells' man, Ger Power, had watched it happening. From the safety of a front row seat the wreckage splayed itself out in front of him. He picked up the loose ball.

The goal was a disaster. Lyons was the first back onto his feet. The two Red Cross men, Sean, our physio Anne Bourton, Doc Finn, McEntee the surgeon - they were rushing around. McQuillan's face was a bloodied mess. His nose had been broken. Cassells' head was bandaged up. Four minutes later the game restarted. We instantly recovered: 0-7 to 1-2. The loss of the goal had been painful, but the lead had been gathered together again. Half-time. I looked at the clock. 4.05 pm The thirty-five minutes were up. Half-time had to be around the corner, after the next kickout.

Kerry scored one point. They scored two more. Tommy Doyle had come upfield. I was surprised to see him so far up, at this stage of the game. The ball was played across to him. He went to move to his right. I had him. He turned back to his left. I still had him, if I really wanted him. But he had no room, no time. I watched Doyle kick the ball over the bar with his left foot, and felt sickened by my own lack of judgment. Thirty-nine minutes. We had been watching them for four minutes. Four points: 0-7 to 1-6, and finally the referee waved his arms for half-time.

0-8 to 1-9.

Fifty-five minutes. We were still playing well. There were chances. McEntee was screaming at me.

'We have them. WE HAVE THEM'.

Finian Murtagh was fouled thirty-five metres out, to the left of their posts. I had scored two frees out of two in the first twenty minutes. Each time I had stroked the ball over the bar with the top of my foot. I hadn't thought about it. This time I had to make sure, and the message had crossed my mind before I could suffocate it. The message was throbbing as I stepped backwards, and stalled, looking at the posts. I didn't think of Lee Trevino's words, his advice to those with a putter in their hand, which goes something like 'If you're going to miss them, miss' em real quick'. I was taking my time, and I struck the ball perfectly. It was over the bar. And then it began to veer, to the right, and more, shading past the post, missing the post by two or three feet. But I had hit it perfectly, believe me. Twenty seconds later Pat Spillane scored the sort of point which only he scores. One minute later Murtagh was wide with a free on the opposite side of the field to mine.

They were wearing blue, not their traditional green and gold, and they had looked like ordinary mortals. Now, they were the Kerry team I had been admiring, and disbelieving, all my life. Seanie Walsh! He had always been my favourite. Such a natural footballer, but still every bit as athletic as those around him, but a pure footballer, sculptured, and set in motion. I was running around, up and down the field, and I was beginning to feel totally disorientated. At one point I found myself deep in our own defence, and I couldn't remember journeying there. My left ankle was getting heavier, and more painful. I had damaged ligaments after falling awkwardly on it three weeks earlier, and suddenly I was leaning on it. It was becoming a crutch. A stick which had been nowhere in sight for most of the first half.

I wanted it to end. I begged for it to end. I was clutching at Moran's jersey and Mick Lyons lunged in our direction. Mick and I both fell to the ground. Pat Spillane lobbed the ball into our large square. Jack O'Shea touched it down. Willie Maher hammered it into the net. I was still on one knee.

0-12 to 2-13.

It was over. Good!

· · · ·

It didn't end there. I had to put the experience into words for *The Sunday Press* the following weekend. I took the paper's readers into our dressing-room with me, and allowed them to look around. Before the game began, at half-time, and at the very end.

'We continued to sit there, as if awaiting judgment, in varying stages of undress and distress, emotions exposed. Losing is a lonely game, loneliest when played before a large audience. The showers offered only temporary sanctuary. So we sat there, and stared, with fixed expressions, with faces calculating the depths of individual defeats. No further judgment was needed.'

The dressing-room was packed with family, friends and perfect strangers. They meant well, most of them. But Cassells was stretched out on the table in the centre of the room, and there was a push to give him air. He had taken a knock on the back from Liston at the end of the first half, and his left side was numb. He just needed air. Privacy was out of the question.

I finally gathered up my bag, stuffed in my damp towel, and made my way towards the door. I walked down the same dull corridor, now reeking of victory as well as defeat, and behind the large steel outer doors were my family, Anne, more friends. I wished they weren't there. They would be good and protective, and they would say the right things to me. But I just wanted to sit on the edge of my own tragic performance for a while, alone. The doors had to be opened. There were still kids outside with their match programmes which they wanted signed. The centre pages with the team lists already had the names of Paudie O'Shea, Charlie Nelligan, Tom Spillane triumphantly scribbled down. They had already left, in the same manner as they had entered, without us seeing them.

Two months later I was on holidays in the Canary Islands with Anne. It was our first trip abroad together and from a distance, with her, the entire year didn't seem to lead into such a deep hole. Also, in the two weeks away, I missed Meath's first game in the National League. Meath easily beat Dublin in Croke Park, and Mattie McCabe had looked very good in the centre of the field with McEntee. Boylan subsequently phoned me at work to tell me that I was being left off the team for the next game against Down. I was surprised, but I told him I accepted their decision.

That Sunday somebody cried off the team on the morning of the game, and on our way to Newcastle, in the team coach, Sean told me that I would be starting at left half-forward. I didn't like the position but I didn't say anything. In the dressing-room the jerseys were given out. The same worn, shrunken set which always seemed to be resurrected during the winter. Actually they were experiencing their fifth winter. I had to pull the jersey down over my shoulders. The sleeves halted midway, between my elbows and wrists. I shouted something, I can't remember what or at whom. Boylan answered. He shouted back. We argued. The game started. Five minutes from the end I was taken off. We lost by one point. The next day I told Sean I wanted to talk to him, and I got to his house at 9 pm.

When he told me that he wished I had been angry when he phoned me the previous week about the selection of the team I began to fume inside. I told him that McEntee, O'Rourke, Cassells, Mick Lyons, none of them would have been left off the team in similar circumstances. That's how our conversation began, and it ended over two hours later, a storm which had been quietened in one of Sean's tea cups.

••••

In our final game before the Christmas break Kerry came back into view again. It was a Kerry team with new, kiddish decorations on it. Throughout that December afternoon, one half of the Kells pitch, the half further away from the centre of the town, refused to alter its frosty glare. I was back at midfield again. We won 1-12 to 0-4. I had played okay. Everyone seemed happy, including Mick O'Dwyer, and those who had travelled up with him the previous afternoon. I don't know why I was content. After six years I was right back, if not at square one, then next door to it.

On that white, gaunt afternoon O'Dwyer had glimpsed into the future. He didn't seem to believe what he had seen, or else he didn't want to believe it. The greatest team of all time was on its knees, and the fresh young bodies racing up behind it were incapable of lifting it up, of taking it to the sidelines where it could happily spend the remainder of its days, without a single regret having taken seed. Kerry would lose to Cork, after a replay, in the 1987 Munster final. The same Kerry team would lose again to their neighbours in 1988 and 1989. A total of four Munster final defeats on the trot meant that in the heaviest treasure chest in the Gaelic Athletic Association there remained a mound of distasteful memories in one corner. Pity!

Some of his players, those who held on to O'Dwyer's every whim with both hands, and refused to let go (even when their own bodies petitioned to be released) limped away from the greatest sports story ever told on this island. A handful of them possess muscles and bones which may not dutifully serve them throughout the remaining years of their lives. That's a pity too. But we shouldn't pity them. They knew good times, great times, and their only error was that they never wanted them to end. It was hard for them to leave the arena, where friendships and egos and business careers had been built. It's always hard for 'The Greatest' to vacate their own altars.

On 11 December, 1981, a sportswriter called Hugh McIlvanney watched Muhammad Ali enter the ring for the sixty-first time in a career spanning twenty-one years. Ali was five weeks and two days short of his fortieth birthday.

'I'm shooting for immortality and I'm on the doorstep,' McIlvanney heard Ali promise earlier in the week

The greatest, proudest fighter lost on points to a middle of the road opponent called Trevor Berbick. McIlvanney watched, and wrote, 'To see him lose to such a moderate fighter in such a grubby contest was like watching a king ride into permanent exile on the back of a garbage truck.' Around McIlvanney, Ali's friends (his subjects) also sat there in the Queen Elizabeth Sports Centre in Nassau, and watched.

Of course, it wasn't quite like that for Kerry. They were amateur footballers. Each player held two lives, a football life, and what remained of his former life, before he bowed to Mick O'Dwyer's fanaticism. But some of them eventually grasped some of the horror which stared Muhammad Ali in the face in his final minutes in the ring, and from which he refused to walk away.

They too took their time, and they paid their dues with those final four defeats.

Mick Lyons

1987

29 January

The first training session of the new year is always hell. It doesn't have to be hell, of course. That choice is always ours. When the National League was stored away for the winter, in early December, I was fit and healthy. In the best shape of my life, probably. But after ten months of continuous football nobody thinks of doing anything over the Christmas break. The clever thing would be to just do two or three lights sessions each week, and then easily pick up the pieces when Boylan calls us back together again in January. But who wants to be clever?

It's vital to throw your football bag into the garage in December and promise to return to it a few days later. I had left mine there, and two weeks later I finally got around to emptying it. When I unzipped it, there was a smell of newly potted plants, that mouldy, earthy smell. Boots, socks, tracksuit, gum shield, towel, shorts, an old jersey, gloves - they had all taken root. I didn't need my boots tonight. We were training in the gymnasium in St Pat's in Navan, and we began the evening with a run around the darker streets of the town. It was less than a couple of miles. After the initial chatter and jockeying and laughter we relaxed into an easy stride. Terry Ferguson and Bob O'Malley maintained the same pace. The rest of us didn't really try to keep up with them. I was sure I wouldn't be able to. I was already short of breath and my lungs were beginning to burn up a little. I wanted to get back to the gym with something left inside. Most of us did!

It's good to be back together and the eight weeks break has seemed more like eight months. There's a novelty about the first session. However, the mood quickly evaporates, and driving home from Navan it seemed like we had never really broken up.

I was partially distracted all night long. I have to fly out to New York tomorrow afternoon, and throughout the evening I was thinking about Eamonn Coghlan. He will be running in the Wannamaker Mile in the Millrose Games tomorrow night in Madison Square Garden, and the *Press* have decided to send me out. This means I will not be around for the GAA All-Stars banquet, which is also on tomorrow night. I don't have to rent out a monkey suit, and I don't have to feel stiff and uncomfortable the whole evening. The All-Star awards are chosen by a group of GAA writers and were a good idea. However, provincial whims and the preposterous manner in which players who have been sent off during the previous twelve months are deemed ineligible, make each All-Star award much less significant than it may seem. They should never be taken very seriously, but they are not quite a joke either. Most players want one. Some players cannot have one, even if they have excelled during the year. However, Mick Lyons will be receiving one. He's the only Meath player selected on the team. It's his second All-Star award, and he deserves it. But so too does Gerry McEntee, and more than a handful of other footballers who have been simply ignored.

1 February

Meath played Cork in the first game of the new year. A challenge match, which we lost. The game was in Cork. I was still 3,000 miles away, but on my way home. I didn't ask how much we lost by? The pitch had been a quagmire, and the game had descended into farce. I was delighted to have missed it. How I hate challenge matches! They tell you nothing. They issue an entire litany of uncertain promises. They are a chore, and even if you play well in one, even if you play out of your skin, you still ask yourself what's the point? Everyone agrees, and it always shows in our performances. In challenge matches the Meath team has always been lazy and undisciplined. The team just doesn't give a damn, and doesn't try very hard to hide it. I don't know why. Normally we are hugely competitive. In the League we try. In the Championship we try even harder. In the Championship we are probably the most competitive team in the country.

Next Sunday the League resumes, and although the tables were frozen over at the beginning of December (and we are nicely placed after beating Dublin and Kerry, drawing with Armagh, and losing to Down) the team is slowly awakening to the thought of playing Roscommon at Dr Hyde Park. We are third in Division One. But, in the dressing-room, in the faces, it's like an entirely new season is just beginning. What happened in the final weeks of 1986 seems like history. The form of 1986 is also old. The team will be picked afresh. We are bright-eyed but weary, and Roscommon are probably the least tempting team in the country. They're just so dull, and they're always a difficult team to play against.

4 February

The team is still re-arranging itself, since losing in the All-Ireland semi-final to Kerry six months ago. The trauma of that defeat shook everything up a little. Everything's a little bit in the air. Bob O'Malley is back on the team after losing the right corner-back position to Joe Cassells last year. Bob had taken that badly. His head was down for months, and it seemed like he might never raise it.

Bob O'Malley had been a full-back on the Meath minor team in 1983, and we became close in the next twelve months. He kidded that he wanted to play midfield for Meath and that anything else was something less. I have a feeling he was also serious at times. Bob is the ambitious sort, and he wants to be whatever he chooses to be. But he was cut out of Sean Boylan's plans early on during last year's championship, and he barely spoke a word for the rest of the year.

Bob O'Malley had definitely been treated coldly, rather than harshly. Meath had won the Leinster title for the first time in sixteen years, but Bob remained in his boots, and everybody else lost sympathy for him eventually. The experience was still showing on his face in the National League games before Christmas, and even now that he is back on the team at the beginning of a whole new year, Bob is still quiet. Yet he is starting to laugh at what happened.

'We'll win nothing, y'know that.'

When he said that to me last week I laughed, but I hope he doesn't keep thinking like that for long.

'We'll never win anything!' Bob's words, and his laughter, are combining to tell the world that he is no longer so uptight, and that he's just interested in enjoying himself. It isn't a bad attitude to have. It's a better one than he had, but neither is it ideal, though he's playing well and he's relaxed.

Bob got straight back into the team because Cassells is not around. Joe decided to rest up for the winter after the injury he received in the All-Ireland semi-final. Colm Coyle and Terry Ferguson have also been struggling through injuries since last August. Coyler had been a half-back against Kerry in August, but is now spending time on the half-forward line. He's adaptable like that and he's doing okay. The only problem is he may not be able to pin down the position firmly, whereas he was very much at home in the half-back line. However, Des Lane and Kevin Foley are being tried out there during the League. Coyler is being switched from chair to chair, and he knows the time might come when all the seats on the team are full, and he's still standing. He knows the risk, but he's not the sort who is afraid of risks.

Training tonight was much the same as last Wednesday. It was tiring. Everybody found it tiring, and not too many of us are doing the sessions on our own which Sean is demanding. That's obvious, but Sean hasn't said anything.

7 February

Ireland beat England in the Five Nations Championship at Lansdowne Road. The match was played in a downpour, and it was a shambles, but the Irish players showed terrific courage. I hate playing in mud! Tomorrow we play Roscommon, and Hyde Park is bound to be a total bog. I never like playing there anyhow. The ground is dismal, and there's a 200 yards walk from the changing rooms to the field, through supporters who are arriving late. I just don't like the place. It's going to be wet and cold and miserable, and I'm not fit. It's a day I'd prefer to leap-frog.

When I entered the press-box, and squeezed my way to my seat and sat down, somebody in the row behind me asked, 'How are the Meathmen for tomorrow?' I turned, and mumbled, 'Oh, I don't know, that's a good question', and smiled. I turned back, and faced the empty pitch. It wasn't a good question! I feel uncomfortable existing as a Meath footballer in the press box at Lansdowne Road. I'd prefer to sit down as another member of the press, not as a GAA man. Besides rugby excites me and is quickly becoming my favourite game.

At 5.15 pm, I was still sitting in the press box. Almost all the reporters were in the press room below, stuffing opinions down each other's throats (and whoever can talk and swallow at the same time wins). It was quiet and deserted in the box at the top of the West Stand. It was also cold and the field was in darkness. The two middle fingers of my right hand had quickly numbed, as usual, which makes it awkward holding my pen. They too, like to remind me of who I am. Two years ago, in a National League game in Navan, they were both wrenched out of place on a dull, grimy afternoon.

8 February
Roscommon 0-12, Meath 2-9, National League
Roscommon were just as we expected, hard, dour, persistent, clawing and honest. Our own performance was unexpected. We dominated the game and had it wrapped up early in the second half, when we led 2-8 to 0-3, though they continued to play all sorts of short, and extremely patient balls the length of the field.

I felt good. Only once did I actually come to a standstill, and that was after running sixty yards with the ball and passing to Colm O'Rourke who kicked a point. That was in the forty-first minute, leaving us that eleven points in front. But we failed to score for the next twenty-one minutes. Roscommon got a grip on the game in the centre of the field, and scored nine points on the trot. I had never quite managed to fill my lungs after that long run, and Mickey McQuillan was kicking every single kick-out in my direction. Paul Earley had come out to midfield from full-forward for Roscommon and his timing was perfect. He caught everything for twenty minutes. I felt dead. Our defence looked dead, and McQuillan should have been shot dead for not changing the direction of his kick-outs. Roscommon just kept coming at us, at the same pace, until they finally ran out of time.

It should have been a good day. It should have been a good win. I would have been happy with a three point win, if I had been promised it before the game. But when you go eleven points up, and are then totally outplayed for the remainder of the game, and you win by three, well, you feel that your victory has been man-handled. Heads were neither down nor up in the dressing-room, and Sean didn't say very much. The good had been sucked out of our performance in the last twenty minutes and what was left was obvious for everybody to see.

Martin O'Connell had played well though. He was back on the team again, and should have been back in his favoured position at right half-back, but the selectors wanted to stick with Lane and Foley on the wings. They had Marty on the half-forward line, and he scored two points and was directly involved in one of our goals when he combined with Coyler and Lane, and Staff got his fist to the ball in front of Roscommon keeper, Gay Sheerin. But Marty was still inhibited by the forward position. He took too long to turn and look up when he got possession, and that simply wasn't him.

21 February

It's easy to wonder about and severely doubt Irish rugby supporters. After the convincing victory over England two weeks ago, the visit to Murrayfield was a precious step which had to be taken towards another Triple Crown. Ireland lost 16-12. I felt deflated after the match. But Saturday evening in Edinburgh was no different than Friday evening had been, and the hordes of Irishmen and women went about their business of eating, drinking and being merry as if a household fly in green had unluckily been swatted. The passion, the fury, the anger and the disappointment which fuel the minds of GAA people don't seem to surface within the great Irish rugby public, which as a giant body acts the part of a gluttonous fool. Their sporting lives and social lives are embraced in a sweaty quest. Often I pity them. Don't they understand, that excellence and beauty and even failure in the sporting arena is something to be respected, to be honoured, something which deserves to be treated with at least a tablespoonful of dignity? I don't think they do.

This evening I ate in a restaurant closer to Murrayfield than Prince's Street, closer to the graveside of Ireland's defeat. I thought about my own weekend. Tomorrow afternoon we play Monaghan in Kells, and we complete our League programme by travelling to Charlestown to play Mayo. Monaghan have a good team, and the disappointment of coming so close to the All-Ireland in 1985 hasn't retarded its growth. David Byrne will be playing midfield. His career and mine, I see as being neck and neck. He is athletic, and extremely skilful, and lacks confidence. I should be able to match him in the air, but I don't want to have to cover too much of the field. Monaghan love to move the ball fast. I'm not looking forward to the game. Mayo will be easier, I think. They have been struggling in the League. We only need two more points to make sure of qualifying for the knockout stages, and of the two games, Mayo look the softer route, even though they are a much more physical team than Monaghan. Their style of play suits us more.

22 February
Meath 0-11, Monaghan 0-5, National League

It was too easy, in a way. Monaghan had no appetite, and it wasn't surprising that they scored only one point from play in the sixty minutes. We've now qualified for the quarter-finals, and the season is falling into place, though we're still not in good shape. It didn't show this afternoon, but I'd be greatly surprised if any more than a handful of players are doing the extra training which Sean Boylan is asking for. I'm not doing anything. It's not laziness. I just haven't got the interest in going out on my own in the evenings, and besides, the season is young. Also, Sean hasn't introduced the stamina training yet, and I know there's enough pain and sweat awaiting me next month.

Despite that, I played very well today. It was probably my best game in almost twelve months, and I had the edge on David Byrne throughout the hour. My best moment was midway through the second half, when we were already leading by six points. He fielded the ball well. I chased after him, and pressurised him and intercepted his pass (I know Sean thinks I'm as lazy as sin. I know it from the way he looks at me, and doubts me without saying anything, and occasionally feels compelled to take me aside and suggest that I do a specific run or a specific training session, something like that). The moment proved that I wasn't just interested in high catches and long solo runs. I was doing my chores around the field too.

Bernie Flynn was in impeccable form, dancing and stopping and darting. He scored five points in the first half. We led 0-7 to 0-2 at half-time. We got two more points in the first four minutes of the second half, and unlike Roscommon, Monaghan never questioned the beating they were receiving.

Today, Colm Coyle started the game at right half-back, and Martin O'Connell was still left in the half-forward line where he didn't do very much. Marty just isn't happy there. Otherwise, everything seems to be looking rosy. Sean's not killing us in training, and the mood in the dressing-room is good. Two wins have seen to that. Now the thought of winning the National League seems more intriguing than it did just a month ago, when I wanted it to end. Then, I wanted the Championship to start. But Meath have not won the League since 1975, and if we keep playing like this we'll probably win the damn thing. It's a nice thought.

8 March
Mayo 0-6, Meath 0-3, National League

Awful! We were awful, and they were awful too. It was two points each at half-time, and I didn't think it was possible for our performance to slide any further. But it did.

The day had begun badly. It was decided to travel to Charlestown by coach. On the way down we talked and laughed, and Jinksy sang a couple of his old rugby songs. Two or three voices actually called for 'more!' We were bright and smiling widely, and happy with the world until the coach pulled up in Charlestown, outside a dull, old-fashioned guesthouse. The Meath County Board are not known for their extravagance. We had sandwiches and tea in a back room which looked like a large scullery. We were told we would be eating back there too, after the game.

When the game finally ended, most of the lads started drinking.

Half of us ate, and were back on the coach shortly before 7 pm. We waited on board for thirty minutes, but there was no sign of the rest of the lads emerging from the pubs. We were angry. We knew they were angry too. I wanted to get to hell home and forget about the entire afternoon. After forty-five minutes Gerry McEntee stormed off the bus and ran into the nearest pub. Most of the lads were there, Mick and Padraig Lyons, Liam Harnan, quite a large group around one table. Gerry Mc rushed in, and kicked the table over. But ten minutes later Gerry was sitting at the same table, which was now upright, with the same lads, drinking. I arrived in soon after, and had words with Mick.

'Don't you L...' he said, though I didn't hear exactly what else he said.

I replied in similar language, went back to the bus, and sat down, thicker than at any point earlier in the whole awful day.

We left Charlestown twenty minutes later. Most of the lads wanted to stop in Edgeworthstown on the way home, and we did. We remained in the village until closing time. A few of us went to a chipper to get something to eat. English wrestlers were advertised as playing in the local hotel. But the show was finishing up and the chipper was filling up. The coach was the quietest place to be, to think. We had still finished second in the division, but instead of playing Clare in the quarter-final, our defeat had landed us Galway instead. We have seldom played well against Galway, and even though they spent the winter in Division Three, they had spent their time winning every match they played.

11 March

We call him James and we call him 'Scubs'. Both names fall easily on his balding head, glasses and happy face. Scubs was standing over me as I changed into my clothes after the toughest training session of the season, and he was explaining why we lost to Mayo the way we did. It makes such utter sense, the way he looks at it. James has been 'driving' Meath players for over thirty years.

Scubs Whyte operates as a hackney driver for the team, but that's not why he lives amongst us. He loves the Meath team. He's a tall, dignified, upstanding citizen and he tells stories about Meath teams in the Sixties and Seventies which make my toes curl up with warmth and happiness.

The way Scubs tells them, they sound like stories about old uncles and grandfathers and cousins. I imagine, someday, he will be recounting funny little tales about the Meath team of the Eighties. The journey to Charlestown will probably be a priceless nugget in his repertoire.

17 March

Sean Boylan asked us to be at Dalgan Park for training this evening. We had been training in Pairc Tailteann in Navan, under the three spotlights attached to the roof of the stand and the street lights which peered over the galvanised fencing on the opposite side of the ground. But Sean wanted us to be at Dalgan for 8 pm which was fine. I was sitting in my car in the car-park, in absolute darkness, wondering what Boylan was up to now. There were no lights in Dalgan Park!

He told us to leave our bags in the dressing-room, and we walked down one of the long corridors of the seminary, behind him. He sat in the middle of the room on an upright wooden chair. I was sitting on the carpet to his right. We formed a semi-circle around him. His voice rose gradually for ten minutes, and then reached a plateau upon which he exclaimed 'I don't mind people shitting on me now and again, but when they start wiping their arses with me, WELL, LADS!' He was angry and emotional - normally, he excuses himself before or after using strong language - and slightly irrational. He didn't want to listen to anybody, that was clear, even though nobody around him was about to open his mouth anyway. He was quitting. That was the bottom line.

He thanked us for the years we had together, and wished us the best of luck in the future, and walked out the door.

I was stunned. Sean's entire speech had taken about fifteen minutes, and when he left there was silence. We were amazed. Things weren't that bad, were they? We had been doing well in the League, and training was being well attended, wasn't it? What was wrong with him? I know we weren't doing what he had been asking us to do on our own, and it probably showed, but he had said 'YOU'RE LEINSTER CHAMPIONS, but you're going to win nothing more. NOTHING!' The Charlestown experience hadn't been that devastating. We are due to play Galway in the League quarter-final in a few weeks. The season is still fresh. We have everything to win.

So why was I feeling guilty and apologetic, and why was the empty chair in the middle of the floor showing absolutely no mercy towards any of us? Everybody was feeling the same, because voices remained quiet, and sentences pulled themselves up short for the next twenty minutes.

We continued to talk.

Our conversation was circling, and footprints were deepening, and I decided to make a good confession. I admitted that I hadn't been doing very much training, practically none on my own and that I probably had been taking Sean for granted. I also said that it was obvious that nobody else was doing much either.

'Has anybody been doing what he's asked us to do?'

My question hung in the air, and drooped pathetically. A voice on the far side of the room said he had been doing everything Sean said.

'You have like fuck.' I replied.

I was getting angry too. There wasn't one other person who was prepared to make a good confession. Not one soul, NOT ONE OTHER SINNER.

Or, perhaps the silence which was being maintained was served up as a show of guilty hands. If so, that wasn't good enough. I didn't make much of a contribution to the remainder of the discussion, and although others in their own time, and in different ways voiced their guilt, I was still feeling pissed off with the lot of them. It was after 11 pm when we all left the room. Colm O'Rourke, it has been decided, will approach Boylan tomorrow, and tell him. Tell him what? I'm not sure. He's not going to say 'We're sorry, Sean.' But he'll talk to him, calmly and sensibly, and I presume he'll assure Sean that nobody ever had any intention of using him as toilet paper. I'm sure he'll convince him that nobody was consciously abusing him. I hope so.

Yeah, he will!

18 March

Great! I heard today that Colm Coyle has gone back to Chicago. That's all we needed! I had spoken to him on our way home from Charlestown. We had been sitting together and he hadn't said a word about emigrating.

2 April

This evening we were back in Dalgan Park, and this time we trained in poor light. Next Sunday we play Galway in Portlaoise, and we're looking forward to it. We owe Galway a beating, and there's no reason in the world why we shouldn't be able to win well, though nobody admits to that. We only think it. Boylan is aware that the Meath team builds a giant Achilles heel for itself whenever we underestimate another team. He prefers to put our backs firmly against a wall, and he has already started building that wall for next Sunday's game.

I fly out to Cardiff on Friday afternoon for the Five Nations Championship match against Wales the following afternoon. I'm due to fly home on Sunday morning. After the game on Saturday afternoon I will have just over an hour to get my thoughts together and write. I want to write well, and an hour is not much time. That's my immediate challenge this weekend. Galway is much bigger, but comes second, and I know I will not be able to concentrate my mind fully on the match until Saturday night over my meal, or maybe even Sunday morning.

4 April

Ireland beat Wales 15-11 in Cardiff Arms Park. The Crest Hotel, where I am staying, was chock-a-block with fans, though the dining room was quite empty, and I ate alone. Thinking about Galway, thinking about Mullin's and Dean's tries, and the richness of the entire day, despite the drenching rain and rising mud which made the game a lottery.

5 April

My morning call had me out of the bed before 8 am and I opened the curtains to see if it was still raining. My bedroom was facing the Arms Park, and on arrival on Friday afternoon I had stared out at the vast oval cement block for several minutes. It was my first time to view it. But, this morning, when I opened the curtains the Arms Park had vanished. I stared into a thick greyness, and couldn't make out one single feature of the stadium. I felt weak at the knees and began to get a little hot all over as I hurriedly got my bags together.

Boylan had suggested to me, early last week, that I get a flight home on Saturday night, in case of fog or some other delay. He thought I could fly out from Bristol or even Heathrow. I told him I would check it out, and I did, briefly, and found I would only be dashing away after the match and racing after trains and airplanes, and even at that, there was still a chance that I could end up in a hotel room in England. I would stay in Cardiff, I decided, but I didn't tell him that. I'm not sure if he would understand that while I am away I exist as a journalist, entirely, and I don't want anything to distract me from that. I can't be part journalist and part footballer. It's got to be one or the other. But this morning I was all footballer rushing in a taxi to Cardiff airport.

The National League quarter-final against Galway was still seven hours away. The fog had firmly squatted on the city, but there was time and hope. A fifty minute flight and a dash from Dublin to Portlaoise would take, what? Two hours? Two and a half hours, max. It was 10 am At 12.45 pm I phoned Sean, and in my panic with a dodgy public phone, I reversed the charges. Sean answered, and I spilled the beginnings of my plight to him. He then told me the game had been postponed because of rain.

I was relieved. He was surprised.

Our conversation quickly wrapped itself up.

12 April

Galway 1-8, Meath 0-9.

It wasn't just that we lost. We lost in Portlaoise, where we will have to return in less than two months to play Laois in the first round of the Leinster Championship. Two games in Portlaoise, and our season could be over by the middle of the summer! That's what I was thinking as I left the ground. One of those games had already been played, and now our season is left on a knife-edge. We were confident of winning, but we were also uptight. Players were fumbling the ball, and with the wind at our backs, passes were going too long. By the nineteenth minute we had two points and five wides. Galway had three points. I still felt good. I was marking Hugh Blehein, and he was strong under the ball, but I was timing my runs well and was catching the ball behind him. Bob O'Malley was also doing very well, and Liam Harnan was sound. In the ten minutes before half-time, our passing suddenly started to come together, and three and four passes were being strung the length of the field. The Galway defence was being pulled apart, and Flynn, McCabe, McEntee and Murtagh (two) had a succession of points to leave us 0-7 to 0-3 in front.

It looked like we had come to terms with them, or rather with the inhibition which always embraces us in Galway's company. I don't know what it was, but I think it was their confidence, their arrogance which has always amazed us in the past. Galway are a strong, physical team, with a hefty tradition at their backs, and they talk loudly on the field. They're probably the loudest team in the country, not at abusing the opposition, but encouraging each other. Their belief in their own ability is surprising, considering they have repeatedly failed to express themselves fully since losing the All-Ireland final in 1983.

Terry Ferguson had his first poor game in our defence, since making his debut two years ago, and in the first half Tomas Tierney gained a great deal of the ball throughout the field. Three minutes into the second half, Tierney had drifted in behind Ter and a superb pass from Val Daly left him with the ball in his hands, and McQuillan advancing. He struck the ball poorly, but it bounced against the far post and spun into the net. Tierney scored two more points after that, and although we held onto our lead until the final ten minutes, something in our gut told us that Galway were going to beat us again. By then, Joe Cassells had been brought on for his first game since the All-Ireland semi-final last August. Joe went full-forward. Mick Lyons, who was also having a bad day, was brought up to centre-forward. We were clawing at a result.

There will be no training on Tuesday, and that will feel weird. Boylan, Pat Reynolds and Tony Brennan have to select a fresh panel for the Championship, but we all know there are very few changes they can make. They can't doubt the team they have spent the last six months building, not now. They have to stick with it, although they will go through the motions of replacing two or three of the subs. They always do that. It's a largely cosmetic exercise, and a ruthless one. Players who have spent most of the winter and spring plonked on the substitutes' bench haven't done anything wrong, but if they haven't played out of their skin in matches on the training field then they are likely to be axed. From Boylan's point of view it's important to have fresh blood circulating through the squad.

After the League there is an immediate void, and then comes a whole clatter of challenge matches as the Championship comes into view. This is the time of year I dislike most, and I hate it even more when I'm playing well. I feel I'm about to pour good performances down the drain in an assortment of different football grounds. Clubs are going to be opening and blessing clubhouses and pitches for the next two months, when all I want, now that I'm possibly in the best form I'll hit this season, is for the Championship to begin. Who wants to wait around for two months, thinking about 14 June and Laois, and nothing else?

22 April

It looks like Martin O'Connell has quit the team for good. I'm surprised, and I'm not greatly surprised, if you know what I mean. I knew how unhappy Marty was. Three years ago he was one of the best half-backs in the country, but Sean, Pat and Tony, obviously have no intention of picking him in defence again. Marty is the most natural footballer on the team, and as a forward he can be good, but he's not happy there, and at a time when the selectors have been trying out several other players as half-backs, Marty's frustration is perfectly understandable. I haven't been able to say anything to him over the last couple of months, only listen to him.

Nobody said he has quit the panel, but he wasn't at training this evening, and the word is that he told the selectors he didn't want to play for Meath again unless it was in defence. He probably never said that himself, but his decision to opt out of the squad has spelled that message out in bold, black lettering. It's a shame, it really is. We can't afford to do without a player of Martin O'Connell's ability. That's two of our best players now lost! Both of them half-backs, born and bred. Martin's absence this evening left me disheartened, because he had spoken to me so often, and I hadn't said much to Sean, or to the two lads.

Most of this evening was spent up to our ankles in sand. Sean brought us training to Bettystown. We changed, and later ate in the Neptune Hotel, but Sean had a course marked out a couple of miles further down the beach, in Mornington. Himself and Mick Lyons, the captain (Sean is big into the captaincy thing this year, and every second team speech begins 'Mick and myself...') had walked over the dunes last night. I don't know how long it is around, and I'm not sure how many laps we did. He just told us to start running. One of those nights!

I'd guess it was seven or eight laps, and a total distance of about four miles. But, the sand is the killer, not the distance. It gobbles up the strength in the legs, and after a couple of laps O'Malley, Ferguson, and O'Rourke (I'm always amazed at his stamina, because he's the most awkward looking runner on the team) were leaving gaps at the front. First, O'Malley and Ferguson and Liam Smith, and then a second group led by O'Rourke which included McEntee. After them, there came one long stringy group, into which I had dropped after two full laps. I took to keeping pace with Cassells. Old Joe! But Old Joe is also a fine athlete, and I was happy to be ahead of him at the finish.

Distance running simply dilutes my will power. My back begins to feel like it will crack, my legs become heavy, and then my stomach starts to cave in. My lungs always feel good, but without the rest of my body, they don't get very far. Middle distance running I like. I'd fancy myself against anyone in the squad over 400 metres or 800 metres, and sprinting too is okay. I'm quite fast, and a lot faster than my long upright strides suggest. O'Rourke is very fast, though that's what I can't understand. He's got excellent stamina and magnificent speed, and I'd only put money on Beggy to beat him. Nobody else would.

24 April

A Friday night! We never train on Friday nights, Sean knows that, and it has always been one of the unwritten rules (a guarantee to wives and girlfriends) since he began five years ago. This is different, it seems. This is our third consecutive evening in Mornington, and on the dunes. Sean is like a little boy. He loves this, the sea, the water and the air and the mountainous dunes and he raced around in front of us and behind us playing peek-a-boo. We're lapping, and he's popping up on our right and disappearing. On the left, on top of a different dune the next time. Where's he gone now?

28 April

Tuesday! Last Sunday, Dublin beat Kerry in the National League final, and from a distance they seemed the two best teams in the country. I was in the Hogan Stand, and I couldn't dispute that view. It was a thrilling game of football, and Dublin's new midfielder Declan Bolger looked the most exciting player on the field. He has good hands, and he seems strong too. After the game, on my car radio, I listened to Mick O'Dwyer leaping overboard in the Dublin dressing-room.

O'Dwyer spoke deliriously about Dublin and Kerry and All-Ireland finals, and I too wondered (though I'm still certain that two or three of the Dublin forwards are lacking sufficient heart and stomach to carry them to an All-Ireland final). Not that I'm worried about Dublin. Laois are still sitting in the distance, and waiting for us.

We are still haunted by the ten points thrashing we received from Laois in the Leinster semi-final two years ago. Sean has made sure of that, and resurrects the smelling carcass of that performance any chance he gets. Last year, we expected to face the ghost of '85, but Laois were beaten by Wicklow in the first round and never entered our lives. This year we have to prove something to ourselves in their company.

But, tonight in Bettystown, as Boylan sent us off on a familiar path, we had O'Dwyer's words for company. It would be foolish to allow them to rub salt into our aching muscles. Instead, we try laughing at his vision, and that helps, especially when Gerry Mc reproduces O'Dwyer's speech, syllable by syllable.

29 April

After each session, Boylan demands ten minutes in the water. No one dares to venture beyond ankle depth for the first couple of minutes, as the icy water cuts through skin and pierces our bones. Sean bullies us further out, and further, until the water splashes against my hips and the pain fades away. Then we eat steak and chips in the Neptune, but nobody is talking about Laois. The Championship is still six weeks away, too far away, quietly throbbing in the distance.

30 April

Getting out of the car this evening, after arriving at the Neptune Hotel, Joe Cassells didn't realise that more than a dozen eyes were fixed upon him. He looked really old. That's what grabbed our attention. He swung his legs out of the car first, and then pulled the rest of his body out. In all, it took about four or five movements. This is our sixth session in nine days on the sand, and some of us are beginning to stiffen up far too much.

With a couple of laps under his belt, Joe began to increase his stride this evening, and I was struggling to keep pace with him. We were midway down the group, and Cass was moving in the right direction. I was just happy to cling to him. There was a wedding in the Neptune Hotel this evening, and we ate in Alfie's Cafe on the seafront, instead.

Bob was behind the bar helping Alfie serve up the chips and burgers.

It was the best meal we've had in years after training, and sitting on the sand, staring out at the water splashing contentedly in the darkness, Laois seemed a lot closer. And that felt good.

3 May
Meath 2-17, Offaly 2-11.

Today is Gerard's birthday. I trained with Skryne in the field this morning, and had the Meath game this evening. It was only a challenge match. Offaly led 1-6 to 0-4 at half-time, and they were holding nothing back. I can never understand that. Who wants to play the game of his life in a challenge match? Or worse still, who wants to play the game of his life, and risk that life and several of his limbs in the same challenge match? Shortly before half-time I collided with Dave Kavanagh in the middle of the field, and we had words, and the remainder of the game turned into a personal duel between us. Every ball in the air was being sought, as if it was the last ball to drop in a Leinster final. We both needed our heads screwed off, and filled with common sense.

It was a bad ending to an evening which had begun badly. We hadn't got fifteen players in our dressing-room, as Offaly went running out onto the field at 7.30 pm. Mickey McQuillan and Bob O'Malley had the 'flu, and I didn't want to hear where everybody else was, even if somebody was prepared to tell me.

We won quite easily in the end, and I should have been really pleased with my own performance. I would have been if I wasn't stuck in a quiet little field, tucked away in a strange parish, on a Sunday evening. There's a time and a place for playing brilliantly, and Ballinabrackey on 3 May wasn't it. There are two things you don't want in challenge matches. You don't want to play out of your skin, and you don't want to get injured. I suppose I shouldn't complain. John O'Sullivan, who replaced McQuillan in our goals, was knocked unconscious near the end of the game.

7 May

Gerry O'Reilly, home from Villanova for the summer, turned up at training tonight, with Sean. He shows up once or twice every year. The first time he appeared at a training session, McEntee asked 'Who's he?'

Boylan replied, 'Oh, he's a midfielder!'

Then Boylan sent us out onto the beach, with the International miler at the front of the pack. This evening, on the field in Dalgan, Gerry is totally at ease amongst us, but as footballers we are intimidated by his slim and tidy athleticism. As we struggle we become increasingly cumbersome and uncoordinated, and Boylan is immensely pleased.

He has four challenge matches awaiting us in the next two weeks. Thanks a lot, Sean! Cork, Donegal, Mayo and Armagh. Armagh will be the hardest, I know that. They'll fight and argue over every little ball, if I know them. Cork should be sensibly laid back, and Donegal and Mayo are unlikely to be looking for glory in challenge matches, are they? I doubt it. They are good games, to have, I suppose. But two of them would be more than enough. If we win two of them, say we beat Cork and Mayo, then everybody should be happy that we are progressing nicely towards 14 June.

12 May

Once again, the County Board are trying to squeeze in club championship games here, there and everywhere, leaving Boylan in a spin as he tries to keep track of his entire squad. Tonight, there were only fourteen of the panel of twenty-four on the field. It was impossible to gain anything from the session with those numbers. It meant Sean couldn't have much ball work, and it meant the rest of us were left dangerously close to empty on enthusiasm.

31 May
Mayo 1-15, Meath 1-5.

We beat Cork last weekend, and Donegal yesterday. The mood of the squad is good, and significantly, Boylan seems more relaxed than he has been in a long time. He gets uptight at this time of year, and is difficult to talk to. He's happy to talk, but at the same time seems weighed down. At times like this, it's incredible to see how much he's changed. He's serious, businesslike. There's still a boyish touch to everything he does, and he's still conscious of treating everyone around him with the utmost respect, and he can often be found tip-toeing on the feelings of others, but Sean has become hugely stubborn. Once a player is labelled in his mind, neither God nor man will get him to think twice. Marty O'Connell was proof of that, but we're all included, we all bear his labels. I'm aware of that. So, too is Bob O'Malley who knows Sean looks at him more than any other defender. Two of the younger players on the panel, Des Lane and Mickey McDonnell played today, but it's obvious that Boylan is uncertain about both of them. Des is a tight-marking half-back, but he looks sluggish in his actions. If Des Lane is labelled as being sluggish he may never play regularly for Meath. Whereas, Mickey, for all his strength and his magnificent hands, sometimes looks confused when he gains possession. He also seems a little slow in his reactions. Mickey McDonnell has everything a young man requires on the football field, but I can see that Boylan doubts him too. I think he has already been labelled.

Barry Ferguson is also new on the panel. He's Terry's younger brother, and Boylan sees something in him which is not perfectly visible to the rest of us. Barry's a good young footballer, but he's inexperienced, and he still has an awful lot to learn. He has been getting lots of opportunities lately, and Sean has obviously brought him to the front of the queue on the substitutes' bench. He played right half-back this afternoon, and did quite well. He looks good on the ball especially, and he's also nimble on his feet. But he needs to be, because he's not physically strong enough at the moment.

Yesterday was not a good day. We beat Donegal, but Mattie McCabe was punched in the face off the ball, midway through the second half, and seemingly his cheekbone is fractured. It's just Mattie's luck. He's been in great form these past few weeks, and has looked perfectly comfortable on the side. I had to work yesterday, so I got the report on Mattie second-hand. The team stayed over in Mayo last night, and I drove to Kilmaine with Joe Cassells and Frankie Byrne this mornmg.

Joe was just closing the front door behind him when we arrived at his house in Navan, and he held one of his sons by either hand. They were going to 11 am Mass together. Joe had promised them, and he told us he'd be back in half an hour. I told him we hadn't time, we had to go! The two boys were brought back inside. Joe wasn't happy.

'You'll know all about it someday, don't worry about that,' he told me.

I still had no sympathy for him. He felt like a dog for letting the kids down, but he shouldn't have told them he'd bring them to Mass in the first place. I was still grinning at him. His two boys were staring out the front window at him.

'Don't worry,' he said, 'You'll find out what it's fucking like too Hayes.'

We met up with the team in the parochial hall in Kilmaine. Most of the lads were quiet. The County Board had agreed with the local club that the players could stay with different families on the Saturday night. Scubs Whyte and the lads in his car, Mickey McQuillan, Bob O'Malley and Bernie Flynn, sensibly booked themselves into a hotel in the nearest town instead. The other players were so annoyed at the sleeping arrangements that some of them decided to drink long and late into the night. One group of Meath players went to a disco, and in the early hours of a rainy morning a Garda squad car came across a bunch of footballers on a country road, and gave them a lift home.

It was that sort of night and everybody was quiet this morning. Boylan was quiet too, but as I arrived at the parish hall, and met up with him, I still didn't understand why. He had us on the field, warming up, for almost thirty minutes before the game started, and with Beggy scoring a goal we deserved to be level with them (1-4 to 0-7) at half-time. I was playing well in the middle of the field, and Joe was excellent at centre-back, but then we had an advantage over the rest of the lads. We had slept the previous night, and had only travelled one hundred miles to the game that morning!

In the second half, surprise, surprise, Mayo scored 1-8 without reply and guess what? For most of the half Denis Kearney had been holding me and pulling me, and I struck back with my fist ten minutes from the end. I struck him on the side of the head, and was booked. I told the referee why, but he didn't say anything. The kickout was taken. I fielded the ball, and as I landed I was punched in the face. Kearney was sent off. I had to leave the field too, and in the dressing-room Jack Finn, our doctor, put four stitches in a cut over my eye.

I was sitting there, stitched, and feeling pissed off with life when the rest of the team came in. There is still one more challenge match left, against Armagh next week. But so far, we have learned nothing much in three matches, and we've lost Mattie.

4 June
Armagh 1-11, Meath 0-13.

It didn't matter that we lost tonight, because we played well. It was probably our best performance of the four challenge matches we have played these past three weeks. We should have won too. They scored their goal in injury time, when Joe Kernan fisted a hopeful lob high to McQuillan's right. That didn't matter. We showed a lot more understanding, and we passed the ball well out of defence and from midfield. We were leading, 0-7 to 0-3, at half-time. PJ Gillic was as sharp as I've ever seen him. He scored seven points from the left corner-forward position, which is not his favourite place to be. As well as that Padraig Lyons played his first game in weeks after being out injured with a broken thumb. He played well.

We needed this performance, because on Tuesday night we learned that Summerhill, Trim, Moynalvey, Nobber, Kells, Kilmainhamwood and St Colmcille's were all playing championship games. A total of eleven players were missing from the training session in Dalgan Park, and the evening was perfectly demoralising.

9 June

The team to play Laois was announced at the beginning of training. The big surprise is that Barry Ferguson has been picked at right half-back. He's eighteen years old. Sean obviously believes he's ready. I don't. I think he needs about two years on the bench first. Des Lane is picked at left full-back, which is also a surprise, even though he has been playing better than anybody else in the defence these last few weeks. I didn't think Sean trusted Des. Besides, Padraig Lyons had reported in, fit and well again, just in the nick of time. Later in the evening, in a practice game Padraig pulled wildly on the ball and tore ligaments in his leg. It looks like he's done a lot of damage.

14 June

Meath 1-11, Laois 2-5, Leinster Championship

In the first minute of the game Gerry Browne sent a long pass from the middle of the field down the left wing of our defence. It had to be a goal! From the throw-up Laois had moved Noel Roe out to the middle of the field as a third man, and the entire left wing of our defence was inhabited by just two people. Two people with a public park all to themselves! Barry Ferguson and Tom Prendergast! Barry is still a boy, and Prendergast has for many years been one of the fastest and cleverest forwards in the country. When Gerry Browne's pass floated over Barry Ferguson's head, Prendergast had already drifted twenty yards inside him. He had just McQuillan to beat. Mickey sprinted out of his goals, and Prendergast tried to chip the ball over his head. It was a point, thankfully. Sean immediately switched Bob onto Prendergast, and Barry Ferguson was sent to follow Roe around the middle of the field. We were lucky, and we remained in that state. In the fifteenth minute Liam Irwin scored from the penalty spot, and they led 1-2 to 0-3. They were on top of us, and although we clawed our way back into the game, we kicked five wides between the twenty-first and twenty-sixth minutes. Colm O'Rourke claimed four of them.

We were nervous and uptight, and in the dressing-room at half-time too many players wanted to speak. Sean, as usual, remained outside the door for a couple of minutes, talking with Tony Brennan and Pat Reynolds. Inside, Colm, Joe and Gerry were all talking. But we needed silence, we needed to calm ourselves. Too many people were talking.

'Why doesn't everybody just shut up', I roared.

The talking continued. We had been waiting for this match for two years, and now that it had arrived, we seemed scared of it. Or, scared of losing to them, again. That thought had left us numb for most of the first half, and although we managed to ease away from them ever so slowly in the second half, the teams were level (1-7 to 2-4) with twelve minutes remaining. A Colm Browne centre from forty-five metres had bounced, somehow, over Mickey McQuillan's left shoulder. He had been waiting for a defender to clear it. A defender should have caught it. But, the entire defence had been waiting for Mickey to claim it.

Then it happened. We began to play. One minute later, Staff played a one-two with Bernie and put us back in the lead. I fielded the kick-out, and passed to Bernie, and he scored. Joe Cassells punched a point. Jinksy took on Colm Browne and for the first time all afternoon got by him and scored from a difficult angle on the right wing. Four points in seven minutes, though in the same seven minutes Colm O'Rourke damaged ligaments in his shoulder and had to be substituted. He joined Kevin Foley, who had also fallen awkwardly on his shoulder, on the line.

Also on the sideline this afternoon was Martin O'Connell. He was asked back into the squad, and was happy to accept. With Barry Ferguson substituted, and his replacement on the half-back line, Kevin Foley being injured, Marty should return instantly to the side.

We play Kildare in Tullamore in two weeks. Marty should be back on familiar defensive turf.

This evening was strange. We had a few drinks with some of the Laois players in the Killeshin Hotel, and they didn't look devastated. They didn't look shocked by their failure. I had imagined they would be. I wished them to be, in a way, because if I was in their shoes tonight I would feel crushed. Didn't they realise that 14 June was destined to be the final date on a headstone for one football team, Laois or Meath? And that the gods were unlikely to be choosy!

When they beat us two years ago I had left Anne back to her house in Dublin around midnight. I was going to stay the night, but I didn't want to talk, eat or sleep. I didn't know what to do. At 1 am I told her I was going to drive home to Skryne instead. Driving through Finglas and into the countryside, I stopped the car, and sat there. I turned around, and went back to Anne's house. I told her I didn't want to see anybody, or be with anybody, and I think she understood. That was only two years ago. This evening the Laois players had been drinking in our company, and they were even managing to smile.

28 June
Meath 0-15, Kildare 0-9, Leinster Championship

We played well, and Kildare played fairly well, but beneath the team's nose these last few months Brian Stafford has blossomed as a rock solid free-taker. He scored ten points this afternoon, from frees and from play. Last year I had been taking the frees, and when Staff was handed the job in October it never occurred to me that he would be equal to Rock or Sheehy or anyone else in the country, within months. Whenever the tiniest hint of a score presented itself, Staff pierced the heart of the Kildare defence and there was nothing they could do about it. We were scoring with every second attack. They were scoring every third or fourth try, and they could have continued playing fairly well until nightfall and they would not have won. It was mathematically impossible, and it's a good feeling to have the power of maths on our side for the first time in our lives.

We were also understrength, but that also made no appreciable difference. Frank Foley came into the team at right half-back, and Martin O'Connell took Colm O'Rourke's No. 13 jersey. Again, Marty was in the furthest corner from our defence, but, once more, he seemed content to be back on the team, though, God knows there's no chance of him ever being picked in his old and familiar position, at left half-back.

14 July

The weeks before a Leinster final are always the toughest weeks of the year. Dublin are sitting in front of us and they resemble a mountain which has to be climbed. If we get over them, then, the whole of the All-Ireland will open itself up in front of our eyes, and the mood in the dressing-room will suddenly lift. Right now, everything is serious, everyone is businesslike. This evening I felt heavy, my legs were leaden, and by the time I finished the opening two laps which are supposed to loosen us up, I was absolutely knackered.

Everyone was breathing heavily, and gasping. Yet, we're in great shape, there's no doubt about that, it's just that everything we did on the field this evening seemed a chore. I don't know why, but I know we're not relaxed. The tension and the doubts and the wondering, they're all draining. Yet, last year, the days leading up to the final weren't as bad, and perhaps the atmosphere in training will be that much lighter next week.

The thought of losing to them makes me want to curl up into a ball and roll away. I'm scared of losing to them, I'm sick at the thought of having to read about them in the newspapers before the All-Ireland semi-final and the All-Ireland final, about McNally and Duff and Rock - especially McNally. He represents everything I dislike about the Dublin team, and yet I don't know him from Adam. He could be one of the nicest fellas you could meet, but from where I'm standing he is large and blue and good when he gets the ball. He's smart but I don't think he's as good as people imagine. But he's confident and cocky. That's Dublin for you too! Losing to them would be like losing your home to your worst enemy, or worse than that.

They're on my mind all the time, and they were tonight, until Sean and myself had a stupid argument. Last week, about one hundred people were turning up to watch us train. This evening there were just six or seven cars facing onto the field, and there was nobody standing around. Sean had told us at the beginning of the session that a funeral would be passing through the grounds at some stage, and that he wanted everything to stop when it appeared.

When the cortege did creep into view from behind the great oak trees, Boylan immediately had us form a guard of honour, of sorts. We formed two straight lines on the field. After that, he was still uptight. He was shouting twice as much as he did last week, which I suppose he had to do in the rain, but he was also demanding that everything be done twice as fast as it had been done last week.

'I'M GOING TO TELL YOU EVERYTHING ONCE, AND LET'S DO IT. I DON'T WANT TO TELL YOU TWICE.'

I don't know whether he simply wanted to get in out of the rain, or whether he just had a bad day. Maybe both. We were doing the usual things with the ball for the first twenty or thirty minutes (Sean tries always to have the ball involved in everything he does on the training field, and it's a good idea. It keeps everyone thinking, and it helps to avoid boredom), and then he divided us up into six groups of four on one sideline. I knew what he was going to do, and I hate it!

He placed six balls on the ground ten yards in from the sideline, and in pairs at the sound of his whistle we had to sprint out and get them. One on one. Whoever got to the ball first, and wasn't rammed into the ground by his opponent as he tried to pick the ball up, had to bring the ball back to the sideline, hopping and soloing. His opponent was a defender. And if his opponent dispossessed him, then, they changed roles. Either way, someone had to get the ball back to the sideline. It's a grinding and tiring exercise, and everyone hates it, and I knew Sean had it in mind. Before he said anything I started taking the top of my wet suit off, pulling it over my shoulders. I ran over to Padraig Lyons, who was injured and hunched under an umbrella beside one of the balls. Padraig said something to me and I answered him, as Sean started giving instructions.

I'd missed what he said.

'What's that?' I shouted.

He was furious.

'What did I say? I want everything done fast, I'm not going to say everything twice.'

I was wet and tired and innocent (I was taking a top off) and before I knew it, I had said it.

'I DIDN'T FUCKING HEAR YOU!'

Everyone else was silent, the bastards, happy with the breather and the bit of entertainment. They watched Sean marching over to me. I couldn't believe it. He took off the whistle which had been hanging around his neck on a piece of string, and he threw the damn thing at my feet.

'Okay! You want to take charge. YOU TAKE CHARGE!'

'Jesus, don't do that,' I replied.

He was already walking away in a huff.

'I didn't hear you,' I added.

I had my hands on my hips, and I was still soaked right through and I felt like an idiot. I took the whistle up and walked over to Sean and handed it back to him. That made me feel a total idiot. I don't know what Sean felt. He was still fuming. It was still raining. Everybody else was dying to start laughing, though they saved it for afterwards, for the two of us.

'How's it goin' coach?' asked Bob as he passed by me towards the showers.

Rourkey also had to say something, 'If you weren't so thick and you'd any sense, you'd have taken the fucking whistle.'

And he also had words for Boylan, 'I wouldn't take that from these young lads Sean.'

When Colm's around you don't need friends or enemies. He can do fine. Boylan wasn't saying anything much, not to me, and I didn't say anything to him. When we speak on the phone tomorrow we'll sound like two long lost cousins. We always do after arguments.

26 Julys
Meath 1-13, Dublin 0-12, Leinster Championship final

Hallelujah, brothers! Marty O'Connell was chosen to play at left half-back. Naturally, he played well there too, and presumably that's where he will remain. He did more then well, he was magnificent. I'm delighted for him, and I'm sure Sean, Tony and Pat are too. God only knows what they have been thinking about these past two years. The job of a selector is always a tough one, I know, but the casebook on Marty should now be torn up into tiny little pieces. In bringing Marty back into defence, however, somebody else had to suffer, and Des Lane was nudged off the team. Des was really good against Laois and Kildare and didn't deserve to be dropped. There was nothing I could say to him. He was wronged by being dropped. Who'd want to be a selector? I wouldn't, and I have no idea what Sean actually said to Des.

The best Meath team was sent out, and we won, didn't we? There was a period at the close of the first half when we seemed to freeze up in their company, just like the old days. We got off to a great start, and we led 1-5 to 0-2 midway through the half. Mattie McCabe got the goal, a typical Mattie goal. He glided through a herd of players, grabbed the ball which was bouncing underneath approximately eleven noses, and side-footed it ever so gently along the ground by O'Leary. We were in total control, and then, I don't know what the hell happened. We started watching them, I think, and we ended up admiring them. They were leading 0-9 to 1-5 at half-time.

It was like the old days. They were playing into the Hill 16 end, and they were so bloody excited. They looked brilliant. At half-time Sean must have revived us. We definitely awoke, and the second half was easy. I was marking McNally in the middle of the field, and Gerry Mc was concentrating on Declan Bolger. McNally got a couple of points, and caught one ball over my head, which he held up in front of my face after I fouled him. We were breaking the ball down most of the time in the first half, and in the second we started to catch the ball. Gerry had heard so much about Bolger, that he took immense satisfaction from distracting him and beating him to the ball and talking to him.

'They're all looking at you Dec, you've got to catch the next ball. Jesus

Dec! You didn't get it!'

Gerry likes to talk on the field, and if his opponent starts into a conversation with him Gerry knows he's winning.

'They'll take you off soon Dec.'

I don't like to talk. Few players do. It distracts me.

I was also enjoying playing on McNally and considering he was our acknowledged 'public enemy No. 1' on the Dublin team, I also found it a novelty. He was talking at me all through. Twice I called him a 'fat fucker', but I couldn't make out what he was saying. He beat me for a couple of balls which I had contested side by side with him, and he was also faster than I had imagined. But in the second half I seldom saw him. I was roaming the field and picking up a lot of loose ball, and he never seemed to be near me. By then we had calmed ourselves again, and were slowly building up a respectable lead. In the last ten minutes they seemed to have accepted their fate, and their spirit had been quenched, even though there was still only three points between the teams. Mattie scored our last point to round off a brilliant personal display, and another surprising hero was Fino Murtagh. He replaced Jinksy seventeen minutes into the second half, and typically ice-cool, he had slotted over two points at a time when we were trying to ease ourselves away from Dublin.

The game had started with a bang, as I gained possession from the throw in and raced at the Dublin defence. Eamonn Heery committed himself, and I fisted the ball over his head towards Staff. Heery kept coming, and knocked me to the ground with a punch on the face. I was dazed. Heery was booked.

A Dublin voice said: 'You'll get the fuckin' same when you get up.'

Obviously Dublin had decided to deliver an early message to me if I tried to race through the middle of their defence. I took it, but more as a compliment really.

It was the first blow. The second time blows were struck I was already on the ground. Bolger and myself had both raced for a low kickout in the middle of the field. I didn't see him. I didn't know what hit me. I was rolled up on the ground and I couldn't breathe. I was begging for air, and was rolling myself tighter and tighter. I began to panic, and then I heard Doc Finn above me. He rolled me onto my side, and in the distance I could see a group of people around a Dublin player. When I finally got to my feet Bolger was still being treated. To my right, underneath the Hogan Stand a group of players were being prised apart. The referee was sending off Kevin Foley and Charlie Redmond, and I asked Marty what had happened. He told me there'd been a fight (seemingly play hadn't been stopped by the referee when Bolger and I collided). I also had to ask Marty the score, and didn't manage to clear my head until half-time when I put it under a tap of cold water in the dressing-room. I was okay, but Bolger didn't reappear for the second half. He's been the most exciting new player of the season, but the season is over for him now.

I wonder how he feels tonight. I wonder how McNally feels, and the other Dublin players. Somehow I don't imagine them feeling as bad as I know I would feel. I think we dislike them more than they do us. Marginally, but there is a difference. We've beaten them in two Leinster finals in succession, and I'm sure that when next we meet they will have changed. They're probably starting to hate us this evening.

Few of the lads arrived back in Ashbourne House for the team meal this evening. Less than half the team actually ate together. I left the place shortly after 9 pm. By then most of the lads had drifted out from the Dublin pubs.

This evening was precious, and I knew that if I remained in Ashbourne I would have been talking to people, and mostly listening to people, and suddenly, the night would be over, and I would wake up tomorrow morning and it would be too late. The day would be over, and Monday would simply exist as the day after one of the most satisfying days of my life. I didn't want that.

2 August

In the early hours of this morning, driving home from Killarney, the thought of winning the All-Ireland flipped from the bottom drawer of my consciousness into a higher drawer. Cork have beaten Kerry in the Munster final, after a replay, and while the Gaelic world is now rid of Kerry and feels free again, the sight of Cork totally outplaying them is worrying. Cork looked brilliant, and Larry Tompkins looks so much at home in the centre of their attack. It's just three months since he returned from New York and we chatted. He told me then that he hoped to play for Cork this season.

That hope had taken root, and late this afternoon Tompkins and Niall Cahalane embraced each other and danced around in a circle like two little boys who had been promised a day at the seaside, boys who had been friends all their lives. It's worrying. And when I met Ger Lynch outside the ground, and he told me that the All-Ireland was now ours, I genuinely found difficulty accepting his words. It wasn't just out of respect for him, and his team mates.

'It's yours now, there's nothing to stop ye,' Ger had insisted.

15 August

Colm Coyle is coming home, I believe. He wasn't able to get to our training this morning because storms or flooding or something prevented him from flying out of Chicago in time. There will be no welcome home party for him. I don't feel angry with him, not anymore, but neither do I feel that he deserves a handshake or a slap on the back or a hug. However, we still need him around, and it's good that he's coming home. Knowing Coyler, he wouldn't want us to pay him too much attention. Nor does he need to be made feel welcome. He's been a member of the team as long as I have, almost, and he has every right to be amongst us now with an All-Ireland final within sight.

I know nothing about Derry, who we meet in the semi-final next week. We've watched a few video tapes of their Ulster Championship games, and they look fast. Dermot McNicholl and Enda Gormley are dangerous, and in the middle of the field they've Brian McGilligan and Plunkett Murphy. I've been told they work together in the building trade. They're both tall and strong, and Colm O'Rourke has spoken quite a bit about McGilligan with whom he toured in Australia last year.

'He's as strong as a horse, so be careful,' he told Gerry and myself at a team meeting.

It made Gerry mad, and it made me laugh. McGilligan may be strong, but we've heard stories from Australia before, and the way they're told they smack of 'Ah, they don't make men nowadays like they did in Australia in '86'. Gerry Mc says it's bullshit, and obviously I agree with him. We've been playing together for six years, and the last thing we need is advice sounding like Rourkey telling us to be careful crossing the road.

23 August

Meath 0-15, Derry 0-8, All-Ireland semi-final

PJ Gillic was the only Meath forward not to score this afternoon. He hasn't scored in any of our four championship games, and it's easy to take him for granted. After the game he sat back in the dressing-room, his face covered in the same satisfaction as everyone else's - we've reached the All-Ireland final. And, it's a strange feeling. I can't tell you exactly what it's like, but I feel as if I have been pushed onto the set of a movie. We're all suddenly playing a part in this great big movie. It doesn't seem for real.

WE'RE IN THE ALL-IRELAND FINAL.

PJ has every right to be happy, although he has received the minimum amount of credit for what has happened this season. Because his name hasn't appeared on any score sheets people conclude that he's only filling in space on the forward line or that he's the best of what's left on the squad but can't score. It's not true. There are better forwards than PJ on the panel. There's Mattie McCabe and Liam Smith and one or two others. But PJ is not only a forward, he's something more, and this afternoon he took a giant's share of possession around the middle of the field and fed the forwards around him with a silver spoon (which doubles as his right foot). PJ Gillic can kick the ball longer and harder and more accurately than any other person on the team. His ability is unique, and it would be a waste to use him merely as a forward.

It's a pity that people don't appreciate him, and it's a pity that he feels their eyes on him and is only dying to score a point. He could have scored today, but he remained unselfish to the end. We led 0-8 to 0-4 at half-time, which left us worried in our dressing-room considering that we had dominated the middle of the field. We sat around and drank the heavily-sugared tea and the bottled water, and nobody said anything. Sean had told us to relax, even though nobody can relax at half-time. You walk back into the same dressing-room which you had occupied forty minutes earlier and you sit down on the same part of the wooden bench. You can't relax. Your work is only half done. The faces around you, each of which had been identical in their concentration and determination when you left the dressing-room earlier in the afternoon, are now different. Some expressions are pained, some are calmer than others, and some are still tensed, and everybody's eyes are searching around them for confirmation that we are going to win the match.

Aren't we?

The first couple of balls which were up for grabs in the middle of the field waited for us to take them. Plunkett Murphy waited too, in line behind me, it seemed. After ten minutes the thought crossed my mind that this was going to be easy.

'THIS IS GOING TO BE EASY'

I couldn't do a thing after that, and although I scored our first point of the second half I ended up giving my worst performance of the season. But then, I suppose not that many of us played well. PJ, Marty, Staff, Bernie, and Cass, and that was about it. And here we are in an All-Ireland final.

27 August

The lawns of the Columban Fathers in Dalgan Park were no longer recognisable this evening. They were overrun by supporters, elderly men, couples in love, mothers and their children and teenagers in leather, and all of them were overjoyed with life, with the freshness of life. Meath haven't been in an All-Ireland final since 1970. I remember sitting amongst adult legs watching the television, watching Meath lose to Kerry, and watching out for my Uncle Denis who somehow had managed to get onto the sideline at Meath's matches.

'There he is, there, THERE, SEE HIM.'

And there was Uncle Denis, squatting up against the wire close to the fifty yard line. We were amazed to see him, there, so close, being able to touch the team, sit in their dressing-room, and talk to the players.

The Meath team, in my eyes, were no less heroic than the Brazilian team which won the World Cup in Mexico City that same summer. They were equally distant, and certainly untouchable. I marvelled at how my Uncle Denis could walk amongst them. This evening, there were little girls and boys shouting and squealing for my autograph at the end of our training session, as I crossed the same lawns I have been crossing for several months now. They wanted the names written on pieces of paper and t-shirts and forearms, and they wanted us to pose for photographs. It took ten minutes to travel the 200 yards to the dressing-rooms, and I was beginning to chill, and my sweaty jersey felt damp and sticky. The kids got everything they wanted, and I was happy for them. It's important. Was it like this in the old days, in August of 1970?

Aidan Keating was there this evening too. I wondered what he must be thinking, watching all the other boys and girls running around, laughing and shouting, playing football on the lawns. Frank, his father, took him home just as the training session had ended and the kids started to cluster around us. Aidan and Frank Keating didn't need to wait around. They both know us now, and we know them. Frank stopped his car in front of me as I left the field, just to say goodnight. He doesn't need to say hello.

Aidan is dying, Frank has told me that. He is wheelchair bound with a crippling ailment I do not even know the name of. I said hello to Frank, and stooped down and looked over and said hello to Aidan who was in the passenger seat, half reclined, his body covered with his woollen blanket, and his head of red hair rigid. He glanced sideways at me and gestured. I said I'd see them on Tuesday, at our next session.

Supporters started turning up at our training sessions in the weeks leading into the Leinster final. July was wet, and often cold, and their numbers were small to begin with. After that the numbers began to double and treble with each passing week. Aidan and Frank were here in Dalgan Park, alone, in early summer. It was damp and grey then, and Frank made sure that Aidan remained in the car. Some nights they would come and go and we would barely see them. It's always good to see them.

30 August

Cork eased themselves past Galway in the All-Ireland semi-final. They won 0-18 to 1-4 and Larry Tompkins looked irrepressible. He spent most of the game around the centre of the field picking up passes and running at the Galway defence, and through it. He scored eleven points. Anthony Davis and Tony Nation also looked brilliant. They constantly attack from their own defence. I wonder what they're like when they are pinned back in that defence?

I watched the game from the Nally Stand, which is not the best viewing point in the ground. There were Galway supporters directly in front of me, and Cork people somewhere behind me. Midway through the first half they started arguing, and even at that stage it was obvious that the Galway man and his son should keep quiet. They'd nothing to shout about, but the more Cork went in front the more abuse they threw back over their shoulders. They didn't notice me. They didn't know me, thankfully, but I wished they'd shut up because they were a noisy distraction. Early in the second half the Galway folk resorted to dismissing the entire Championship.

'Yer no fucking good, and neither are Meath. Two of the worst teams ever played in an All-Ireland!'

I left before the end of the game. I'd seen more than enough anyhow. Shay Fahy and Teddy McCarthy also looked good. McCarthy's fielding is incredible, and if he's gets any sort of short run up to the catch he'll be difficult to stop. Fahy is the more solid of the two. I know Shay well enough, and I think I know that he's very one-paced. He does everything well, but in his own time. We first played against each other in the Leinster minor final in 1980, and Tompkins was also playing for Kildare that day. We won by three points, and I missed two penalties, one in each half. We've played against each other a lot and I'm sure we'll be marking each other in the All-Ireland final, because Gerry Mc's going to insist on marking McCarthy. He'll see him as the biggest threat. Gerry always chooses who he wants to mark, that's the way it's always been, and that suits me. The bigger the challenge, the taller the mountain, the more excited and determined he becomes.

It'll be a risk, I know, because if McCarthy gets running at the ball Gerry is unlikely to beat him in the air. I'd fancy myself against McCarthy, but if Gerry wants him he'll have him. I know what he'll try to do, he'll work so hard around the field that he'll drive McCarthy to distraction, and he'll try to tangle with him at every kick-out. That's what Gerry does best. He tangles with his opponent, and at the same time manages to keep his concentration on the ball. He does it brilliantly.

31 August

Because of the training and the build-up, I worked today, Monday. Normally it's my day off, but I wanted to talk to Cyril Farrell about the All-Ireland Hurling final. And the journey down to Woodford and home was certainly going to take up most of the day. Cyril's home, where he lives with his mother, looks down upon the village. We talked, and he was quite uncomfortable when I took my notebook out and threw some formal questions at him. I stopped after ten minutes and put my pen and paper away, and we chatted about Galway, Meath and Kilkenny for most of the afternoon.

Galway have lost the 1985 and '86 All-Ireland Hurling finals, and Cyril knows that if they lose again his team will exist as an historical curiosity, and nothing more. It doesn't bear thinking about for him. He told me that on the Monday evening after the last two All-Ireland finals he walked up the road from the village, and every step he took was being viewed. He felt the eyes of the entire village, each neighbour and every Galwayman, on his back.

3 September

There were two coaches full of kids at training this evening, and there must have been about 400 or 500 people standing around, mostly silent. It's weird, and suddenly the bumpy little field in Dalgan Park is no longer a penitentiary, or a private place of learning. Boylan doesn't seem to mind this sort of thing. It excites and inflates the little boy inside him. He's in great form. He has told us to concentrate on what we're doing and not to mind the people. They're just people, he says.

Larry Tompkins was just another player, although another very good player, when he played for Kildare. Not too many people gave him the credit he possibly deserved because Kildare were never around long enough in the Championship to attract a great deal of attention. When Tompkins went to New York, where he played for two years for the Donegal club, nobody seemed to miss him. Now he's back just three months and everybody is talking about him. He has captured the imagination of the entire country, but I still think he's the same player I've known for the last eight years.

His free-taking is superb, it always was, and if anything, he's even more accurate now. He's probably practising a lot more, and he's getting more games than ever before, so he probably has improved. But Larry is still Larry. We've played against him too many times to think of him as anything else. Anytime anyone is fouled in training, in match-type situations, the guilty party is christened 'Larry.' Throughout the field this evening lads were shouting 'Well done, Larry!' to make sure that we all get the message. Any free given away to Cork within fifty yards of our goals will be as good as chalking up another point for Larry Tompkins. Twice, I was called 'Larry' this evening.

6 September

Galway won the All-Ireland Hurling final. Good! I stayed at home and watched it, although I had a ticket for the game. We had a trial match tonight in Walterstown and I wanted to rest up for it. An afternoon in Croke Park would have left me deadbeat. I'm delighted for Cyril, and I know that he'll be watching us for the next two weeks.

10 September

It was crazy tonight. It was like a bloody circus. There were people everywhere, inside and outside the low wire which surrounds the field. It's taking longer and longer to get to the dressing-rooms after training. I don't want to walk through herds of kids and their parents who are looking for autographs and photos, nor do I want to get another cold. I'm just feeling better now, and my chest is clearing. Still, it must have taken me about twenty minutes to get to the changing-rooms. Staff and Mattie were the only two behind me. I'm worried. We don't seem to have done anything in training in the last week, and the circus ring is getting bigger and bigger.

12 September

We trained at 10.30 am. It was warm and humid, and difficult working up a sweat at that hour of the morning. It's the same every Saturday morning. Everyone feels stiff, and everyone looks lazy and it took about thirty minutes before the session got up and running properly. Sean had a trial match, and nobody was holding anything back. That's what Sean wanted. It was perfectly acceptable. He wanted us to think and play in exactly the way we will approach the game tomorrow week.

Ten minutes from the end Liam Harnan, who'd been throwing himself about too much and taking too much satisfaction from it as far as I was concerned, came running up field with the ball. I went to tackle him, and I didn't expect him to kick the ball. He did. I continued with the shoulder charge and I meant to hit him hard. I didn't think he was completely off balance.

He fell to the ground. He didn't get back up. Sean and Gerry and Doc Finn and Anne Bourton were quickly around him. I stood there too. Nobody was saying anything, and everybody else on the field stayed where they were, sitting down, talking, bending and exercising. I stood there, and felt an absolute fool, a thick country fool. Harnan had fallen on the point of his right shoulder, it seemed, and he was taken off the field. The match continued for a few minutes, and then Sean ended it. Rourkey said something nicely insulting to me in the dressing-room, to make me feel better.

'Y'know you're a horse of a man Hayes. Who're you going to kill next week?'

And I did feel marginally better. But I also felt like apologising to every man in the room. I didn't. I didn't say anything to Harnan either. What could I say? I don't know whether he'll be okay for the All-Ireland, but I doubt it. Shoulder injuries are normally long-term, and even if he does improve, Harnan's performances are based on solid tackling. He plays a totally physical game, and anything less might leave him much less a player.

15 September

This evening was better. The craziness was mopped up. The supporters were still around, probably a thousand or more, but we noticed them less. The session was lively and fast, and I felt a lot better for it.

Harnan didn't train. He sat on a bench on the sideline, and a radio reporter sat down beside him and asked him if he knew if Liam Harnan was about? Harnan told her he hadn't seen him all week. He seems relaxed and his shoulder has improved, though it remains serious. He's our only injury worry. Everybody else is fine, and the team, when it was announced, was as expected, same as the semi-final, which leaves Mattie McCabe on the bench. He's played brilliantly for most of this season, yet he's had absolutely no luck, and now he's in the wrong place with no time to do anything about it.

Coyler and Padraig Lyons are also on the bench, which will be difficult for both of them. Padraig has also had bad luck this season, but even if he had been wrapped in cotton wool the entire summer the selectors wouldn't have picked him. That's the way it looks. He's been labelled as slow, that tiny bit too slow. Himself and Coyler were both on the team which lost to Kerry in the All-Ireland semi-final last year. Coyler, unlike Padraig, denied himself the opportunity of playing in the final. Instead Kevin Foley will play right half-back. He doesn't look half the player of Coyler and he never has. We played in secondary school together, and even then he read a game brilliantly and turned up with interceptions and catches in the unlikeliest of places. But I never thought he honestly cared enough about football to make it at the highest level.

19 September

Liam Harnan had the 'flu but was recovering fast. That was the official story! And, this evening it was announced that he would be fit to take his place. In truth, Harnan's shoulder is still troublesome, and although he is certain to start, several layers of strapping are unlikely to take his mind away from the pain. It is also true that we need him. He is, we think, perfect for Tompkins who has been brushing past defenders all season.

Dalgan Park was quiet, for the first time in months, at 5.30 pm. The great solemn building watched over our final training session. It watched us doing very little. There was a peace and calm which nobody wanted to disturb. We showered and dressed happily - despite the doubt shadowing Harnan there is a mood of well-being mixed with the tension - and the Columban Fathers provided us with a Mass as usual. A greater number than normal took Communion.

We spoke about Cork for almost ninety minutes after training last Thursday evening. This evening was darker and wetter, and I ran from my car into the large stately home of the Sisters of Sion, which gazes across at Dalgan Park a couple of miles away. We have been eating there after training for two years, and the composed, still atmosphere soothes us. The house often has Americans and other foreigners on retreat, but this evening it was deathly respectful of our needs. We ate - soup, followed by beef, potatoes, carrots, cauliflower, fruit salad afterwards, and adjourned up the winding staircase to the large lecture room on the first floor.

We talked, saying the same things which had been said on Thursday evening, about Tompkins ('Keep with him. Don't commit yourself'); about Cahalane and Davis ('Stop them! If they try to run out with the ball just stop them'); about McCarthy ('He'll come forward, but he doesn't like running back'), and through the team. Sean and Mick Lyons had agreed on the schedule for tomorrow, and shortly after 10 pm we were handed sheets of paper which had been typed and photocopied. At the bottom of the page it said that the team would return to the Grand Hotel in Malahide in the same coach it took from the hotel that morning, and that a separate coach would be provided for wives and girlfriends. The argument started! It had to. The night had been too calm, and everything about the game had been ironed out several times, and there was nothing else to argue about.

Two or three of the lads wanted to have their wives with them on the coach travelling back to Malahide. Sean and Mick were irritated. Sean was silent and Mick spoke for him, 'Wait a second, I don't honestly give a fuck where the girls go as long as we win the game.' That was agreed, and we left.

It had stopped raining, and walking over the gravel towards my car Marty O'Connell grabbed me around the neck.

'Sleep well,' he said.

'We may as well,' I replied.

I drove home to Skryne. Dad had already been up to the city to get the Sunday morning newspapers, and they were there, spread across the breakfast table when I walked into the room. I started to read them. *Some Like It Hot* was on television and I sat back in an armchair and watched Jack Lemmon and Tony Curtis and Marilyn Monroe instead. Dad told me I'd better go to bed. Three times he told me to go to bed. He went up about 1 o'clock, and I followed him up the stairs about half an hour later.

20 September
Meath 1-14, Cork 0-11, All-Ireland final

Cork led 0-7 to 0-2 after twenty-one minutes. It could have been worse. Four minutes earlier Jimmy Kerrigan had a clear shot at our goal from fourteen yards, but Mick Lyons courageously dived full length to block the ball. PJ scored our opening point, his first point of the season, but Cork were faster to the ball, and they were sweeping downfield in clusters of three and four men. Niall Cahalane, whom we had promised ourselves would be caged in for the entire game had raced through midfield and kicked one of their points from forty yards. It wasn't just that promise which was failing us. All our promises were being broken. Cork were leading by five points, and they should have been leading by a goal and five points. Then, something happened.

Seldom, in games, does something happen to turn the nature of the game on its head. The way you start is predictably the way you finish. We had been sluggish and heavy-footed after the first five minutes. We were winning an even share of possession in the middle of the field, but Staff and Bernie seemed elusive targets in front of us. Only PJ was locating Meathmen within the maze of the Cork defence, and one of his passes had swept over the head of Denis Walsh and into Colm O'Rourke's hands. His angle wasn't great, but Colm took one solo too many and in the two seconds it took for the ball to come back into his hands, John Kearins had rushed from the Cork goalmouth and obliterated the target. Behind me, Harnan was getting close to Tompkins but not close enough, although he hadn't scored from play. Bobby was inches from John Cleary. Terry had already watched Colm O'Neill turn onto his right foot ('O'Neill only kicks with his left, he's got no right foot') and score.

The game was drifting away from us, as games can, and usually there's not a damn thing to be done about it.

We had arrived at Malahide at 10.30 am. Everything had happened as Sean said it would. We ate, and strolled on the beach, and posed on the lawns in our official jackets and slacks. The coach, the Garda escort, the arrival at Croke Park! The entire morning and early afternoon was tense and immaculate! Our dressing-room was clean, and smelled of disinfectant, as I suppose it should with an All-Ireland final at its feet.

I sat in a familiar corner of the room, the same place I sat for the semi-final, and the Leinster final too. With Mick Lyons and Liam Harnan and Padraig Lyons on my right, and Colm O'Rourke and Gerry McEntee on my left - our corner. The same faces on either side of me - peas in a pod. At that moment it felt like the pod was at the bottom of a bucket of water. It was like being in a concrete submarine on the seabed. It was like Croke Park and 65,000 spectators were balanced on the ceiling. The dressing-room was long and angular, almost oval. It was small and desperately quiet there, and outside?

I had forgotten about outside, and the thousands of people who were sitting and standing, and the large empty pitch, and the All-Ireland final of 1987. Outside was outer space. My own family were out there, somewhere, but I had forgotten about them too. I stood up again, and thought about going to the jacks again. It would have been my second time since coming into the dressing-rooms. That was twenty-five minutes earlier. It had hardly seemed worthwhile then. Maybe? I went. I didn't feel much different, or any lighter, when I returned.

I started doing some more exercises. Hamstring, groin, calf, thigh, stomach, shoulders, a little more hamstring, and the calf again.

SEVEN OR EIGHT MINUTES.

I waited for Sean to start talking. I was already wearing my shorts and socks. The County Secretary, Liam Creavin had handed them out to everybody last night. I had put them on soon after I walked into the dressing-room, before I went to the jacks the first time, and before I did some earlier stretching. That seemed a long time ago. Not too many people were talking. The full-back, the manager, the physio, the left half-forward and the right corner-back. I wondered what they were talking about?

It was small talk, nervous talk, I knew, but I wondered nevertheless. The Chairman and the Secretary, the centre-forward and Sean, four substitutes in the corner - what are they thinking?

SIX MINUTES.

I decided to take my boots out of my bag, and the secretary threw me a jersey as I bent down beneath the bench. The jersey landed on the ground beside me, still in its plastic wrapping. I tore the plastic off, and threw it on the floor and watched it join an idle tangle of plastic wrappings and pieces of cardboard. I removed the couple of stickers from the cloth and slipped it on over my head. It felt smooth and fresh, soft, silky.

My sister had wanted to clean my boots yesterday morning. We had laughed over it, but I decided to wash and shine them myself, the first time in years. Thinking about that again, I made sure to have the laces tight, not too tight, but nice and tight. I stood up. The left boot didn't feel exactly right. I did it again. My legs had already been oiled and rubbed by Mochie (Martin Regan, one of Sean's men, and the team's very best friend).

Everyone else was doing something. Nobody was just sitting there. I would have preferred to sit and think, but I felt obliged to do something, anything. I did some more stretching, talking, tucked in my jersey again, not tightly, but with just enough looseness around the waist. Sean was talking to Cass. Others were still being oiled and rubbed. I started stretching again, and asked PJ to beat my stomach with his fists. He hammered hard. I returned the compliment. I wandered into the toilets. Bobby was there in the corner as usual, doing his exercises on the tiles, meditating. I didn't disturb him. Coyler was also in there and Staff. Doing their own things. Nobody spoke.

THREE MINUTES.

I popped my right leg up on the table in the middle of the dressing-room floor, keeping it straight, bending my body over it, forward, resting my forehead against my knee, and leaving it there for a couple of seconds. Then my left. The stretch felt strong. Someone said something to me. It was Bernie. He was telling me to kick the ball into his corner early on, low and fast. We spoke about the same thing this morning and on Thursday night. We agreed again. Sean told us all to stand up, and we started doing the final few exercises together. There was a knock on the door.

An official popped his head in, and asked us if we were ready. The door closed again. Sean called us all into a circle, and we joined our arms, and formed one tightly clenched fist, as Sean spoke. I wondered did I need to go to the jacks again, just in case, for the last time. What harm would it do? Why carry anything onto the field? I waited. I didn't need to listen to Sean. I just needed to look at his face. He sounded loud and confident and emotional. Incredibly emotional, and he asked us questions and questions and questions, and he wasn't looking for answers.

THIRTY SECONDS.

There was more banging on the door, but nobody opened it. Mick Lyons joined Sean in the middle of the circle. Somebody opened the door, saw who was there, and closed it immediately.

TIME.

Mick's voice raced through my body and I felt charged. I wanted to shout. I wanted to run. I wanted the game to start now. Mick finished, and marched towards the door. We seeped through the opening behind him, grabbing each other's shoulders and waists, clenching each other's arms. We ran down the long grey corridor, and suddenly there was an explosion of colour. I ran onto the field, and felt lighter than I had ever felt in my life.

And, then? By the time the game began I felt alone. How many of us felt alone? The game started and we played like strangers. We were losing by 0-7 to 0-2, and were lucky at that. Then, it happened. It may have been Mick's brilliant save from Jimmy Kerrigan, or it may have been Rourkey's goal. Jinksy had intercepted a crossfield pass by Anthony Davis, and he had passed to Colm. He raced towards the goal and slipped the ball to Bernie, who tried to tap it by Kearins. The ball was blocked, and Colm, falling, punched it into the corner of the net. Jinksy danced around three defenders to score the equalising point. We were one point in front at half-time. 1-6 to 0-8.

I'm not sure whether it was Colm or Mick who changed the course of the game. Or, maybe it was Cork themselves. They had been waiting for us to respond to their lightning start, and waiting, and waiting. They had been looking over their shoulders. When we did move, they found themselves unable to react. They had their problems too. Their full-back Colman Corrigan tried to shoulder charge PJ as he gathered a pass, and had come off worst, and didn't start the second half.

In the second half Tompkins, who had scored four points before the break, missed with six shots at goal, including five frees inside our fifty yards line. Cork had switched John O'Driscoll to midfield for a time, and Tompkins also joined us in the middle for a spell. We were in control there, and although I was voted RTE's 'Man of the Match' later in the evening, anyone of our half-back line or Mick or Bobby could have taken the award home. Our forwards were also finding time and room, when in the first half the Cork defence had each of them deposited in cardboard boxes. Staff was drifting to the right and left wings, and with the amount of possession at our fingertips, the choice was his. He scored four points from play, seven in all, and in truth was our most valuable player.

The last ten minutes of the game were ours to enjoy. We were leading by seven points. They would lose by six. Ten minutes and each minute was more enriching than the last. They were incredible. The coach ride from Croke Park to Malahide, with wives and girlfriends aboard, was numbing and fulfilling, and the banquet in the hotel was a distraction and allowed us time to breathe. Yet everything was happening too fast. I wanted to call a stop. I wanted to feel something. I wanted to be able to reach out and actually touch those around me, friends and strangers, the Sam Maguire, my family. Finally, at 3 am, I decided to retire to bed early. I ordered ham sandwiches and tea, and Anne and I closed the bedroom door behind us, and sat down in the quietness, and told each other exactly what had happened today.

We needed to.

In the days and months that followed, the team was slowly carried back down to earth, very gradually indeed. Over the next twenty-four hours the team and their wives and girlfriends were carried through the city, over the heads of a remotely curious people, in a luxurious coach. Then, we left Dublin behind us, and inched into the embrace of our own people. But they were not allowed to touch! At crossroads and villages and towns we briefly left the coach to stand on makeshift platforms, sometimes the sides of trucks, and smile and wave. Forty-five miles were stretched out over seven hours. Navan's Fair Green was populated by 15,000 people by midnight. And still, they were only allowed to look!

Finally, the coach reached the Beechmount Hotel and we were hustled between two firm rows of Gardai into a private restaurant and bar at the rear of the building. We had a quiet meal and a few drinks behind the locked glass doors. It was soon 2 am The thousands of people who had followed us through the rainy evening squeezed into the corridors, foyer and bars. They were beginning to fog up the windows and doors with their breath. A pane of glass suddenly cracked. That signalled others to start thumping the doors. Obviously, they had enough. We had been dangled in front of their eyes for too long. They wanted us back - and the funny thing was, some of them were neighbours, and players from other parishes who had probably tried to kill most of us on the football field earlier in the year, and perfect strangers who would hardly cast us a second glance a week later.

Sean Boylan asked some of us to go outside, amongst them, onto the disco floor, through the foyer, into the bars and out through the carpark. The doors opened, and a bunch of us were grasped by a giant pair of hands belonging to several thousand people. They shook us, grabbed at our jackets, snatched handkerchiefs from three or four breast pockets and slapped our backs. Young girls wanted autographs on their forearms and young mothers wanted to be kissed on the lips. Their little boys waited patiently to shake our hands. A father put his hand on my shoulder, and said 'Thanks' (and that I remember more clearly than anything else that entire weekend!).

It was exhilarating and it was tiring. It seemed that we had reached ground level. We hadn't. Five hours after the team's dramatic entrance I was seated on a low wall outside the front door of the hotel. Anne was still inside the hotel trying to phone home, asking some one to come into town and collect the pair of us. Thankfully, the attention was down to a trickle, and a great deal of interest was now being shown in the fish and chip van on the opposite side of the road. It was cold, and I had my collar raised high around my neck.

A neighbour's daughter enquired if I needed a lift home?

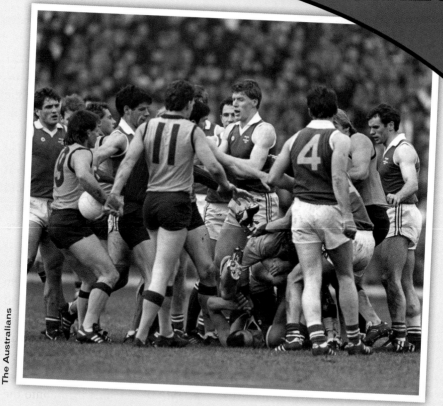

CHAPTER 8

The Australians

MY **COUNTRY** NEEDS ME?

30 September, 1987

Often, I wonder why I play this game. Often, when I'm on the field, I start thinking about it, wondering what I'm doing out here. I mean, even in the All-Ireland final there was lots of time to think. Other athletes in other sports say the same, and even the fastest sport on earth affords the participant at least one single moment to dwell on what he's doing, what an opponent is thinking, or why the hell Jack Lemmon and Tony Curtis didn't just disappear with Marilyn Monroe in the middle of the night (in *Some Like it Hot*, the film I watched the night before the game). The craziest thoughts can float through your head when you're out there!

Sometimes, I find it hard to concentrate, and there are occasions when I've literally found myself wandering around the field. In those moments I'm not entirely vulnerable, because I zero in on my opponent instead and keep one eye on him while my mind is temporarily occupied with other things. I especially find myself watching the game, analysing it, admiring something which Bob or Rourkey might just have done, or looking really closely at Tompkins or Fahy and guessing how they are feeling at this precise moment.

If all that sounds like my mind is usually elsewhere, then I'm being unfair to myself. The thoughts I have might last for five seconds or they may extend for fifteen, twenty seconds, and the rest of the time I know where I am and what I'm doing. But fifteen seconds on the field can be a long time. You can think about a lot in fifteen seconds.

Other players are different. Gerry Mc? He's just so engrossed! Mick too. Harnan and Foley and some other players are like Mick. I always find that PJ and myself have much the same thoughts during games, and much the same experiences on the field. And I expect Staff and Bernie are similar.

There are also occasions when I feel totally, completely and utterly immersed in the game - often when I have taken a heavy blow, especially a thump on the head. I wonder what it would be like to feel like that all the time.

In his book *Paper Lion*, the award winning writer George Plimpton spent time with the Detroit Lions football team and he discovered how some players could actually prepare themselves for specific moments on the field. The Lions' star defensive tackle Alex Karras told Plimpton how he psyched himself up during games by imagining that the opposing quarterback was the sort of person he hated most, the sort who didn't smoke, drink or swear, the clean-cut type who came from an eastern school and had a hoity-toity voice. John Gordy, who blocked for the passer on offence, admitted how he psyched himself up by pretending that the passer was his own six month-old son asleep in his basket with monsters rushing in trying to destroy him.

For me, there are special moments on the field. I think they are the moments for which I play, especially when the final whistle sounds and you've won, and for a split second you experience a sense of peace, within a great shell of satisfaction.

That moment is total contentment, and how many times in our lives do any of us feel one hundred per cent content? Not ninety-nine per cent, one hundred! That's why I play, and there are other moments too, the moment on the training field when I feel like a little boy surrounded by my best friends, the moment I walk out the dressing-room door (before I run down the corridor and run out onto the field), and the moment in the game when the opposing goalkeeper is taking his kick-out and I know I'm going to catch the ball and I'm waiting and nothing in the wide earthly world can prevent me from catching that ball. It's an incredible moment, waiting there in the middle of the field and loving every second of it.

George Plimpton actually trained with the Lions and played for five minutes in one of their pre-season exhibition games. He was the quarter-back, and discovered what it felt like to be in the middle of a huddle of players calling out the next play.

'Everything fine about being a quarterback – the embodiment of his power – was encompassed in those dozen seconds or so,' he wrote. 'Giving the instructions to ten attentive men, breaking out of the huddle, walking for the line, and then pausing behind the centre, dawdling amidst men poised and waiting under the trigger of his voice, cataleptic, until the deliverance of himself and them to the future. The pleasure of sport was so often the chance to indulge the cessation of time itself – the pitcher dawdling on the mound, the skier poised at the top of the mountain trail, the basketball player with the rough skin of the ball against his palm preparing for a foul shot, the tennis player at set point over his opponent – all of them savouring a moment before committing themselves to action.'

The cessation of time! When I'm waiting for that kick-out and I know I'm going to catch the ball, time stands still, and I'm on my own, and I love it.

A couple of days after the All-Ireland final my name was added to the Irish squad which plays Australia next month in the Compromise Rules series. It's the third time the games are being played between the two countries, and I want to be involved. I want to play. I want to play for Ireland, and I suppose, I want to be able to look my grandchildren in their wide and hungry eyes and know that I played for my country. Does that sound corny? I know it does. Probably the real reason I want to play is because I've sat in the press box at Lansdowne Road so many times, and watched the Irish rugby team racing out onto the field, and I've always wondered exactly what they feel? I can guess, of course, but I want to get closer to that experience.

This evening, in Belfield, the Irish team trained, and I was part of it, though it wasn't exactly a momentous occasion. It was dark, and John O'Leary took the training session. He's Irish captain for the Series, and he's taking the Dublin based players while Eugene McGee, who's managing the team, took a training session in the midlands someplace. We used a darkened pitch, twelve of us, mostly Dublin players, O'Leary,

Gerry Hargan, Ciaran Duff, as well as Bob O'Malley, Bernie Flynn and myself! There was a long run, and a series of sprints, and a certain amount of nervous laughter in the dressing-room. It's strange being together. Hargan had us in stitches, telling us about the Galway player who took him to one side last month, and told him 'Listen Gerry, there's a lot of dead wood about. It'll be better in a couple of weeks, believe me!' The same player is now nowhere to be seen, though he is in the woodpile.

This is my second time to be involved in the Series. I was on the squad in 1984, when it started in the GAA Centenary year with the Australians touring. I also tried out for the 1986 tour, when Ireland travelled 'down under', and was cut from the panel after three months of training. That reads like it seems I'm quite desperate to play in the Series, and I suppose I am. 'The Honour' and 'The Glory' - those sort of things - appeal to me. 1984 was a total disaster though. It was a meeting of two pre-historic creatures. Peter McDermott of Meath and Liam Sammon of Galway were joint Irish managers, and it wasn't their fault that their team waltzed into a street-fight.

Nobody knew what to expect before that first meeting in Pairc Ui Chaoimh on 21 October, 1984. Eamonn Young, the former Cork player, was one of the selectors, and on the previous evening, at the end of the team meeting, he showed how to stand for the National Anthem before the start of the game. Nobody said anything. When he was finished someone at the back asked 'Would you mind showing us that again?' There was, of course, some sniggering at the back of the room and stiff faces at the front. However, everybody was smiling the following afternoon, in the cramped dressing-rooms (with some of the team togging out in the jacks). There were smiles all round. Eoin Liston was the life of the party atmosphere, but everybody was in good form. They had never played with a round ball in their lives, and there's no net in sight in Australian Rules football, so it had to be easy.

Mick Lyons was stretchered off the field after a couple of minutes, after leaving his jaw on the end of one of the most blatant uppercuts I had ever seen. And, the rest was an unfortunate piece of sporting history. The Australians won 70-57, but representatives from both sides met forty-eight hours later to try to concoct some set of rules which would allow the GAA and Australian Rules football to live in each other's boots, without standing on each other's toes all the time. I'd watched most of the game from the sideline. In the second quarter I was brought on at left half-forward, and I didn't get a touch of the ball for ten minutes. I was taken off at half-time, but about a minute from the finish, Liam Sammon told me to go back on.

'Run everywhere,' he ordered.

My final memory of the 1984 series was acted out in the lobby of Jury's Hotel in Cork shortly after midnight. We were leaving and longing to have the journey over us, to have the entire experience at our backs. There were a large number of people still in the lobby at that hour, laughing at us, and at the entire Irish team, telling us we should be ashamed of ourselves. We talked the whole way home, about what had happened and what we had learned. We agreed it would be different the following Sunday. The following evening I learned that Joe Cassells had replaced me on the squad. In the end Australia won the Series two games to one.

18 October
Ireland 53, Australia 51, International Rules, first Test.

In the dressing-room, ten minutes before taking the field, I overheard Ger Lynch regretting the fact that he had forgotten his gum-shield. The Kerry wing-back was searching his bag, and couldn't find it. I was glad, because I'd also forgotten mine. It was good to have somebody else in the same state.

It seemed an absolute necessity to wear one against the Australians. I don't know how I managed to forget mine, since I started using a gum shield over two years ago, and I don't even run onto the training field without it nowadays. It's part of my kit, and I can hardly believe that I played almost all my life with my teeth bared and prepared to be knocked in, or out! As it turned out the game was fast and fiercely contested, and nothing more than that. I started as a substitute, but was soon introduced into the game. I was marking Jim Stynes, the former Dublin minor player who was then a star with Melbourne Demons. I did well on him, even if I did find myself predominantly in a defensive role. I got plenty of the ball, and dispossessed him once or twice, and in the jacks in the dressin-groom at half-time I thought to myself, that's it, I've proven myself in an Irish jersey!

It felt good wearing the green jersey, even if there were no sleeves and the material was coarse and extremely tight (as the Australians also wear them, so as to deny their opponents extra cloth to grab at). I was back in the dugout during the third quarter, and finished up the game in the full-forward line.

Yet today's game still possessed a rebellious character. The rules still allow the Australians to grab us and shove us to the ground, and while that may appear small compensation for forfeiting their oval ball and their oval pitch, it allows them great latitude in their tackling which we on the Irish team are incapable of seizing upon. They see it as a legitimate strength, a prized skill. Most of the time we take their tackles as personal assaults. It's annoying, but it's something we've got to live with. Besides, Eugene McGee is putting a great deal of emphasis on allowing the Series a clean bill of health on this occasion. He'd watched the Series in 1984 and in 1986 develop into a back-street brawl, and he wants to take it out of there. I agree with him.

25 October
Ireland 47, Australia 72, International Rules, second Test.
Most of the lads were in the Ashling Hotel on Friday evening, as we checked in for the weekend. Then some of them went around the corner for a drink, and two cars went into the city centre to see a film. I hung around the hotel, as neither a smoky Friday night pub nor a tightly-packed cinema appealed to me. I was in bed by 11.30 pm, and I watched a late film. I was sharing a room with Frank Foley, who is a sub on the Meath team, but who is acting as assistant-physiotherapist to the Irish team. We watched *True Grit* with John Wayne as the one-eyed marshal Rooster Cogburn.

Yesterday morning was bright and sunny, and we clogged up the foyer in our green, white and gold tracksuits with IRELAND stamped across each back. It felt good. On the team coach, which glided through the city towards Belfield, I sat beside Stephen Mulvenna, from Antrim. We small-talked, mostly about our work, my writing, and his workmates who are drawn from both sides of Belfast.

Most of the players and I simply acknowledge each other, and not much more than that. I can't fully relax amongst them. The training session in Belfield was far too long, and too tiring, and I'm not sure what McGee was trying to achieve. He had a short trial game which was tough and useful, but apart from that, the ninety minutes we spent on the field were more or less a waste of time. We had lunch back in the hotel, and I had to go to work. There was a team meeting at 10 pm, but the players had the evening to themselves. I brought Val Daly and Seamus McHugh and Paul Earley into town, and left them at the Adidas headquarters. They wanted to collect some gear. I didn't wait around. I had to be in the office from 4.30 to 10 pm.

The office was quiet. There were no late stories, nobody twisting ankles, or pulling hamstrings, and I got out of the place an hour early. I wanted to get something to eat, because I knew I'd missed the evening meal in the hotel. The streets of Dublin were as they always are on Saturday nights, interesting and noisy, though at that time they were mainly populated by couples leisurely making their way to the pub or cinema. The night was still warm and almost humid, and it smelled of a mid-summer's evening in the city. Or, maybe that was just me. I felt happy, but the realisation that I was locked into a twenty-four hours journey which would carry me into the arms of another game against the Australians was unnerving. I ate in a Chinese restaurant off Grafton Street, and rushed back to the hotel.

Eugene McGee was waiting around in the lobby. There was nobody else about and we had to talk (even though we had spoken less than six or seven words in the last eight days). He told me that I would be playing midfield, alongside Tom Spillane. I said good, and he talked about other bits and pieces, and then Micheal O'Mhuircheartaigh arrived. Micheal and myself shook hands and I left. Obviously he had been promised the team, and would be able to spend the night preparing his radio commentary for the next day.

Back in my bedroom, Frank wasn't about, but there was a sweet and heavy stench in the air. I opened the windows, and turned on the television set, and lay down on the bed. It was damp, sticky. There was massage oil on the quilts of both beds. I knew Frank had been using the room to rub down the lads after the training session, but, fuck it! The team meeting began twenty minutes late. Some of the lads had been at a late film, and others had lingered over a couple of good pints. McGee and his assistant Sean McCague sat at a top table, and McGee did all the talking. He seldom looked up. He must have spoken for twenty minutes, and I found it difficult to listen to him. I know he's been a good manager, and his record with the Offaly team which defeated Kerry in the 1982 All-Ireland final speaks volumes about his ability.

This morning, Frank was rubbing down more players in our room. I went out to buy some newspapers, and took a walk through the Phoenix Park, but when I came back into the room Tom Spillane was lying on my bed, his legs freshly oiled, and there were three more waiting in line behind him. I went down to the foyer. I was tense, and spent the next hour sipping a glass of Seven-Up.

The dressing-room was quieter and more business-like than it had been last month when I undressed for the All-Ireland final. We were one game up in the Series, and the Australians had nowhere left to go. They had to win. I felt good, less nervous, more excited. We listened to McGee, even though he still did not look at us very much, and John O'Leary said the last few words. We raced onto the field. The afternoon had remained dry. The ground was subdued, however and there didn't seem to be much more than a whimper as we took the field. The place looked full, but the stadium was either holding its breath, or else it was breathing very softly.

The ball was thrown up, and I was at the back. I'd told Spillane that I'd knock it down to him, but as I jumped I was shoved to one side. The Australian had the ball and threw it, awkwardly, into the air to kick it. As he swung his leg I flicked the ball away and kicked it up the field. It wasn't what I had wished for, but it wasn't a bad start to the worst day I have ever spent in Croke Park in my life. The Australians were faster and stronger than they had been seven days earlier. We were chasing after them and failing to cling to them from the beginning.

I didn't get the ball into my hands again in the first quarter, and at the change of ends for the second quarter I was moved to full-forward. There I met Danny Frawley, a sheep farmer and a semi-professional footballer with St Kilda's FC, and a total pain in the arse. He was the same size as me, and just as fast, and every ball which was kicked in between us I got to first. That was the way he wanted it. Three times I chased after long balls which were kicked down the sideline beneath the Cusack Stand, and grabbed them. And he grabbed me. Under the Compromise Rules if I am caught in possession of the ball (and don't make a clean catch) the free is against me. Each time he grabbed me, I released the ball. I dropped it, or flicked it away towards a green shirt. But he kept holding me, and each time we wrestled on the ground for a few seconds while play continued without us. He was enjoying himself, I could see that.

In the third quarter, he grabbed me by the jersey as I grabbed the hopping ball. I turned sharply to his left, but couldn't get away from him, and we both ended up in a heap on the ground in the middle of the field, about thirty yards from the Canal End. The ball was to one side, and as we remained in each other's grip, another Australian defender scooped it up and raced back down the field. Frawley wouldn't let go. I broke out of his grip and swung a fist across his chest. It was a warning. I had to let him know that I wasn't going to take any more of it.

He took my punch as an invitation for a fight, though he didn't do anything. He jumped to his feet, and with his fists raised, bobbing up and down on his toes, he started shouting.

'Come on, what ya gonna do about it? WHAT YA GONNA DO ABOUT IT?'

My own fists were somewhere between my knees and my waist, but they were clenched. I stood there.

'WHAT YA GONNA DO ABOUT IT THEN?'

He wanted to fight. I thought about it. My own pride, his fat ugly face, the honour of my country, the eyes of 30,000 Irish supporters, and suddenly I was struck from the side by another Australian defender who had come running from nowhere. Niall Cahalane was hot on his heels, and there was a brief scuffle.

The game continued. Frawley was muttering away to himself for the remainder of the afternoon. I got a couple of balls late in the game, and made a total hash of one easy kick. We were being outplayed throughout the field, and I just wished for the entire sorry afternoon to end. There was one moment of amusement however. The Tyrone defender John Lynch, who likes to play the game recklessly, ended up behind the end line in a clench with an Australian. From the opposite end of the field all I could see was Lynch's blond spiky head and about half a dozen crew-cut Aussies. I couldn't believe it. Lynch was in an egg box with six Aussies and he seemed to take the one immediately in front of him by the ears, and I thought to myself 'Don't fucking do it!' Lynch did. Holding the Aussie's ears, he head-butted him.

'The fucking cunt,' roared Frawley, as he raced past me.

I followed Frawley down the field, as was my duty! Behind me I could hear an Irish voice laughing.

'This is another fine mess you've gotten us into Stanley!'

We were both laughing and trying to keep up with the Australians.

Afterwards, nobody said very much in the dressing-room, but nobody looked very disappointed either. Anger, and some other emotions were in evidence, surrounding a mountain of frustration. I didn't bother going back to the hotel for the team meal and meeting. I had to travel down to Carlow instead, where I was due to speak at the Knockbeg College annual dinner dance. My parents and Anne were also invited. I sat in the back of the car on the way down, and thought about my brief appearance as an International player in 1984, and my lengthy performance this afternoon. Both memories rubbed shoulders, and it finally occurred to me that I had allowed my entire life as a Gaelic footballer, seventeen years, to be dragged along on its belly by an Australian sheep farmer. As well as that, I had received a kick between my legs and the most valuable part of my anatomy had turned black and blue, and I had difficulty walking when we finally got out of the car.

Coming home, I tried to sleep, but the pain was deepening, and I was worried that perhaps I had lost more than my self-respect this afternoon.

The afternoon had already been a failure, and there was nothing to be gained from decorating it with a bloodied nose – Frawley's, or most probably mine. That wasn't why I dwelled over his invitation though. I felt an absolute fool out there this afternoon. I felt I was in the middle of a circus ring, and that the thousands of curious eyes around me wanted to be entertained. They are used to 'free-for-alls' (or 'dust-ups' as the Australians fondly refer to them) in this infant game, and they would love to have seen one more big one added to the dozen or so they have witnessed since 1984.

The game is an interesting spectacle, I know that, and there are times when the ball is played fast and furiously. At times it can be thrilling, but it has no future, and it is obvious to me now that it is an entertaining little monster which should never have been born. It molests too many of the true skills of Gaelic football, and detests long solo runs or forwards swerving around defenders or a midfielder leaping within a cluster of bodies and racing away with the ball. It also leaves Gaelic footballers ragged and brawling.

The International Compromise Rules game is dragging Gaelic football back in time, by the scruff of its neck! Thanks to Kevin Heffernan and Mick O'Dwyer our game has become fast and skilful and highly articulate in the last decade. Though you wouldn't think that, looking at this afternoon's International stage. Australian Rules football is bar-room football, and that's the way the Aussies like it. It can be spectacular, but most of the time it's downright ugly, and the only thing it has in common with Gaelic football is its lonely existence these past one hundred years.

Australia 59, Ireland 55, International Rules, third Test.

I didn't give a damn whether I played in the final test. In this morning's *Sunday Press* I wrote about what happened last weekend, and how, as I stood in the middle of the field being asked 'WHAT YA GONNA DO ABOUT IT?' I realised that my pursuit of an Irish jersey had led me up the garden path, and into a field, where the little boy inside me got lost.

I admitted in print that my desire to do the decent thing for my country, and my desire to have the sheep farmer doing an impersonation of Little Bo Peep, had frozen over. It wasn't that I walked away from Danny Frawley. I've never had second thoughts about putting my face on the line for Meath. I walked away from the falsehood that by being chosen to play for Ireland I had actually dipped my toes into an international arena.

I wrote the article on Thursday morning. The team was announced on Saturday night. I didn't really care whether I was chosen or not. I felt I wouldn't be, and I was right. Last night I didn't stay over in the team hotel, but returned this morning for another team meeting at 11 am. Most of the players were seated when I entered the room, and I sat down without saying much. Pat Spillane and Noel Roche both turned to me and congratulated me on what I had written. Spillane felt it was spot on. They were both on the team this afternoon, but the same frustration and disillusionment had surfaced within them these past two weeks. Except, they still wanted to play for their country.

Bob O'Malley, Bernie Flynn and Mick Lyons were also on the Irish team and they played brilliantly. Particularly Bernie, who bobbed up and down in the Australian defence. He was Ireland's best player. Bob seemed to enjoy himself, and was calm and assured in everything he did. In the middle of the field, Mick was partnered by Brian McGilligan and they pushed the Australians around, and behaved like two grown men in a school yard. It was good to watch, and there were times when I wanted Ireland to win. Most of the time however, I wondered what the hell I was doing sitting in the lower deck of the Hogan Stand.

Earlier in the afternoon, as I parked my car on Clonliffe Road, there was a moment when I regretted not being able to reach for my kitbag and head for the dressing-room. I was locking up, when a boy of about ten walked past with his father. The boy wore an Irish scarf, and he had a hundred questions impatiently waiting on the tip of his tongue. He was going to see Ireland play! For a second I wished I could share his view of Croke Park, and I wished I was about to play for my country.

8 November
Dublin 2-5, Meath 0-11, National League

Today, the 1987 All-Ireland final officially became history, even though it remains alive and kicking in our minds, and even though the Sam Maguire Cup is still wandering all over the county and drawing us towards it, on dark, awful nights, in grotty, smoky pubs. The magnetism is still strong.

It was wet and grey and morbid in the shadow of Croke Park. I tried to imagine the Dublin players standing outside the tunnel to the dressing-rooms, in the rain - tradition stupidly insists that the All-Ireland Champions receive a guard of honour onto the field in each of their games prior to Christmas - and that warmed me a little. They were nowhere in sight when we raced out of our dressing-room though. Instead they could be found down at their normal end of the field beneath a drenched Hill 16 warming up in the mud instead.

We would have provided them with a guard - I know that - if the positions had been reversed. Not because we would have wanted to. We simply would have done so. We did it in 1983 when they visited Navan after winning the All-Ireland and Gerry Mc insisted 'Let's clap them onto the field, and then kick the shite out of them'. It's a fine theory. A little extreme, but then it's not meant to be taken literally. Is it?

We were two points behind in the final minute of the game. Liam Harnan scored our equaliser. It was important not to lose to them. There are young Dublin players, Bolger included, who have never known what it is like to walk off a field having defeated a Meath team, and the more they wonder, the greater the weight of each defeat they suffer at our hands.

6 December
Meath 0-13, Armagh 2-6, National League

By the end of this deathly cold afternoon we were playing like demons, and arguing over every single ball in the mud, and all because of a ridiculous incident shortly after half-time. The former Sligo footballer Mickey Kearns was refereeing the game, and it had started off in a pleasant enough atmosphere, although Armagh are always a very physical team and whenever we play them a large dose of tension is quickly injected into the game. But the match had been sauntering along, quite smoothly, until Kearns decided to send off Colm O'Rourke and Jim McKerr. They had been in a bit of a tangle, but the referee didn't like what O'Rourke had to say to him. It wasn't complimentary, though I've heard worse. It began with 'Fuck' and ended with 'bollocks' I think, but obviously Kearns felt mortally offended. He should have turned around and told Rourkey what he thought of him, and then slapped his wrist.

The remainder of the game was played in front of 8,000 supporters, mainly Meath supporters, who were shouting for blood. Our one point victory didn't quench their thirst enough, and as we made our way to the dressing-rooms (Kells is one of those awful grounds in which the players must walk about 200 yards from the changing rooms to the entrance to the pitch) it was obvious that the crowd weren't happy. O'Rourke had been sent off, for nothing; they thought! As I squeezed through them to the dressing-room I could sense that their anger was still intact. O'Rourke wouldn't be eligible for an All-Star award now, and they blamed Kearns. He had been certain to get one of the awards, for his excellence throughout the previous eleven months.

In the dressing-room we sat down, and nobody was saying very much. We had to struggle really hard for our victory, and this morning there was hardly a Meath footballer who had any wish to stretch himself for a couple of National League points. If they came easy, fine! If they didn't come, pity! The last thing we wanted was to get ourselves into an all-in wrestling and football match. After the game when Boylan arrived into the dressing-room he seemed fussed, and anxious. He wanted six of us to go back out onto the field with him. Mickey Kearns was still in the middle of the field, and the crowd were not going to let him out. He was frightened, and he had every right to be. Respectable men and their sons were behaving like ravenous savages on this Sunday afternoon.

Boylan led us back onto the field, and at first Kearns was still reluctant to move. Boylan insisted that he should. After a couple of minutes we made our way to the gate behind the goals, and edged towards the jaws of several hundred frenzied supporters. Three or four Armagh players also surrounded the referee. With a handful of stewards, and about fourteen or fifteen of us around him, Boylan was promising Kearns that nobody was going to get hurt.

Oh yeah?

The gate opened. The roaring of the crowd rose, and we began to edge our way through. After about twenty yards, the crowd began to shove and push. Somebody jumped over the top of the human shell and aimed a punch into the middle, in the direction of the referee. Kearns crouched down. Somebody else was struck on the back of the head. A lump of mud splattered past my left ear, wiping its feet on the side of my face. By now we were running towards the dressing-room, and the crowd were still roaring, but nobody got hurt. Mickey Kearns was deposited in his own dressing-room with a guard of officials. He was shaken, and still scared. He had yet to leave town. It was decided that it would be foolish to allow him to drive home alone.

December 13
Meath 0-12, Kerry 0-8, National League

Being received in The Kingdom as All-Ireland Champions is something I have never dreamed of. Yet, strangely, they were the perfect hosts. It was a role which was new to them, but which they carried out with dignity. It was like being received in the home of Muhammad Ali, with a World Heavyweight Championship belt tied around my stomach.

They formed a guard of honour as we jogged onto the pitch - Charlie Nelligan, Tommy Doyle, Seanie Walsh, Tom Spillane! I wondered what they were thinking as we ran past them, as they clapped. Were they thinking of kicking something in particular out of some of us?

We won, easily, and the only tense moment came in the forty-fifth minute when Jim Joe Landers, the referee, went to book Bob O'Malley for a foul on Donal McEvoy. Bob had already been booked in the first half, and it looked from where I was standing with my hands on my hips in the centre of the pitch, that Bob was going to walk the same sorry road as Colm O'Rourke. He too was about to have eleven months of excellence erased with one stroke of a pen. Bob held his hands over his head. For some reason the referee put his book back in his pocket, and continued talking. Bob was lucky. Five minutes later he threw the ball at a Kerry player after being fouled himself. He was both foolish and lucky this afternoon.

The season is over. He will win his All-Star, and by the middle of winter every one of us will be wishing to win one. But this evening, as we took the early evening train back to Dublin, I was just happy to lick the envelope closed on the best season of our lives.

CHAPTER 9

Liam Hayes

THE **HONEYMOON** SUITE

17 April, 1988
Dublin 1-8, Meath 0-11, National League Final

Humiliation comes in all shapes, sizes, and depths. This afternoon, it was vast, for me, and for Gerry Mc too, though we didn't talk about it after the game. We happened to glance at each other several times as we stripped off and showered and dressed.

Declan Bolger and Jim Bissett had given us a thorough lesson in football, and in life, just when we thought we had the pair of them in our pocket. Last year, after one game, we thought that Bissett was definitely finished. All through the first half Gerry had been telling him how badly he was playing. Ten minutes before half-time Gerry started telling Jim that they were going to take him off if he didn't catch a ball soon.

'You'd better catch one, because you won't be around in the second half,' Gerry had advised.

Gerry and myself were standing in the middle of the field as the Dublin team emerged from the tunnel for the second half. We looked up and saw Jim Bissett making his way behind the goals with the rest of the Dublin substitutes. After the game Gerry told me he felt lousy, and he wanted to apologise to Bissett. I told him it was too late.

This afternoon, I felt physically sickened. Meath had drawn with Dublin in the National League final, and the team had shown great courage, and calmness, in scoring four points in the last seven minutes of the game, after Mick Galvin had punched what looked like a match-winning goal one minute earlier. We led by one point, and with the last kick of the game Joe McNally snatched the equaliser. That McNally score encapsulated my entire afternoon. Gerry Hargan took a long free from their half of the field. The ball stalled in the air, perfectly. I had it, and then I discovered, at the last second, that I was too far underneath it. I got my left hand to it and it fell behind me, at Joe McNally's feet! Mick Lyons had him covered. I had him too, but I didn't want to foul him, and rather than tackle him I tried to slap the ball out of his arms. I'm sure he didn't even feel it. Mick was afraid of fouling him too, and had given him a little bit too much space. It was a good point, and McNally gorged himself on it, as he usually does. He had his fists clenched, and then I think he blew a kiss to heaven - something like that. I felt like kicking my own arse, not his.

That was my day. Gerry's was not much better, and Declan Bolger and Jim Bissett must have caught three balls for every one that we swatted. It's the first time Bissett has outplayed me. And it was the best game Bolger has had since last year's National League final when he lorded it in the middle of the field against Kerry. The worst part was that I felt fresh in the dressing-room at the end of it all. I would have loved to walk back out onto the field and play the replay, there and then. I would have given my right arm for that opportunity (and I probably could have, because I'd only been using one arm the entire afternoon anyway).

18 April

This evening, I heard on the radio in Anne's apartment on Collins Avenue on Dublin's northside, that the game has been postponed. There were two or three reasons and I didn't listen to them. Anne knew by the look of me how I felt. She already knew how important, absolutely vital it was for me to bury my memory of the National League final. I left her place shortly after midnight, and drove through Finglas, into the countryside and home, still a beaten man.

The game has been postponed for five weeks. I can't believe that! The Meath team travels to the United States in seven or eight days' time on the All-Star tour, and the replay will take place on the team's return, on 22 May, two days after I return from my honeymoon. Luckily, Anne and I are also going to the US where we'll spend a few days in New York, and meet up with the team in San Francisco (the thought of playing for Meath on tour in the States is irresistible). So, we're going to meet up with them for three days, that's all. After that we're going to get a car, and travel south.

7 May

It rained and rained in New York for the three days, and I loved it. Anne didn't. We were married, happily married last Sunday. Only two of the Meath team were present, Rourkey (Patricia's second child was due today) and Gerry Mc (overworked). This morning we flew to San Francisco, and this evening we ate in an Italian place with Sean Boylan and Mickey McQuillan. Tomorrow Meath play the All-Stars for the second time. The Cathedral Hill Hotel is spacious and quietly luxurious, and I think it's costing $120 a night. We're going to stay five nights and the team will be under the same roof for three of those nights. It's going to be expensive for Anne and myself, and certainly, in our three weeks' trek across the US we're going to be spending most of our time in less comfortable bedrooms. But I wanted to be with the team.

I don't expect the Meath County Board to pay for our room. It's our honeymoon, and why on earth should anyone subsidise it? The Meath County Board, as it happens, have already paid my airfare. I was presented with a cheque for £500 a couple of days before the team left (only after Colm O'Rourke persuaded them to pay). The rest of the Meath team have their airline tickets, and hotel rooms, and they have also received an allowance for the two weeks. I didn't ask anybody how much it was. It was something like $800, I think. Part of me feels that I've been guilty of holding my hand out, on my honeymoon!

Another part of me, to be honest, feels annoyed that O'Rourke had to make several requests before my airfare was covered. I haven't thought about it for too long, but when I do, and when I think that I've offered up the greatest part of my life to this team over the last eight years, I feel like splitting on tomorrow's game, and driving off down Highway 1 instead.

The thought of touring the United States with the Meath team has always excited me. Okay, it was hidden behind the winning of an All-Ireland title, but nevertheless, to travel across the Atlantic with the team would probably be one of the most memorable moments of my entire career. I want to play in tomorrow's game, and I will, because it's the ultimate enjoyment for a Gaelic footballer, to play for his county against the All-Stars, to play for the All-Ireland champions against the All-Stars! I've always imagined that to be a moment when you know you are perched on top of the Gaelic football tree.

I want to play tomorrow because I want to satisfy something within myself. In the process, I've been prepared to disrupt my honeymoon, in order to wear the Meath No.8 one more time. I want to be with the team, my team. And I feel a little bit disgusted that I should have to pay for the roof over my head and the mattress beneath my back in order to be part of that team. Honeymoon or no honeymoon!

Interestingly, while the Meath officials were ignoring Anne, Dermot Power of Bank of Ireland, who sponsored the tour, presented us with a crystal glass decanter. It was a really nice gesture.

We're having a good time. Colm O'Rourke and Gerry McEntee are at home, working and probably thinking about what the Meath team is doing, and trying not to think about it for too long. Neither of them could make the tour, for good reasons. McEntee has been playing with Meath since 1975, O'Rourke since '76. They have sacrificed their families and their working lives for the Meath team, and they will continue to do so without question, I know.

They have missed out on two weeks of basking in the glory and the sunshine of the All-Ireland. Other players, some of them good young players who have offered up less than twelve months of their lives to the Meath team, are enjoying the holiday of a lifetime, all in, a holiday worth slightly less than $3,000. O'Rourke and McEntee will hear about it when the team gets home, and O'Rourke and McEntee will be expected to carry their own weight (and extra weight if necessary) in the National League final replay against Dublin one week later.

I can see the day (a day when my own boots will have been well and truly hung up) when inter-county players will be suitably compensated for playing the game. If that day doesn't arrive, Gaelic football will simply begin to stagnate, and that would be a pity. But the signs are already there. Only a handful of teams, in both football and hurling, hold any prospects of winning All-Irelands these days. The other teams are badly organised or poorly motivated. They're not serious about winning, and they're definitely not serious about dedicating their lives to the pursuit of football excellence. What other reason can anybody give for a county like Cavan suddenly nose-diving? It won nine out of ten Ulster titles in the 1940s, a few in the 50s, and three or four in the 60s, and then, nothing! Don't try telling me that they haven't got the players, that with the best will in the world they would be unable to win one more Ulster Championship in the near future. A county with such tradition and pride doesn't suddenly dry up overnight.

There are other anomalies within the GAA, in the larger and more powerful counties, which are also pitiful. I've always been amazed that Dublin players are handed tea and milk and biscuits after training. In Meath we have been receiving substantial meals after every training session, since shortly after Sean Boylan was appointed manager. I know the official explanation for a lack of knives and forks in Dublin is that the players have shorter distances to travel, and they have time to eat at home before training or after training or something like that. That's ridiculous! Even after championship games in Croke Park the Dublin team is regularly denied a dinner together. I've often seen the players walking away from the ground in different directions, and I know they probably meet up later in the evening in smaller groups in different pubs, but it hardly helps team spirit.

Small things like that are important and considering Dublin are the strongest and most colourful asset the GAA has, the treatment of the team is utterly shameful. But it suits us in Meath to see them like that. We have fewer complaints, but they are still genuine complaints. The treatment of O'Rourke and McEntee, in this instance, has been disgusting. Lesser irritations come in the form of travelling expenses.

Only those of us who drive to or bring players to training sessions and matches receive mileage, which is something like fourteen pence or sixteen pence a mile at the moment. I'm not sure, I've never bothered to check it. For the difference of one or two pence it's hardly worth my while. I know other people in the GAA get much more substantial mileage rates. I've heard figures twice as high, sometimes three times as high, but I've never taken any interest in finding out exactly what the difference between the rates is. I'm too busy playing and training, and I'm too busy with my own life.

That's the problem. That's why GAA players have never bothered to stand up for themselves and demand a fairer deal. They don't think they have the time. That includes me, we're all guilty. I remember attending a meeting of a Players' Association in 1983. Robbie Kelleher of Dublin and Johnny Callinan, the Clare hurler, were at the top table. There were less than twenty players in the room. The Players' Association had been in existence for a couple of years, but due to an appalling lack of interest, it was quickly abandoned. It's a pity that none of us think we have the time.

I know that for the National League final replay later this month I'll be handed one ticket, probably the evening before the game. The same as I was handed just one ticket for the drawn final last week. When that happens I'll get angry, and I'll probably say something to whoever is left with the task of handing it out to me. A few of us will make a few caustic remarks, but we will not do a damn thing about it. Most of us have wives or girlfriends, and a great many of us have parents with whom we are on speaking terms, so one ticket to the game is an insult. But I'll take it. The night before the game will not be a good time for an argument. We're all supposed to have our minds on the game, and we will have them there, and the ticket will be slipped into a back pocket.

I'm not sure how players will be compensated in the future. But the time will come when they will be able to ask for the basic things in any athlete's life. I think that county teams will soon have a pool of money, from sponsorship and a share of gate receipts, which will be shared out at the end of the season. Until then, some teams will prosper and some teams may never prosper again, and football and hurling will continue to wander aimlessly down a much too predictable path.

8 May
Meath 0-10, All-Stars 1-9.

This evening, there was a banquet somewhere for both teams, but we didn't feel like going. Anne and I ate in a nice little restaurant at Fisherman's Wharf instead. While we had been waiting in the foyer of the hotel for a taxi to arrive, we bumped into Colman Corrigan and John Kearins. The two Cork players were also looking for a taxi. They were late for the team coaches, and yet they stopped and we talked for five or ten minutes, about the All-Ireland final and about today's game. More importantly, they both took time to talk to Anne too, and I thought that was good of them. I know the All-Ireland final is seven months old, but they've got to have bad memories of it. They were winning the game by five points, and they lost by six, and Corrigan finished up on the sideline in a concussed state. It was the first time I had spoken to any Cork players at any length since the All-Ireland, and they were dignified, even charming I suppose.

Midway through, the game had turned a little bit rough. Again, for what? I managed to hit Ciaran Duff with one perfect shoulder charge which sent him spinning. He'd been getting on my nerves earlier in the game, talking too much, and coming in with one or two late tackles. So when the opportunity came to hit him I grabbed it. He went to slip by Martin O'Connell on the left, and I'd expected him to try it, and had built up a bit of speed and struck him squarely, and fairly. It hurt him, and it shook me up too.

Duff and Mick Kennedy were the only two Dubliners on the tour, and I don't know why Duff was so intent on making himself heard. The National League final wasn't on my mind, and from the stories I've heard from last week it hasn't been on the minds of many other Meath footballers either. Sean is calling a training session every morning, to make sure the team make the most of the trip and are prepared for Dublin immediately upon our return. But he also wants everybody to have a good time. There are no rules. However, one morning last week, at the very beginning of a training session one of the younger players chased after a ball twenty yards in front of him. He was fine for four or five yards, and then he fell over his own feet. He couldn't get back up. The poor lad was sozzled. The training session went progressively downhill from there, so, Sean called a halt. He had the lads do laps instead, lap after lap, not saying anything, lap after lap after lap. Until everybody had reasonably sobered up.

22 May
Meath 2-13, Dublin 0-11, National League final reply

Yesterday evening Sean had insisted that I take a fitness test. I told him that I had trained on my own in the States, but he wanted me to 'work up a sweat'. I spent fifteen minutes with David Beggy, and with Sean kicking balls to the left of us and to the right of us. I couldn't move. On Friday, after flying into Shannon from Los Angeles I didn't bother going to bed, and decided that anytime I was tired to take a long walk instead. I wanted to get back into a reasonable sleeping pattern. I felt fine for most of the day, but after fifteen minutes with Jinksy yesterday, I couldn't move.

'Come on Liam, I want you to work up a sweat fella.'

Sean kept on shouting that, and I wanted to work up a sweat, but I couldn't move. Thankfully, he believed me when I said another night's rest would have me right.

I've also heard stories about the tour, but I haven't had time to find out what everybody's talking about. Seemingly, earlier in the week, there were a couple of stories in the daily newspapers which claimed that there were a few incidents between Ciaran Duff and various Meath players. I asked a number of the lads about them and they seemed touchy about it. They seemed angry. They insisted that nothing happened, that Duff had words with one Meath player at one post-game function, but the pair of them had shaken hands by the end of the evening.

When I met up with the tour there was no ill-feeling. Everybody seemed to be having a good time. The only incident of note occurred when one of the Galway party got into trouble in the hotel swimming pool, and Mick Lyons, who is not the strongest swimmer as it happens, leaped in and pulled him out. But word of that act of heroism hasn't reached home.

It was a good game for us, almost the perfect game. We won by eight points, and with only fourteen men. On a personal level, Gerry and myself easily got the better of Bisset and Bolger in the middle of the field.

Immediately after half-time I scored the goal of my life. McQuillan's kickout cleared a group of us in the middle of the field, and I turned to find PJ collecting the ball, and falling. He passed to me as he fell, and I had a clear run at the Dublin goal. I was running and I couldn't hear anything behind me. It was strange. John O'Leary was shouting at his full-back line to keep their ground, to mind their men. He was roaring at them. I was getting closer, and when I thought I was virtually on top of him I shot into the top right-hand corner of the net. I couldn't miss but when I watched it on video tonight, I was surprised to find that I had actually kicked the ball from the twenty-one yards line. The ball went into the very corner, but, on television, it looked too close for comfort. At the time I had been running for so long, and looking at the goals for so long that they seemed huge as I shot. We had been leading by four points. Suddenly, we were seven points up, and with Bernie Flynn causing absolute mayhem in the Dublin defence we looked like scoring a lot more.

The game ended with both teams playing out time, almost leisurely. It had begun with a bang. The first few minutes were tense and nervous, and furious.

In the eleventh minute Kevin Foley fell on a loose, hopping ball. Duff fell on top of him. They tangled and a couple of punches were thrown.

Duff got to his feet, and as Foley raised himself up off the ground Vinny Murphy struck him - quietly - but the entire Meath defence caught him in the act. Thirty seconds later, when referee Pat Lane sought calm, two Dublin players were sprawled on the ground. Once more, McNally, was nursing the side of his face. One of those on the ground was Murphy. He had been hit with three of the sweetest punches I have ever seen on the field. They were sweet punches because each one of them was totally deserved. Murphy, by his action, had asked for the fight. Kevin Foley was the only man sent off.

He'll probably miss the first round of the Championship on Sunday week against Louth. Certainly on this occasion he is unfortunate. In the past Kevin has brought all sorts of misfortune down upon himself and he is probably the most aggressive player on the team, not only in matches but in training too. Yet he did virtually nothing on this occasion. Certainly he didn't start anything and by the time he got to his feet so many punches had been thrown there was nothing left for him anyhow! Afterwards in our dressing-room, after his shower, Kevin was asked by a reporter if he threw a punch?

'I did' said Foley.

'Was it the first punch?' asked the reporter.

'The fourth, I think,' replied Foley.

'Who threw the others?'

'I don't know.'

'How do you feel now?'

'Bad.'

'Was it a good win?' continued the reporter.

'You're standing on my fucking towel,' murmured Foley.

The fight will probably get most of the attention tomorrow morning, but we'll have to live with that. I'm sure we can.

We're National League Champions. That doesn't mean much to me now, as I sit here and write. We're also All-Ireland Champions, but the Championship still seems a long way off. It's only two weeks away, I know, but at this moment the thought of playing Louth in Navan is tiny.

CHAPTER 10

Larry Tompkins

WINNERS **ALL** RIGHT

31 July, 1988
Meath 2-5, Dublin 0-9, Leinster final

Last night, a pin could not have dropped on the floor of our dressing-room in Dalgan Park without screeching for the attention of twenty-six pairs of ears. Between 6.30 and 7.0 pm there was silence. There were no pins, only one boot, the property of Colm O'Rourke which was sent crashing into the solar plexus of a locker as Staff walked back into the room after failing a fitness test. Staff had a hamstring problem all week, but Sean had decided not to say anything about it. Whenever anybody asked they were told that Staff had a bit of a cold, that was all. I too had to lie, which made it difficult at work, because there were a lot of rumours about him and I had to scotch every one of them. It's not something I like. I can't understand what Sean and the lads (like Gerry Mc, for instance, who always thinks there's everything to be gained from singing dumb) are trying to achieve by pulling a cloak of secrecy over an injury like this. But, they always do. Despite the fact that word always leaks out anyhow, because the selectors or the players tell their wives or a mother or a father, someone! And it spreads.

Dalgan Park was once a bustling seminary. It opened for business in the 1940s, when several hundred young men strolled the corridors and lawns and played on the fields, and the Columban Fathers sent handfuls of missionaries in a wide variety of directions around the world every year. These days, the proud granite building serves as a retirement home of sorts. It has accepted the changing times with great dignity, though scarcely more than a dozen elderly men now breathe life into the long corridors. They walk the wooden tiled floors, and say hello to us. They watch us.

I wonder what they think? Those men, their bodies shrivelled and painful, their minds littered with memories from other lands of suffering and joy. They looked at us last night, at faces which were tightened and scared, and I suppose those old men would have to be forgiven if they burst into laughter, at the sight of strong, able men left uneasy and in some cases numb at the thought of a football match! Maybe they do laugh, inside. Maybe they howl, though they are always so respectful towards us.

After learning about Staff, we waited for him to shower and change. We walked two long corridors, and entered the church. After Mass we ate in Bellinter, as usual, in the home of Our Lady of Sion Sisters. The huge, nineteenth century home in Bellinter is also quiet and private, but as we waited for our food last night greater attention than normal was directed towards the pool table in the corner of the dining room. Staff was playing with Mattie, Marty and Mickey McQuillan. For a moment I wondered how he had the stomach for it, but I suppose that's Brian's style. He is always so relaxed and perfectly laid-back He never displays very much emotion, so I suppose it was just like him to play pool less than half an hour after learning that he wouldn't be playing in the Leinster final. It wouldn't have helped to have him sitting around with a long face on him and I'm sure he knew that too, though he didn't say very much at the team meeting. Since the start of the year Sean insists upon having the chairs forming a circle. Nobody can hide. Everybody feels obliged to say something, even something small. We talked for about half an hour, though most of us were still thinking about Staff

Staff has always been a total mystery to me. He is the most valuable member of the team, and his free-taking, in addition to his sharpness and accuracy, also make him the most inspirational player we have. There is nothing quite like watching a long-range free go over the bar, especially when you've been working your arse off and you know you deserve a point. You stand with your hands on your hips, and you tell yourself that it may not go over, and deep, deep down inside you're on your knees praying your head off

Staff? I don't know him, though it's easy to accept him, and totally relax in his company. He doesn't say very much, but if someone like Rourkey starts slagging him off Staff always defends himself, and frequently turns the tables. In the same situation I prefer to sit and hope Rourkey runs out of steam. I don't know Staff, and I don't even think about him very much, even though he gets over fifty per cent of our scores in every game. I should know him!

I know he seems dog lazy. I know he couldn't do more than ten press-ups when he first appeared in the dressing-room three years ago, and I doubt if he could do any more now. He's got a big arse, which gets bigger in winter, and yet, in summer he can cover ten yards faster than anybody else on the team. He can look awful, and he's too good to be true, and maybe I'm right not to think about him too much.

Sitting in the circle, we went over the same things, which we had trampled over the week before that, and the week before. It's important to hear them again. But it's even more important to hear voices, each other's voices. I'm never sure how much anybody listens. It was difficult to concentrate last night, as it always is before a Leinster final, and Sean knows that. He also knows that the act of sitting together is sufficient in its own way. There had been a long drawn-out discussion over one particular point last night, and in the middle of it there was a difference of opinion as to where we should leave our cars the following afternoon. We were all meeting in Ashbourne, but we were sharing cars into Croke Park because of the limited parking facilities in the ground. The discussion continued and circled for five minutes, then ten minutes. It had started out with someone suggesting that all of the cars should be left in Ashbourne, where they could be collected that evening. But that suggestion had been flooded out of it by several others. Sean started talking about the game again, and about ten minutes later, after discussing Colm O'Rourke's role and agreeing once again on what Mick Lyons should do if his man wandered out towards the middle of the field, PJ Gillic suddenly burst into the conversation. In a loud, angry voice he demanded, 'For God's sake, let's leave the fucking cars in Ashbourne, AND FORGET ABOUT

IT!' The place erupted in laughter, and PJ begged to be told what he had said wrong. I know what he had been thinking about - Staff.

Mostly, I thought about Staff, and PJ, who would be taking the free-kicks in his place. In the 1986 Leinster final I had been our free-taker, and I finished the game with one point from three attempts, but ever since then Staff has taken that role, and he has been impeccable. With his amazing accuracy, Barney Rock is no longer a threat, whereas in the past Rock's brilliance in free-taking left us chasing Dublin every time we played them.

Today we started off with a flourish. We scored two goals in the first fifteen minutes and Dublin were floundering. Staff's absence gave Colm Coyle the opportunity to get back on the team. He lined out at full-forward, but didn't spend much time there. Coyler is such a valuable footballer, he can literally play anywhere. It's a big advantage to him too, because the team really has a settled, solid look about it now. Terry Ferguson and Joe Cassells, who is captain this season and was troubled with different leg strains earlier in the year, are both on the outside looking in. Nor can their hopes be too high. Terry and Joe know there are only certain roles they can fill. Coyler can fit himself anywhere.

He started the movement for our second goal. The first goal by Mattie had looked simple - as Mattie McCabe's always do! I kicked a long sideline ball from beneath the Hogan Stand, and Rourkey and PJ both went to catch it with three or four defenders. The ball dropped, and Mattie just drifted (glided!) through a passageway in the square, collected the ball, and casually side-footed it along the ground to John O'Leary's left. The second goal was morale boosting, and especially sickening for Dublin.

Eamonn Heery was running with the ball into our half of the field. Heery always holds onto the ball too long, and we've said it to each other so often at team meetings. 'If Heery gets the ball follow him. He'll always try to solo it.' It's also easy to take the ball off him, because the ball is very loose in his possession. For our second goal, Coyler ran after Heery and took the ball off him. Rourkey gathered it, and passed to Bernie who knocked it across the goalmouth to PJ. He blasted the damn thing. It went too much to the left and too high, but squeezed itself into the top left-hand corner of the goals.

PJ finished the game with a personal tally of 1-3 (he scored two vital frees late in the second half, at much the same time as Rock was wide with two scoreable kicks at the other end). Mattie got 1-1, and I got our other point. It's hard to imagine! We got seven scores in the Leinster final, and Rourkey and Bernie, and Staff naturally, didn't score anything. But our seven scores also illustrates how well they played. They regained their composure after that bad start, and they pulled themselves together a second time when Synnott was sent off midway through the second half. They also missed a penalty with the final kick of the game. But, if those facts give the impression that they dominated the game, then ignore them.

We were on top in the middle of the field, and we probably had our best game together in over twelve months. I took Declan Bolger. And Gerry marked Tommy Conroy, who is a beautiful footballer, but who never quite recovered after failing to play well in the successive All-Ireland final defeats by Kerry in 1984 and '85. It was a last chance for Conroy, and Gerry knew that. Tommy Conroy is a magnificently creative player, but Gerry didn't allow him to breathe. We also feel that Bolger is close to the end, even though he just started out on the Dublin team last year. To us Bolger, because of his unfortunate likeness to Brian Mullins I suppose, represents the birth of a new and winning Dublin team. He's good, and has a great deal of presence on the field because of his blond hair and his high fielding, but if we finish him off before he has even started out on his inter-county career, then the entire Dublin team will struggle to mature.

As it turned out, Bolger was taken off the field with two minutes remaining, and watching him go was one of the most satisfying moments of my career. I know that may sound cold-blooded and cynical, but Gerry and myself have agreed, so often, that Bolger cannot be allowed to become a man on the Dublin team. If he does, he could also develop into a father figure, who knows? There is no such figure on the Dublin team at the moment, whereas we have three or four of them. That's the greatest difference between Dublin and ourselves.

Their uncertainty displayed itself at the very end when Vinny Murphy was taken down in our square, and Dublin were awarded a penalty. There were three points in it. Mick Kennedy is their normal penalty taker, but he was hobbling after taking a knock ten minutes earlier. In the old days Rock took their penalties, but he wasn't volunteering this afternoon. In the end, after much confusion, Charlie Redmond stepped up. Charlie went to place the ball and Gerry Mc helped him.

'Jesus Charlie, they're not asking you to take it, are they?'

Charlie side-footed it over the bar. I didn't want to look, but I did.

I was sure he would score, and I was all set to kick myself, because we had been in total control of the game for the previous ten minutes and shouldn't have found ourselves in such a situation. It had been the last kick of the game. Charlie Redmond lay on his back next to the penalty spot. Mattie was bent over him with a fistful of his jersey. He was shouting at Charlie.

'Give us your jersey, give us your jersey.'

It wasn't very good timing on Mattie's part, but afterwards in the dressing-room he told everybody he met that the 'fucking bollocks' wouldn't give him the jersey. Mattie thought it was really bad form.

Gerry McCaul, the Dublin manager, was squatting on the sideline with his back to the kick. I looked at him, and then I looked at Redmond kicking the ball over the bar. I didn't feel sorry for McCaul. He is an intense man and refuses to visit our dressing-room after games, as tradition suggests opposing managers should. That's his business, but the Meath team has decided to take his absence as a direct insult. Like we talk about Bolger, a few of us talk about McCaul. I don't know him, though Gerry Mc and Rourkey played with him in UCD for a while. But even they don't know him very well. He is included in the handful of ambitions which the Meath team holds. I want to see him replaced as Dublin manager before things start coming right for him. You've got to understand that every team needs to feed itself, and it doesn't matter how you do it. You've got to be hungry, you've got to be very hungry, and after winning the All-Ireland last year Gerry McCaul is very important to us.

21 August
Meath 0-16, Mayo 2-5, All-Ireland semi-final

Without doubt this was a weird game. We played fairly well for forty-five minutes and Mayo watched us. We were leading 0-12 to 0-2. It was too easy. Then Liam McHale got a good goal, from nothing really; then Anthony Finnerty got a second goal, after Mickey McQuillan fumbled a high centre and was left crawling after a ball which had been momentarily in his grasp; then McHale scored a third goal, beating Liam Harnan in the air and flicking the ball to the net. The third goal, thankfully, was disallowed because McHale had at least one foot in our small square. But, on some other day that same sort of goal would have been allowed. Mayo could have won the bloody match. Yet, in the final few minutes we regained our composure, and started building up our lead again which had been whittled down to four points. Mayo were also back to their old selves by then.

I can't explain it, but we wanted to win more than they did. It doesn't make sense, but I'm sure we want to win more than any other team in the country. We want to win more than we did last year, and that too seems hard to believe. But, it's the truth. We want to experience that same feeling again. We want to relive every moment of last year's All-Ireland victory. We have to. Winning the All-Ireland last year was amazing and surprising. Winning it this year exists as something natural. It's got to be ours.

17 September

This morning Martin Breheny's wife Rosemary called into our apartment in Sandymount. She had a letter from their two year-old son Alan which I'm being entrusted to carry to Martin who flew out to Seoul for the Olympic Games last Wednesday morning, with Jimmy Meagen. I'm the third part of the Press Group's team, but because of the All-Ireland final tomorrow I've delayed my flight out until Monday morning. Actually the Games opened today. I didn't see the ceremony because we were meeting up in Bellinter as usual this evening. My bags are packed, tickets, accreditation, travellers' cheques, Alan Breheny's letter to his Daddy.

I'm going to have to bring my bags to the Grand Hotel in Malahide tomorrow morning. There's a banquet for the team on Sunday night, and on Monday afternoon the team coach will inch into the arms of the Meath people. I'll miss that, and I hate missing it. Last year, as our coach crept towards the centre of Navan the entire Fair Green, a meadow of green and gold, slowly came into view, and I remember somebody shouting 'I don't believe this. I DON'T BELIEVE IT'. That's what winning this All-Ireland is all about, for us. It's about believing that we are the All-Ireland Champions. But, I've got to fly out to Seoul at 8.15 am on Monday morning.

18 September
Meath 0-12, Cork 1-9, All-Ireland final

The same forest of yachts, which we viewed as we walked Portmarnock beach twelve months ago, were still standing this morning. It was a dull morning. We'd met at the hotel in Malahide at 11 am and taken the coach to the beach. We walked, and kicked about a dozen footballs up and down the thoroughfare of hardened sand (and when a ball occasionally sailed towards the water one of Pat Reynolds' lads was commissioned to retrieve it). I don't know for how long I stared out at the yachts, imagining who was on them, and wondering what they were thinking. If they were racing, were they having fun? Their faces, were they smooth with satisfaction? Was the skin pulled taut, in concentration, determination? Whatever their faces were like they couldn't be like ours, and I think I envied them in a small way. They were sailing through the water. I felt stranded on the beach, sick in the stomach from tension, and squinting out through my death mask. On the morning of the All-Ireland final there is a huge variety of death masks, but they don't reveal anything. It's just that you don't know how you're supposed to look. You don't know what's about to happen, and you don't want to look happy or sad. You don't want to allow anything to surface on your face. So we all wear masks.

We ate a salad, and then retired to our rooms to nap for half an hour, and to change into our official clothes for the team photograph. I had the Sunday newspapers on the floor, and I'd flicked through *The Sunday Press* earlier this morning. I didn't want to flick through the others, but I did. I didn't want to rest. I didn't read. I glanced at different paragraphs, picking and choosing, and I stared at the front page of the *Sunday World* for ages. There on the front page, in colour, was an attractive blonde model; a sometime topless model, whom I'd often noticed before. And there she was wearing a Meath jersey. I was staring at her, and it meant something to me. Seeing this model in a Meath jersey told me that we were All-Ireland Champions, that we'd made it. I felt foolish for thinking that, and I felt foolish looking at her, staring at her just a few hours before I raced out onto the field for the All-Ireland final. But she was beautiful, and she was wearing our jersey. And I felt aroused. The jersey was cut in half. One portion she wore on top, and the second piece was tied around her waist like a mini-skirt. I shouldn't have been looking at her, I shouldn't have been thinking what I was thinking. I realised that then and I realise that now.

It's quite natural though to feel aroused at moments like that. I don't know about the other lads (it's not a subject we discuss very much) but I don't believe in having sex in the days and nights leading into a championship game. It's just something I don't allow myself, and Anne, thankfully, is understanding most of the time! There may be no good reason for not having any, and there may even be lots of medical evidence to insist that a steamy night doesn't have a negative effect, and cannot possibly leave your legs weak the following morning. So be it. I still refuse to indulge myself in anything the nights before an important game.

The entire Meath team is a fairly disciplined group. Nobody drinks too much during the course of the Championship, and nobody smokes but Jinksy. I have also tried to get my diet in order in the last few years, mainly trying to stock up on fruits, pasta, fish and white meat.

When you're training your backside off all through the summer, and making other sacrifices here and there, restricting your love life doesn't seem such a huge deal, though it can be difficult at certain moments. I remember watching an old boxing movie, in which the contender was resting on his bed and his wife (or lover) was walking through the room in her underwear. The contender grabbed her, and they kissed and passionately fondled each other and he threw her to one side, grabbed a bucket of ice and emptied it down the front of his shorts.

I believe an ice bucket is important in the life of an athlete. Not to reserve the strength in the legs, but to keep the mind right. I know I would not feel right having sex three or four days before an important game. I'd feel guilty. I'd feel distracted the following morning, and in the game, at a precious moment, it's just possible that I might imagine my opponent having the tiniest edge on me.

I'm not flying out to Seoul for the Olympic Games tomorrow morning either. I spent two hours in discussion with my sports editor Michael Carwood, and my editor Michael Keane tonight. I still can't believe that the game was a draw. We should have lost, and I was prepared for that defeat midway through the second half. They were the better team. They were the more aggressive team, and we were clinging to them. When the final whistle sounded I felt numb. I walked towards the dressing-room, and Brian Smyth, my uncle, was one of the first to reach me on the pitch. He asked me what I was going to do? I told him I wasn't going anywhere, and he seemed surprised. In the dressing-room, I kept repeating myself, telling anybody who asked, that I had to make a few phone-calls. By the time the team coach reached the hotel in Malahide there was some confusion about whether the replay would be in two or three weeks' time. Several phone-calls later it was decided to have a meeting with my editors in the Park Hotel on the southside of Dublin. Anne came with me. I was nervous, and I needed her there. I needed to tell her, repeatedly, what I was going to do, and I needed her to tell me that I was doing the right thing. As we went in the front door of the hotel I told her 'You know, I mightn't have a job when we walk out of here.' I'd given my word that whatever the outcome of the game I'd be on my way to Seoul, and I was reminded of that as I spoke with my editors. Michael Keane also made a couple of phone-calls during the meeting. To make a long meeting short, we finished up in agreement, and I thanked them for their support. Back in Malahide, at 2 am Anne and I sat down for our first meal since early afternoon.

I was happy, though the mood in the hotel befitted a beaten team. We had drawn with Cork, but they had beaten us. They were the better team, but they had also beaten us physically. They were far more aggressive than we were, and it showed. Rourkey climbed the staircase to his bedroom like an old man, having taken a shoulder charge from Barry Coffey in the chest and head. A tackle by Niall Cahalane had resulted in Staff having five stitches inserted between his nose and mouth after the game. An elbow of Dinny Allen's had connected with Mick Lyons' jaw, and he too retired to bed early suffering from severe headaches. He had played through the remainder of the game in a state of semi-concussion. They were the scars which were visible, but each of us felt inside, as though we had taken a beating.

Cork also played very good football from the opening bell. Dinny Allen gained possession on the right wing and made enough time and room for himself, and brilliantly chipped the ball across the field to Teddy McCarthy, who had somehow lost Gerry Mc. McCarthy also allowed Kevin Foley to slide past him, and slotted the ball into the net, between Mickey McQuillan's legs. Mickey, however, was the only member of the team who had been wide awake. The rest of us had been taken by surprise. Cork had played well, and still, we led by one point at half-time. 0-6 to 1-2. Staff had scored four points (three of them from frees) and Rourkey had launched two mighty points. Michael McCarthy and Larry Tompkins, from a free, scored Cork's two points, but it was McCarthy's score which stayed with me in the dressing-room. He had taken a short pass from Paul McGrath on the right wing, and ducked inside one desperate tackle before shooting over the bar from a narrow angle. It was a point which was taken quickly and brilliantly, and oh, so easily. It was a point which was already haunting our dressing-room.

We were leading because we had just about scrambled a share of the possession in the middle of the field. Cork brought Tompkins into the middle in the second half and I thought that suited us. The further Tompkins was from our goal the more defenders there were between him and scores, and that had to be in our favour. In our minds Tompkins wasn't a threat in the middle of the field. We then proceeded to watch

Larry Tompkins delivering one of the greatest performances of all time in an All-Ireland final. By the end of the game he had scored eight points, and he had also missed two or three frees which he should have scored, but in between he was quite breathtaking. The entire Cork performance was first class, a combination of skill and aggression which is often hard to balance, but of which Cork were totally in control throughout the second half. Gerry Mc had collided with Shay Fahy at the end of the first half and was subsequently barely able to trot. He was moved into centre-forward, and PJ was with me. With ten minutes to go Cork were leading by three points, and they took a breather. We suddenly realised what was happening and in the last ten minutes myself and PJ started winning practically every ball in the middle of the field, and three minutes from the end I made a thirty yard run into the Cork half of the field. I didn't look for anybody. I just decided to keep soloing until I was stopped. Stephen O'Brien and Tompkins both obliged. Staff scored from the free, and we were level. One minute from the end Tompkins struck a magnificent point from a free, and in injury time Martin O'Connell hit a long sideline kick from beneath the Cusack Stand. Rourkey went to catch it and the ball fell to the ground. Jinksy grabbed it and lost it, and in between he fell over Dave Barry's leg. It was a free, but it was the sort of free which teams seldom get, and which we never expected to get in the final moment of an All-Ireland final.

After Staff levelled the scores again, and Tommy Sugrue from Kerry blew the final whistle straight after the kick-out, the Cork players were incensed. I felt nothing. I walked by them as they crowded around the referee. They were behaving like men who had been cheated, but Tommy Sugrue had no hand or part in it. It was us.

19 September

Sean asked for a meeting at 11 am this morning. We sat in the bar where the air was still heavy with smoke and stale beer and Sean asked us, 'What happened?' We all told him what we thought, and Finian Murtagh was one of the last to speak. Fino had been on the bench yesterday, and wasn't one of the three substitutes who were used, but he was angry, and the more he spoke, the madder he became. There were lots of sore heads and painful faces around him. Mattie was sitting next to him, and in the middle of Fino's piece Mattie jumped onto his feet, walked around his chair twice, and sat down again. It took a couple of hours for everybody to sober up, and go home. Fino is normally one of the calmest and most level-headed individuals on the team. He said that we had been pushed around and bullied and punched, as well as being outplayed, and we didn't do a damn thing about it. Fino also said what we would have to do in the replay. Then he stopped and nobody had to say any more. Tonight I had to unpack my two suitcases. Tomorrow morning I will have to bring my travellers' cheques back to the bank. Tomorrow night we're training.

1 October

The Ballymascanlon Hotel, beneath the Cooley Mountains, was chosen by Sean as a place where we could quietly complete our preparations for next weekend's replay. It hasn't quite worked out that way, or maybe it has. I don't know. There was an argument this evening. Some of the single lads on the team started grumbling about the fact that they weren't allowed to bring along their girlfriends for the weekend. All the wives were present, and Boylan felt that was necessary. The season has been long and tiring, and he didn't want lads going back home tomorrow night to be met by wives who had been locked up on their own all weekend, or worse still, locked up with their kids all weekend. That would be totally counter-productive. He wanted us all to relax, and let off a little steam. The tension has been like a knife-edge for the last two weeks, and on the training ground two or three players are getting slightly injured every night. That's the way we decided we should do it. We decided to train like we planned to play, and on the first Tuesday evening after the drawn match Harnan had thudded into Mattie and left him heaped on the ground. That set the ground rules, and nobody had complained. A couple of the younger lads went missing later tonight though, and there'll probably be more words about that tomorrow morning.

Sean wanted everybody to stay put on the premises, but after that, the night was ours. None of the lads drank too much, but everybody stayed up late, and most of us stayed around for the disco in the hotel.

At 2 am, in the jacks, I was at a urinal when two lads unzipped either side of me. They asked me if I was Liam Hayes. They were from Armagh. They couldn't believe that I was at a disco the week before the All-Ireland final. They thought I had sneaked off for the weekend. I told them that Lyons and Harnan and the rest of the lads were outside. They started laughing. They didn't believe me.

2 October

The television set in the hotel bedroom wouldn't do a damn thing for me. I had got up early because I wanted to see John Treacy in the Olympic Marathon, but the damn television set was spluttering and coughing, and after fifteen minutes I gave up on it and went back to bed. That about sums up the Seoul Olympics for me. For the last two weeks I've been setting alarm clocks for the middle of the night, or lowering mugs of coffee into the early hours, but either way I've missed most of the action. A tiny part of me tells me that I should have been there, that I could have flown back two or three days before the replay and nobody would have been at a loss.

A final trial game was played in the grounds of Cooley Kickhams later in the morning. It was raining heavily all morning, and although there was a length of grass on the field it was still difficult to keep our feet. The game was, well, as we had agreed it should be, to be honest. Coyler and Kevin Foley had to be pulled apart in the opening minutes.

They hadn't thrown any punches, but there was something about the way Coyler was shouting and Foley was staring, which suggested that they didn't like each other very much at that moment. There were more tackles like that, and Sean who was refereeing let most of them go. I was up-ended by Padraig Lyons, and was blatantly pushed in the back twice by Gerry Mc. We were playing on opposing teams, and I was getting pissed off. Ten minutes from the end, Gerry went to catch a ball close to the sideline and I chose not to contest it with him. Instead I timed my challenge late, and knocked him over with a late charge. Fuck him!

But, he didn't get up.

Seemingly he hurt his shoulder, and nobody knows how bad it is, not until he gets it checked out in hospital tomorrow morning. I felt an idiot after it, and all afternoon while the lads swam or played tennis, I walked around like a sulking schoolboy. I wanted to tell everybody that it wasn't my fault. But it was my fault. Maybe there hadn't been any rules these past two weeks, but I still should have known better. For that moment on the field only one single thought gripped my mind. I had wanted to hurt Gerry, and I'd succeeded.

The team was announced this afternoon, and Padraig Lyons, Kevin Foley and Mattie McCabe have been sacrificed. They've been replaced by Terry Ferguson, Colm Coyle and Joe Cassells, and there were good reasons why they were replaced. But there were reasons why practically any one of us could have been dropped, and I feel sorry for them. I do. Especially Mattie. He'd played reasonably well in the drawn game, and had gathered up a good deal of possession, but obviously Sean felt he had to make some tough decisions.

Joe Cassells will be starting his first Championship game of the season, and he will assume his captain's role too. His patience and his support all summer long is being rewarded, and Mick Lyons doesn't mind a bit handing the captaincy back to him.

9 October
Meath 0-13, Cork 0-12, All-Ireland final replay

Nobody tried to wrap our intentions in secrecy these past three weeks. We said we were going to be a more aggressive team, and Cork had overheard us, there's no doubt about that. Nevertheless, it was important to tell them personally in the first few minutes of the game. That's all we wanted to do, let them know that we weren't going to be shoved around. Up to the last minute before we left the dressing-room Sean voiced his approval, but he also held the ball up in the air in one hand, as he spoke.

'This is what will win the game for us. Nothing else!'

Those were his final words.

'Controlled aggression.' That is what Sean has demanded almost every day, for the last three weeks. He had a picture in his mind of how he wanted us to play, and we all saw that picture. It was a picture remarkably similar to Cork's performance in the drawn match, and if we could reproduce that performance we knew we would win. Six-and-a-half minutes into the game, Gerry Mc was sent off. He walked to the sideline, and was met there by Sean who, at that moment, looked old and weary. Gerry had stopped Niall Cahalane from rushing out of his defence with the ball, and in the presence of the referee he struck Cahalane on the side of the face. It was a slap with his open fist, which was worse than a proper punch, because it made more noise. Cahalane fell. All the Cork players jumped in Gerry's direction, as we knew they would, and even though Gerry was in trouble with the referee we knew we had to do what we said we would do. We had to match them man for man, outnumber them, push them back. I struck Shay Fahy, Cass hit Teddy McCarthy. Everybody else was pushing and shoving. Then, Gerry was gone.

The game continued to descend into a physical and untidy squabble, which suited us while we regained our composure, and reorganised. Cork led 0-6 to 0-5 by the interval. By then, there had been one further knockdown, and one which was perfectly legal. Ten minutes before half-time, Cahalane was once again coming out of his defence with the ball, marching out of defence as he likes to do, and Rourkey met him flush on the shoulder. Cahalane fell back on his arse, and was eventually penalised for over-holding. It was a perfect charge by Rourkey, and not only did it set up Staff for a point from the free, it also assured each one of us that we could beat them even if they had an extra man.

One of their half-backs, Tony Davis was the extra man, but it was Martin O'Connell who made all the difference between the two teams. His fielding and charging up the field was inspirational, and it was the sight of Marty, more than anything else, which made us believe we could win the game. In the fiftieth minute it was 0-8 each, when Bernie Flynn, who had swapped positions with Jinksy at half-time, latched onto a crossfield ball, beat his man and stroked the ball over the bar from thirty yards. Dropping a point behind seemed to totally dishearten Cork, who had already been struggling to locate their extra man when they had possession. We were three points up with nine minutes left, four points up with seven minutes left, and began to bravely (and stupidly) defend. Allen, Tompkins and Coffey scored points, and if an extra minute remained Cork would have levelled the game.

We had received a second bite of the cherry, and we had sharpened our teeth and taken a mouthful. We had played the same way Cork had chosen to play three weeks earlier, but in the intervening period they seemed to have changed. They never managed to summon up the desire which had left us virtually beaten and definitely sore when last we met. In the midst of our happiness there were several heroes. My own choice was PJ, who had watched over the threat of Tompkins for most of the afternoon. He will not be near the front of the queue when the credits are being handed out tomorrow morning. He did nothing spectacular, and neither did Larry, and that's all that needs to be said in PJ's case.

As he left the field, Tompkins was struck by a Meath supporter. I didn't see it, but I heard about it, and it sickened me. I've always felt that supporters shouldn't be allowed onto the field at the end of games. It leaves the players in physical danger, and frankly I'm amazed that somebody hasn't been hurt in the past. I've been verbally abused after matches myself. Nobody should ever be allowed onto Croke Park after matches again. I only hope that what happened to Tompkins doesn't overshadow our achievement, though, in honesty, it should.

We're All-Ireland Champions, and allowing that thought to seep down through my body is all that matters to me at this moment.

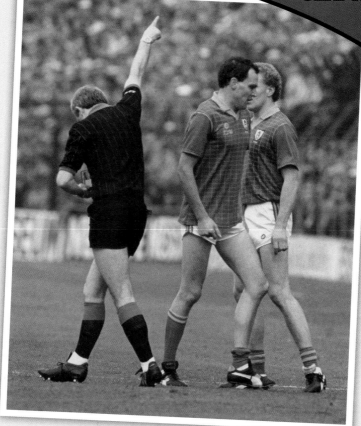

CHAPTER 11

Gerry McEntee

BAD LOSERS AND BAD WINNERS

10 October, 1988

It didn't have to be a beautiful morning, and yet, it was blue and mild, warm even, and there was a faintly freshening breeze coming in off the sea. Or was that the way I wanted it to be? I walked with Anne for a mile or two along the beach, neither of us saying very much. I hadn't slept well. Every time I twisted or turned on the bed I seemed to discover a different bruise on my body. It was good to get out of bed finally, eat a quick breakfast, and stroll along the beach. I was thinking about Gerry Mc a lot. He'd been quiet and withdrawn yesterday evening.

Gerry is someone whom I've always felt close to, although we rarely talk or meet outside the dressing-room we've shared for the last eight years. We're all friends, but how many good friends will we have when it's all over and we walk away in a variety of directions?

That's a question which is easily answered. In my case I know I will have very few, though Gerry might be one of them. Who knows? There's nothing anybody can do about the loneliness he is feeling, and Gerry is such an intense creature at the best of times that anybody who tries to reach him will probably end up empty-handed. I was thinking about him as I walked the beach, and at the same time I was feeling very happy for myself. I also felt guilty, I felt bad because a certain portion of my happiness had its roots in Gerry's misery. I was thinking that now that Gerry had been nowhere in sight for almost an entire All-Ireland final which we had won, maybe I was finally freed from beneath his great wing.

That's where a great number of people feel I have been residing for the last few years, and perhaps they're right. It's difficult to escape Gerry's incredible presence and I'm up closer to him than anybody else. We've been together for eight years, but sports writers (my colleagues) have a nasty habit of insisting that Gerry Mc is more than a partner in the middle of the field. I can see it in Sean Boylan too, and other lads on the team. Gerry is a father amongst us, and I will always be one of the boys. Most of the time that doesn't bother me, but yesterday PJ and myself played together at midfield on a Meath team which won the All-Ireland title, and that makes me feel good, even better than I should feel. I'd hate anybody to know that.

I feel like a free man, and that my sympathy for Gerry is overshadowed by the satisfaction of my own performance. That was important to me on the beach, but everything changed this afternoon at the Royal Hospital in Kilmainham. The traditional lunch for both teams is an uneasy alliance at the best of times, a bit like deciding to party in a funeral home. Everybody is happier when it is over, and the winners and losers can stand up from the table and take their separate paths. Very few of the Cork players turned up for the lunch, as it turned out. Barry Coffey and Conor Counihan were there, and one or two others, but I was told that the remainder of the Cork party was scattered in a number of pubs around Heuston Station waiting for the train south. The food was good, and the speeches began.

The president of the GAA, John Dowling, told the gathering that he was not happy with the game he had witnessed yesterday afternoon and stated: 'I will deal with it at the appropriate time and place.' I found it surprising that he should consider the replay any different from the drawn match.

9 December, 1988

The darkness which sat heavily on the large car-park didn't hide the fact that there were only a handful of cars present. It was almost 10 pm, and there was frost in the air and the deeds of autumn 1988 had been glazed over for a couple of months. But the knowledge of what we achieved this season still remains. That's all that matters. The Leinster and All-Ireland medals, and the National League medal presented to us tonight don't matter at all. I haven't examined last year's medals, not once in twelve months, and tomorrow morning I doubt very much if I'll be exploring the three little boxes I took home with me tonight. Tomorrow morning I'm going to wake up and my immediate thoughts are going to confirm that this evening was a disaster.

It was bad enough that there was nobody present. The County Board hired out Warrenstown College, one of the largest halls in the county, for the All-Ireland presentation and by the time I arrived, which was purposely one hour late, about one hundred people were glued to the walls and some country and western band was dying on its feet in front of half a football field of unwanted space. That was bad! From there, the remainder of the evening and the early hours of the morning sped downhill. I left at 1 am, angry and disappointed.

Gerry McEntee and Liam Harnan refused to take the stage to receive their medals from John Dowling. After three months on the receiving end of sermons, editorials and abuse, the last thing we needed was a provocative gesture like that. I know that Gerry and Liam felt they were acting on principle, and I know that in their eyes the rest of us acted like hypocrites. But, this team has taken enough abuse since beating Cork in the All-Ireland final replay, and there's a time to walk away. We should be able to stroll into the distance as champions, and not give a damn. Yet, it's not as easy as that.

There was no problem backstage when the time came to receive the Leinster medals. Jack Boothman, the Chairman of the Leinster Council, held them in his giant hands and everybody had a bigger smile for Jack than for the pieces of silver. Jack Boothman is a very rare and large creature in the GAA's animal kingdom of officials. He understands players and likes us, and spends most of his time socialising with players, but a large share of traditional blood also pours through Big Jack's veins. He's a good friend and as soon as he had finished his job for the evening, John Dowling took his place centre stage. There had already been some discussion among the players in the last week, but as soon as Dowling came into view there was a definite proposal in the air that not one single player should be seen on stage with him. He was seen, rightly or wrongly, as the person who had first criticised out performance in the replay when he spoke at the Royal Hospital dinner. Since then, so many other voices had echoed his sentiments. Anyhow, when the MC called for the team captain, Joe Cassells, to come forward there was still no agreement among us about what we should do.

Some players wanted to leave Dowling frozen to the spot. A few of us were adamant that such a gesture wouldn't do the team a damn bit of good. Joe's name had been called out twice. When he was called the third time, Joe was still being tugged and pushed. In the end I shouted at him to get out on stage. I promised him I would be right behind him. As it turned out most of the players followed Joe, and I took my turn in the middle. Only McEntee and Harnan refused to budge. I suppose that's their right, and they have definitely been courageous to the bitter end, but they've achieved absolutely nothing. It's like insulting someone in your home. It's not going to look good.

It might not do a great deal of harm though either, and who am I to admonish Gerry and Liam? One week after the All-Ireland final replay I refused to bottle up my emotions, and wrote aggressively and arrogantly, I suppose, in *The Sunday Press* in a piece which was headlined 'No Apologies'. I explained why we played the way we did against Cork, how we knew our tactics would be successful, and generally I told anybody who didn't like our style to go stuff themselves. Much of what I wrote still holds true in my heart, but it was bad timing, and perhaps insensitive towards Cork. Then again, they hadn't bothered to show up on the Monday morning and some of their players chose not to be gracious in defeat. They had set the physical tone of the All-Ireland in the drawn game, and we set out to match them in the replay. That's all that happened.

In casual conversation, and even in formal interviews before the replay we admitted that we had been physically outplayed by Cork, and we had the injuries to prove it, although we didn't talk about them. Nor did we ask for sympathy. Since winning the All-Ireland title it seems to us that the Cork team has been soaking up all the sympathy they can get. It was up to them to admit that we had beaten them, if not fairly, then on their own terms. I can't say that all the Cork players are guilty, I'm sure they're not, but too many of them indulged themselves in the roles of victims for our liking. Meanwhile, we have been cast as a group of thugs.

It hasn't spoiled our satisfaction. As I've said, we're very secure in the knowledge that we are All-Ireland Champions, and that we deserved to retain our title. But everything else, the warmth, the ringing applause, the bearing of prized adjectives at our feet, all that was reduced to a trickle within days of our victory, and that has left a certain amount of anger and resentment amongst us. It has showed in our performances since. We have lost four straight games in the National League, beginning with our opening game against Monaghan in Navan two weeks after the All-Ireland final when there were only ten players in the dressing-room fifteen minutes before the start. We've been distracted since, and disorganised, and some of the older lads, Gerry Mc and Joe and Rourkey, have opted out for the winter. We've been in a dishevelled state since early October, and it showed in our last game before the Christmas break when Dublin totally outplayed us. It's the first time in over two years that we have lost a game to them, and the victory is likely to remain centre stage for them until we next meet. It's something we can't take away from them, and even though we consider the defeat meaningless they will convince themselves that it is of incredible value. To them it probably is. The last two months should have been the greatest of our lives, and instead they were something less than that.

Rourkey, Coyler and Larry Tompkins were named as the principal villains in the All-Ireland final, and in a long-drawn-out investigation they were asked to explain their performances in the game. Then they were warned about their future conduct. It was all so ridiculously dramatic and unnecessary, but obviously since John Dowling himself asked for the disciplinary committee to peer into the game, they had to be seen to do something to some players. How they came up with Coyler, Rourkey and Tompkins alone, is anyone's guess. The entire exaggerated inquest has been a farce.

CHAPTER 12

Billy Morgan

BEACHWEAR

26 January, 1989

This afternoon some of us decided to go to Puerto Rico, a resort about thirty minutes from Playa del Ingles. It's smaller and quieter and cleaner, and there was less chance of meeting up with any Cork footballers. That's not why we went there this afternoon, but it is one good reason. Cork and ourselves have been on the same island now for almost a week, and I suppose it's not a huge coincidence that we should both decide to holiday in Gran Canaria. At this time of the year there's not much of a choice when it comes to sun and sand, and some decent heat. We also holidayed here last year, and although most of the team would have preferred to go somewhere else this time, it's just within our price range. Each player can bring his partner and still pocket more than enough spending money. It's a good feeling being handed a little brown envelope with cash in it.

We knew that Cork were going to the Canaries too, but it was only in the last couple of weeks that it was rumoured that they were also staying in Playa del Ingles, and less than seven days ago it was confirmed that we would be staying under the same roof, in the same apartment complex. However, their fortnight began a week earlier than ours, and by the time we arrived last Saturday night some of them had already gone home.

Last Sunday morning, the morning after we checked in, Anne and I decided to walk along the beach front and we hadn't gone half a mile when we came across Cork manager Billy Morgan, Colman Corrigan and John Kearins walking towards us. I saw them about one hundred yards away, and while I didn't know quite what to say to them, I knew I had to say something. When they were upon us I said, 'How's it going lads?' and held out my left hand and patted Kearins on the stomach.

He was the one nearest to me. He seemed uneased by my touch and mumbled something back. Morgan and Corrigan just kept on walking. Anne thought they might not have seen us. Both of us had met Corrigan and Kearins less than twelve months ago, when we were on our honeymoon in San Francisco and had a friendly chat in the hotel lobby for ten minutes. But they must have seen us! I had stalled for a moment as they passed, and I looked around and Morgan was still walking on, but at the same time he was looking back over his shoulder, staring, just staring for several seconds. I told Anne they had definitely seen us, and that they could go to hell.

That's twice that Billy Morgan and some of his players have turned their backs on us since losing the All-Ireland, and obviously they just can't come to terms with the two defeats. That's their business, and it's also their problem. What happened didn't annoy me, but it made me wary of being too polite to any other members of the Cork party we might meet. There was no need to be. I've bumped into Shay Fahy, Teddy McCarthy, and Stephen O'Brien since and they appeared perfectly comfortable with us, and more importantly, with themselves. Then this afternoon, we hadn't been lying down on the beach in Puerto Rico fifteen minutes when I heard Cork voices in the distance. I had my eyes closed. I hoped they would pass by. Instead they stopped directly behind us, an arm's length away.

In the next ten minutes we managed to nod greetings to each other. There was Larry Tompkins, Conor Counihan and John Cleary and their partners. I wasn't bothered crossing the tiny divide of sand to chat to them. The entire Cork party are going home tomorrow, and it will be good to see the back of them. Because then, everybody can relax further. That's what I was thinking when Tompkins suddenly sat down beside me, which took me by surprise. He was friendly and seemed totally relaxed and I thought myself ridiculous for having felt in any way awkward in his company. We talked for twenty minutes, about all sorts of things, and even tiptoed across the All-Ireland final too. In the middle of it, Mick Holden also plonked himself down in our company. Mick, who has played football and hurling for Dublin, has been around all week, and he's one of the best lads you could meet off the field. He's always himself, which means he is laid-back and good-humoured and always thoroughly likable. I've heard that he's been giving Meath lads and Cork lads a hard time whenever he's met up with them, and on one occasion in which a group from both sides were in his company and stubbornly refusing to meet each other halfway, Holden launched into one of his tirades. 'Jaysus lads, ye'll all be dead and there won't be a football in sight.' Typical Holden. 'And if there is one, it's mine, and ye can't play with it!' By the time he was finished both sides were stumbling over each other in their attempts to be chums.

Tompkins and I should be the best of friends. And despite our talk this afternoon, we're not. It's a pity, but it seems it's just not possible. This afternoon he made it his business to be decent and friendly towards me. In the past I've always treated him likewise, and I've always written about him in the highest possible terms. I've stated many times in *The Sunday Press* that Larry Tompkins is the best footballer in the country at this moment in time, and I stepped further than that last year when I suggested that it would have been proper for him to receive the Texaco Footballer of the Year award instead of Brian Stafford. I don't know what Staff thought of that but I've had the impression that he was a little less than pleased, though we've never spoken about it. Other lads have spoken to me about Tompkins, and wondered why I'm willing to act as his publicist. It's difficult for me to reply to that. I know Meath people, and a large section of the Meath team view, Tompkins as the epitome of everything they dislike about the Cork team. All I can say is that I think he is a magnificent player, and perhaps the most complete footballer of his generation.

I believe that, and I've stated it. So why should I feel uncomfortable in his presence, ever so slightly uncomfortable? I suppose it's because we both belong to two different groups who have made enormous sacrifices chasing the same prize in life. Both of us have dedicated this part of our lives to winning the All-Ireland title, and it's not easy to be friends, even though we've come a long way together. Larry and Shay Fahy, myself, Colm Coyle and Finian Murtagh. We played against each other in the Leinster Minor final in 1980, when I missed my two bloody penalty kicks, and we beat them by three points. We had also beaten them in the Leinster Minor semi-final the previous year, and we continued to meet up as we all found our feet on the Meath and Kildare senior teams. Meath won most of those matches, and now Meath are winning against Cork.

I've met up with Shay more than Larry in recent times. He's a strong, big-hearted individual. Last year he was unfortunate on holiday because he travelled out with Kerry midfielder Dermot Hanafin to the Canaries, and also ended up amongst the Meath team. But Shay can cope with those sort of things. He was taken off in last year's All-Ireland final, and the following afternoon I was sitting quietly at a corner table in the Burlington Hotel, and he made it his business to seek me out and congratulate me, even though I had been directly responsible for the greatest disappointment in his football career. That sort of style I could only imagine being matched by a man of Mick Holden's stature.

30 July
Dublin 2-12, Meath 1-10, Leinster final

The final whistle of a game sometimes seems to last a lifetime. That's when you've lost. I've always compared it to a traffic accident, when you know you're about to crash, and a hundred thoughts somersault across your mind. It's always seemed the same to me. Initially, when the whistle sounds, you think this cannot be happening, that it is definitely a dream. Then you admit to yourself it is happening, and you accept you've lost, and you're left waiting to see what's going to happen next. Except that nothing happens. You walk off the field, and into a serene, deathly chamber and sit there, and think, and stare.

It wasn't quite like that this afternoon when Dublin won the Leinster final. I didn't walk anywhere. I listened to the final whistle, and I shook hands with Paul Clarke, and sat down! I don't know why? It just occurred to me to sit down. Two or three of the lads walked off the field. Most of the team stood around in a misshapen huddle while Gerry Hargan received the Leinster trophy on the Hogan Stand. I sat and my view of life, my view of my football career was interesting. I played well this afternoon. It was probably the best and certainly the most complete game

I've ever played for Meath, and my catching was close to perfection all through. Not that any of that means anything now, and it's not as if my own good performance allowed me to view Dublin's glory through a pair of spectacles which deflected the pain of defeat. It still hurt, sitting there, watching Hargan smiling and shouting.

Yet, for some reason there wasn't a trace of envy in my body. I didn't feel happy for the Dublin captain, but the thought that Hargan deserves this moment was already surfacing within me. It hasn't surfaced yet, but it will, soon. Dublin deserved to win, and Gerry Hargan especially deserved to captain them the day they finally beat us. I've watched him, so many times, himself and John O'Leary coming into our dressing-room and congratulating us on our victories. They have both been dignified and brave in the past, and they have walked through our dressing-room, and home, and got through the following week without voicing a word of resentment.

That's why I could sit there and watch Gerry Hargan displaying his happiness as if he was pasting a giant poster across the face of the Hogan Stand. Hargan and O'Leary, Paul Clarke and Ciaran Duff and Barney Rock, they have known how to behave as losers, and it would be petty of me to deny them their moment as winners late this afternoon. We've had our problems this season, and midway through Mick Lyons broke his leg, and to talk of them might be seen as an attempt to steal away a tiny portion of Dublin's hour of contentment, but it's not. Believe me, it's not. They played very well this afternoon, and better than any performance I've witnessed from a Dublin team since the 1984 Leinster final. They were strong and forceful, and they believed they would win. That showed in their faces from the first minute, and it displayed itself in Keith Barr's face more than most. He's a new half-back whom Dublin have 'discovered' in the last couple of months, and he, more than anybody else, fathered this victory. It felt like we were playing the Dublin team of old, and like the old team they scored two goals this afternoon.

We've always assured ourselves that if we deny Dublin goals we will always beat them. The first goal they scored in the opening minutes of the game was one of Duff's greatest. He overcarried the ball. He took about eight or nine steps, in fact, but that's irrelevant now. Duff's shot from twenty yards, which riffled into the top left-hand corner was such a magnificent score that everything which occurred before it was reduced to petty complaints. I think it inspired what followed.

Dublin were the better team from that moment on, and although we clung to them until the final five minutes of the game, on the score card of any boxing judge they would have had a healthy points advantage. As it happened, at the beginning of the twelfth and final round, I managed to gain possession on the end-line beneath Hill 16. I tried to squirm between two defenders, which wasn't pretty. Tonight one of my many good friends on this team told me that I looked like a lug worm in heat. At the time I thought I might win myself a penalty. We were two points down, that's all. I hit the floor and there was no whistle, and I quickly got back onto my feet again and blindly punched the ball across the Dublin goalmouth. Mattie McCabe was there, and he punched his third goal in his third successive Leinster final. We were one point up. One minute later at the opposite end of the field Vinny Murphy did well to make a clean catch in the middle of our square. He tried for a chipped point with the outside of his right boot, but the ball struck Martin O'Connell's hand and left Mickey McQuillan stranded as it entered the net. Dublin were back in front, and they won by five points in the end. Two goals! As we've always told ourselves. 'Dublin win matches with goals!'

I came home early from Ashbourne House Hotel, and at ten minutes to midnight Sean Boylan called in, and we spent the next four and a half hours sitting in the kitchen. There was milk, cheese and tomatoes on the table. That's all we needed. We told each other things, about ourselves and others, which we had never told each other before. He knows that he must largely shoulder the blame for what happened this season, but on Sean's team, in which everybody speaks and whispers and shouts, every single one of us must accept equal blame to the manager. Nevertheless, I don't know what he'll do next. The lads didn't respond to him this season, not like we have in the past. I didn't, and I know that I am beginning to discover more and more faults in his ways, whether they are there or not.

We've been together a long time, and I'm wondering if we're tiring of each other's company on the training field, without knowing it, and without wanting it to happen. Sean has looked old this summer. He has been irritable. There have been times when he has looked distracted. Yet all through he has never quit acting like a best friend to each one of us. We should have given him more, and we didn't.

The year ended much like it began - rushing around, and trying to be somewhere at the last minute. Gerry McEntee left the United States last Friday morning to play in the Leinster final. This year he's working in the famed Mayo Clinic in Minnesota, and he could only manage one weekend off. By the end of the game he was sitting on the sideline, exhausted and in the company of Colm Coyle who had been sent off midway through the second half. As soon as the game was over Gerry had to rush from the ground without showering. There was a helicopter waiting for him in the grounds of Clonliffe College, and a private plane brought him to Heathrow for a 6.30 pm flight to New York. He's due back at work tomorrow morning.

On 3 May, the date of my brother's birthday, David Hayes, my son, was born. He made Gerard's birthday by fifteen minutes, and this afternoon's defeat shrinks rapidly when I put it next to his sleeping body.

We're no longer Leinster Champions. Dublin are back, and in the morning it might feel like they've never been away. When they're champions they play like champions and I imagine we will have to start off at the very beginning again. We were close to finishing them, putting them down for a long time.

Last night, outside Bellinter House, Gerry, Colm and I agreed that one more defeat would see the end of Gerry McCaul. Then Dublin would have to start from scratch with someone new. They would enter the Nineties at our feet. Twenty-four hours ago that was believable.

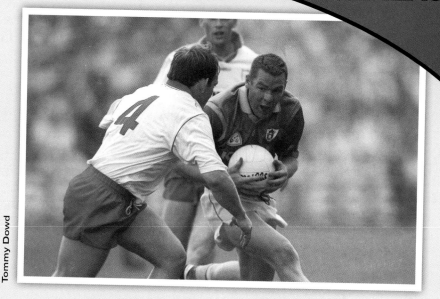

CHAPTER 13

Tommy Dowd

STARTING OVER

29 July, 1990
Meath 1-14, Dublin 0-14, Leinster final

This morning, in *The Sunday Press*, I broke all the rules and bared my soul as I have never dared to in the past. Athletes are not supposed to exhibit themselves in public in this way, I know, but I may never experience the morning of a Leinster final again. It was an opportunity for me, Liam Hayes, sports journalist, to dissect Liam Hayes, Gaelic footballer, and I seized it.

'I hate this, and I don't know why. I should be used to it by now, the thought of spread-eagling myself on this page and wondering if any Dublin footballers will take pleasure in watching me in all my nakedness on the morning of a Leinster Football final.

'Honestly, there is a large knot in my stomach as I write. If anything, it has grown over the years and here I am twenty-eight years old, six feet and three inches, fourteen stones and nine pounds, and I'm scared of telling how I feel. It should be getting easier. Dammit this will be the sixth time we will have played Dublin in a Leinster final and it's the fifth time I'm writing about it.

'I shouldn't feel nervous and tense. Not now, on a Friday afternoon in the comforting silence of a back bedroom, perfectly insulated from the sound, the taste and the smell of Sunday afternoon. I shouldn't feel like rolling myself up into a ball and waiting until Sunday morning to peek out, like the other

guys do. The other players, they snugly hide within their own bodies or else they politely hand out familiar, respectful, anaemic thoughts. Twenty-nine footballers. Twenty-nine bony, muscular balls. And me, with my eyes closed, but wide-legged. . . .

'. . . I'm afraid. There, I've said it. I've opened a chamber of my heart which was last examined when I was eleven years old and made the Skryne under-fourteen team for the first time. I didn't want to know, and minutes after the game I was told to shut the chamber door. I threw away the key myself.

'But why? Now that I'm older, and still nervous, and twice as uncertain, I find myself wondering why Gaelic footballers are scared silly of peering into their own hearts. I see nothing wrong in grasping my fear, balancing it on the palm of my hand, patting it on the head, generally getting to know each other. It's good. Without it we might all become mindless torsos and arms and legs hacking each other to death. No, it's very good. It's strengthening and calming, and most importantly, it's always there.

'We're all afraid, even if we refuse to talk about it. I'm scared of losing, and especially scared of losing to Dublin. I'm scared of playing badly. I'm scared of every sentence I write about the Leinster Football final. I'm scared of waking up tomorrow morning. I'm scared of watching the team die. What are you afraid of?

'I'm scared of losing to Dublin, even if this is our fifteenth time to meet in League and Championship since 1983. The thought exercises itself in my mind every morning and every night, and regularly in between. At lunchtime, when I'm helping my fourteen-month-old son flick through the pages of his first book or sometimes as I stare blankly at the television set. This is 'Rocky XV', but I feel I'm watching the movie for the first time.

'It will not go away and I wouldn't want it to. It's stimulating and sends a nervous charge into every crevice and dead end in my body. I know it's the same for everybody else too. . .

'. . . I'm also scared of the team playing badly. Even though the attitude on the training field and over the dinner table and in front of the television set is different. It's just different than last year. It's as though over the last twelve months a huge brick wall has been built directly behind our backs. If we lose there will be nowhere left to hide. We will be left at the foot of the wall, a large green and gold mound of bodies, a team decomposing in full view. If we lose? That's another word with which football teams refuse to identify. Fear and losing. Everybody thinks about them, but keep your mouth shut!

'What do you mean LOSE?

'It's funny too. Footballers prefer to doubt themselves rather than agonise

over someone else's performance. There is no such thing as a team game, not in a pure sense. Gaelic football is fifteen games which overlap, within one large green board game. Everyone wants to win and everyone wants to play well and everyone wants the guy next to him to play well. That's the order they come in.

'And the guy who's missing? The guy who's injured? Liam Harnan? He will be missed. Though he will cease to be missed once the game commences. Someone in the dressing-room will shout something about 'doing it for Harnan' and everybody else will agree. Just like they agreed when Mick Lyons was absent in the past, and then everybody will run onto the field and forget he ever existed…

'…But why should I worry? Footballers don't read newspapers on the morning of a game. Well, few of them do. They prefer to wait until that evening, when they have won and then they can taste every word and digest them or spit them out, whatever they choose. I know I don't want to read what any other players say in any other newspaper this morning. I don't want to see their pictures. I don't want to see them. I don't want to meet them in the corridor leading to the dressing-room because I know we'll ridiculously try to ignore each other or briefly stare at each other out of the corner of our eyes without saying anything.

'I don't want to see them when I run onto the field and they're at the other end. I don't want to peer over my shoulder during the kick-around. I just want to walk to the centre of the field, and shake one of their hands and wait for Paddy Collins to throw the ball into the air.'

I can hardly remember Sean Boylan as uptight as he was last night. He's been in bad form for a long time it seems, and everyone is entitled to their time in the dumps, but it's unusual in Sean's case. Normally he turns up, out of the blue, one night in a month like a tiny bear with a sore paw. The rest of the time he measures out his moods to fit different occasions. Like the week before a match he'll be getting on everybody's back, but most especially Bernie Flynn or Bob O'Malley (they are two pupils he turns on most often when he feels irritable), and then on the Tuesday before the match he'll jog amongst us, telling us individually how well things have picked up.

'It's going to be just right, fella. It's just right.'

But for the last couple of months he has been edgy every second evening. I'm sure he has his own reasons, and I haven't asked him what they are.

Last night was one of those nights when Sean and myself banged heads in full view of the entire panel. It seems amusing and mostly embarrassing twenty-four hours later, but we always seem to turn on each other only when there is an audience present. We were having our normal team meeting, and there was a lot of tension in the air. The subject on the floor was Tommy Dowd, and how he should play against Keith Barr. Sean knew what he wanted Tommy to do, but it sounded a tiny bit complicated to me. Other ideas were being thrown at Tommy's feet from different corners of the room. I hadn't said very much during the previous thirty minutes, but without intentionally storming the conversation, I barked that we were probably only going to succeed in messing Tommy Dowd up. I also mentioned that the last time I'd heard so much talk being shoved down a player's throat was before the 1986 All-Ireland semi-final when Marty O'Connell was playing full-forward, and was sick with indecision. Sean went to interrupt me, and I told him I was talking. He slammed his pen on the table, and he stood up and I think he motioned to leave the room.

'I've got the floor,' I reminded him, once again too loudly.

I was far too emotional, and probably touching upon the irate, and thankfully Joe Cassells doused the incident with calm words.

Tommy Dowd was outstanding this afternoon, as it turned out. He ended up taking on Barr, one to one, and he beat him several times in the first twenty minutes. That was inspirational. To have a young player, in his first Leinster final doing that was so uplifting, and Barr and the Dublin defence looked quite shocked by Tommy's fielding and his bullish strength. After thirty-five seconds Colm O'Rourke had opened the scoring with a freak goal. A centre from Colm Brady - another twenty-year-old who has been playing midfield in his first season - was dropping down on John O'Leary and Rourkey challenged him on the edge of the small square as he went to catch the ball. Whatever happened, the ball ended up in the net, and Dublin were chasing us for the remainder of the game but they never quite caught up. We were leading 1-7 to 0-2 ten minutes from half-time, and held a five point advantage at the change. The goal left them stunned. We were fortunate, because I must have seen the same sort of goal scored twenty times over the years and it has always been disallowed. Sometimes rightly, sometimes wrongly, but cancelled nevertheless!

We were totally on top in the middle of the field too. My catching was really good. Fingertip stuff, which meant that my timing, the five or ten yards run and the leap, was inches away from being off. I'd have been happier if I was under the ball more, but two of the catches were two of the best I've ever made in Croke Park so I wasn't complaining at half-time. Colm Brady was meeting with less luck from the kick-outs, and was giving Paul Clarke too much space in front of him, but around the field Colm was working himself to a standstill. He is a magnificent athlete, and in Gerry McEntee's absence we have formed a good relationship together on and off the field.

I'm not sure what happened in the second half. Bernie Flynn chipped over a sweet point after thirteen seconds and Staff and Rourkey made it 1-10 to 0-5, and we relaxed ever so slightly, I think. Not purposely. We just couldn't help ourselves, because nothing in our preparation and our thoughts before the game had included a runaway victory. And when a team's momentum dies, no team or no man can restart it from the grave. Twice, in the final five minutes, Dublin reduced the margin to one point, thanks to a series of brilliant free-kicks from Barney Rock. Staff and Jinksy got the final points of the game, and Gerry Mc came on with three or four minutes remaining and made a superb catch. That's the one catch that everybody is talking about this evening - Gerry Mc's! There is a moment in every game when the stage is emptied and one man can fill it on his own. Gerry did that this afternoon, and Colm Brady and Liam Hayes were suddenly relegated to the chorus line. But that's unfair to Colm who maintained his performance all through. I allowed Dave Foran to dominate for a crucial ten minutes in the second half. I can't say anything.

Gerry McCaul came into our dressing-room after the game. He spoke with dignity and honesty and explained that pure superstition prevented him from appearing among us in the past. I'm sure he's finished now as Dublin manager. Whether he wants to continue or not, this is the end for him. We've succeeded in our aim. We've witnessed the last act of McCaul's failure. The only problem is, the pleasure of witnessing that act was left sterile by Gerry McCaul's personal appearance and friendly words.

August 8

The Mardyke Athletic track in Cork was as quiet and peaceful a spot as I could have wished to spend the afternoon. Yet, I was uncomfortable. There was nobody around, and only the squeals and the scraping of runners on tarmac on the adjacent tennis courts served to distract me. I felt uneasy because I was in Cork city. I felt like a foreigner. That's crazy,

I suppose, but it looks like we might be playing Cork in the All-Ireland final again, next month, and I shouldn't be here in the weeks leading up to that possible match. It just doesn't feel right. I felt tense, and by the time Sonia O'Sullivan walked in the gateway, twice I had considered leaving and heading home. She was over an hour late, and although I phoned her home from a telephone box and was told she would definitely arrive, I seriously wished to disappear. Sonia is a middle distance runner, who's on scholarship in Villanova in the US. She's good, quiet-spoken, and she didn't seem to know a damn thing about Gaelic football, which was perfect. The interview went well, and it was worth travelling to Cork to meet her.

We're on the doorstep of an All-Ireland final, and I'm not exactly sure how we've reached this point. Last year, Colm O'Rourke and myself sat in the Cusack Stand and watched Cork beating Mayo in an All-Ireland final which was good-natured, ever so polite and not decently competitive. That game buried the tempestuous finals of 1987 and '88, and throughout the winter it had never dawned on me that our 'business' with Cork would quickly recommence. That might be about to happen. Meath had played poorly in Division Two of the National League, losing to Louth, Roscommon and Antrim.

The final two defeats were by 16 and 10 points respectively, but Division Two was brimful of mediocrity this season and we squeezed through to a quarter-final meeting with Donegal on April Fool's Day!

The year started off normally enough, playing challenge matches in which nobody took any interest, and on one occasion, on a wet Saturday morning playing UCD, Mattie McCabe had his ankle broken. Some things, including Mattie's ill-luck, never change. We beat Mayo by three clear goals on a perishingly windy day in Navan, to restart the National League with a quick shot of encouragement. We looked very good that day. Then all sorts of weird things started to happen. A few hours after Buster Douglas beat Mike Tyson for the World Heavyweight Championship, we were seated, shivering, in an icy dressing-room in Kiltoom watching Colm O'Rourke arguing with local officials who wouldn't allow him out to inspect the field. Colm was ill and wasn't playing, and he was also furious and totally irrational, and eventually he walked the pitch in his wellington boots. It had been raining continuously for twenty-four hours in Roscommon and the pitch wasn't playable.

'Maybe he'll drown out there,' somebody said.

'Yeah, he's definitely going down,' added someone else looking out the window.

'Thanks be to God for that!'

Colm thought the pitch was fine. We all wished he thought it wasn't, but nobody said anything. The feeling was that the team was finally coming around after twelve months of tiredness. The Roscommon officials and team didn't want to play either, but their guests insisted they were going to play, and that was that!

'Let's show these cowardly bastards,' someone shouted as we left the dressing-room.

It had to be someone who was standing beside Rourkey. Roscommon won by sixteen points.

We had to beat Antrim to keep our interests in the competition alive and well, and to prove that Kiltoom was a very damp aberration. The day before the game I was in Paris for the Five Nations Championship match between Ireland and France. Ireland were stuffed, and I was in no mood to go to bed early after the game. So, Vincent Hogan of *The Irish Independent* accompanied me out on the town, and up the Eiffel Tower. I had to be out of my bed at 4 am the next morning. I couldn't get into the same bed until 2 am because the teller at my hotel didn't report in until that time (something like that, honestly), and that was my only opportunity to get money changed. At 6 am I arrived at de Gaulle Airport. The plane I was supposed to be taking to Heathrow was there before me, and we stared at each other for two hours. It was too sick to go anywhere, and I managed to get a flight to Gatwick in London instead. There I got on stand-by, onto a plane, and arrived in Dublin three hours before the start of our game against Antrim. Brian Smyth rushed me to Belfast. The team bus was already in the grounds of Casement Park. It was forty-five minutes before the game. I jumped out of Brian's car and a Meath fan walked by me, and demanded, 'Will ye ever get the lead out of your arse today!' We lost by ten points.

After that Sean announced at training, in the icy air and semi-darkness of Pairc Tailteann that as far as he was concerned the Meath team was finished, and a new one had to be created. He started his building programme by dropping Mickey McQuillan, and unfortunately he stopped it there too. Donal Smith has been in goal ever since, and Donal's an exceptional goalkeeper, but Mickey should still be on the team. He has as much right to be there as any one of us. As he himself likes to remark dryly, 'If it gets past fourteen of ye, why do you think I should save it!' Four goals flew past fifteen Meath players in Casement

Park, but only one player, only Mickey McQuillan has paid the price. He says he will retire at the end of the year, and I'm telling him he can't, but I'm having difficulty convincing him why not.

On 1st April, against Donegal in the League quarter-final, we looked foolish for forty-five minutes. We also looked lazy. We knew that and we couldn't do a damn thing about it, or wouldn't do a damn thing about it, I'm not sure which. Is there much of a difference? They were winning by five or six points, I can't remember, and there were ten or twelve minutes left. Who cared? And then something happened. To them or to us?

We scored two goals. Twice Rourkey offered David Beggy two good opportunities, and twice Jinksy obliged, and then four or five points were scored with the confidence which is normally reserved for the training field. Confidence which none of us had witnessed, anywhere, in the previous eighteen months. I'm still not sure how the team managed to relax for so long. Deep down, we no longer cared. We were tired I know that. We felt wronged, angry and tired, and it's not easy to play football under those three spotlights.

Then, something else happened. We beat Donegal, and Cork in the semi-final, and Down in the final, and we were National League champions, but champions who had been christened on April Fool's Day. I'm not sure how that happened, but we obviously began to show a little bit more pride in our appearance and our performance, and pride has a magnetic force. All sorts of other positive things can attach themselves to a bit of pride.

I'm not saying that we haven't played really well when it mattered in all the vital matches this season. We did and we also surprised ourselves by just how well we played at times. We deserve to be Leinster Champions again. Then, last Sunday evening, we played Galway in a challenge match in Summerhill and half the team dragged its feet into the dressing-room. The other half didn't. They didn't even appear. Some of them had excuses and some of them had awful excuses. It's been that sort of season. It's like we're scaling a mountain and we're not exactly sure how we have reached this point. At times, I'm not even sure how we're holding on.

Last night, Sean Boylan talked about last Sunday's effort against Galway, and then he listened as we talked amongst ourselves. Rourkey and Harnan had decided that the facts of life had to be laid down for some people. Colm Brady was amongst those who didn't show up. I don't know why he didn't show. It's been rumoured that he was at a party on

Bettystown beach, but I don't know for sure. Nor do I know what he told Sean. But it was decided that Liam Harnan should deal with him. What followed left me attempting to seek sanctuary beneath my own seat. Harnan immediately started belting Colm Brady with the facts of life until he was black and blue. I was on the opposite side of the room to Colm. For ten minutes Harnan took him apart, and Colm didn't offer up a single word in his own defence. It was far too much. By the time he finished, Colm Brady may as well have been deposited in tiny little pieces in the small tin bin in the corner of the room. Tonight I phoned Colm to see how he felt. He was better than I expected (he was asleep on the couch, in fact). I still felt as if I was rummaging pathetically through the same bin and trying to piece him together again. I should have at least raised one word in his defence last night and I didn't. Colm and myself have come a long way together this season, and I owed him that. Before every game I've reminded him that it's him and me. That we've got to look after each other.

'We've got to be there for each other all the time.'

'The defence will look after itself, and the forwards will look after themselves.'

'We've got to look after each other.'

That's what I've been saying to him.

'It's you and me. Remember that.'

And where was I last night?

I know Colm Brady is a bit scatty. For instance, he's never at home when Colm O'Rourke calls for him before training. He's always supposed to be at home, but he's usually somewhere else, or else he arrives home half an hour late. Maybe he needed his head twisted around a few degrees, but it shouldn't have been put into a spin, not now. He's the kid on the team. And he's done as much to get us this far as anybody else. I don't know what's going to be left of him.

19 August
Meath 3-9, Donegal 1-7, All-Ireland semi-final

This morning I took the readers of *The Sunday Press* into the circle which the team forms on the field before every game. I didn't ask Sean Boylan's permission, and I have no idea how the rest of the lads felt about having strangers amongst us, observing what lies behind the team's mask.

'Out there, in the open, it's not as if anyone listens. We gather around Sean,

but nobody hears him and he knows that. He knows that it's important to be together, briefly.

'*Not too close. Nobody attempts to wrap their arms around each other. The team is surprisingly reserved in public. We just stand there, somewhere between the twenty-one and forty-five metre lines, arms folded, hands on hips, and seem to listen, intently.*

'*Anyhow, in the dressing-room Sean Boylan has already climbed up onto the tiny pulpit in the middle of the floor and spoken, quietly, with dignity – a friend, calming, and especially reassuring.*

'*His team stands around him with arms stubbornly linked, hanging on every word, watching them drip individually from his lower lip. In the privacy of the ugly, misshapen room the players hold each other, forming one anxious being, one giant insect trapped in a creamy cement box with all its feet nervously twitching.*

'*And for a few minutes, the team's heart and soul, and its stomach, are bared, when nobody is looking, where nobody can hear. Then, and only within that intimate and stifling circle, can the character of the Meath team be perfectly observed.*

'*At that moment the chain breaks, and the team gains a voice. One link, team captain Colm O'Rourke joins Sean in the middle. He says little, but he says enough. He speaks for all of us, and we listen to our own thoughts, our own promises, our own demands. And we listen to our fears being smothered. . . .'*

I continued in that vein. I'm sure the lads didn't like me making a home movie of them. Nobody said anything after the game. If we had lost it may have been different.

Donegal had two great chances to score goals. Seven minutes before half-time Joyce McMullen was racing through our defence after taking a good pass from Martin McHugh, and he could have scored a goal. He should have scored a point. He didn't know what to do, and muffed his shot. Midway through the second half, when the teams were level, McHugh mis-kicked the ball from ten yards and Kevin Foley batted it away. Though Donegal did score one goal. It came on the stroke of half-time from the penalty spot, and left the score at 1-4 each.

PJ Gillic was easily our best player this afternoon, and the rest of us played as though we were still damned tired. We would have been on our knees only for PJ, and our two goals within sixty seconds of each other in the final ten minutes of the game gives the impression that Donegal were well and truly beaten. They were not. But they were never going to win the game either. The team has always relied far too heavily on Martin

McHugh's strong, but small shoulders and he wasn't given more than a couple of sniffs of the ball by Foley. Donegal played well, and they kicked twelve wides, and still they were lucky to score 1-7.

Staff and Bernie, his second, scored the killing goals, and significantly both of them were largely created by Rourkey. He had an awful game, and midway through the second half it looked like he was being taken off. It would have been the first time he has ever been taken off a Meath team. Anyhow there was a great deal of confusion on the field for two or three minutes, after Gerry Mc came on as a substitute. Gerry was coming on in the middle of the field, and he insisted afterwards in the dressing-room that he was told Rourkey was the player going off. He remembers hearing Sean distinctly say that. But Rourkey didn't budge when he was told. In the end Sean ran onto the field, and called Colm Brady off instead.

I'm still not exactly sure what happened, but it looks like Rourkey refused to go off, which was just as well in the light of the last ten minutes. Brady was unlucky to be hurriedly sacrificed in the confusion. He did well.

Donegal started the match by shoving their weight around, and trying to convince us that they wouldn't take any bullying. With the mood the Meath team was in they needn't have bothered, but in those early minutes Brian Murray threw a few punches in the middle of the field, and in one incident where he threw a punch at Kevin Foley who was getting up off the ground, it was Brady who was first in to stand up for his team mate. I was proud of him at that moment, and I'm sure everybody on the team, and especially Liam Harnan, shared that feeling.

It's surprising, as well as a relief, to be in another All-Ireland final. I wasn't aware of the tension which was gripping my stomach though, not until this morning. We were having our chicken salads in the hotel in Ashbourne, and as we were finishing up at about 1 pm, Liam Creavin came around handing out car passes, (the County Board receives only a limited number of passes from Croke Park for parking inside the ground). He was handing out those few tickets, and other tickets for the grounds of Clonliffe College which is about 400-800 yards from the entrance to the ground. Most of the players were receiving the Clonliffe College passes, as usual, and would be left making their way through the rival bands of supporters on our way into the ground.

It's wrong, it's crazy and most dangerous to have players making their way through the crowds in that hectic and tension-filled hour before the start of the game. But, I suppose it's hardly Liam Creavin's fault. He has been County Secretary for over forty years, and he's a mild-mannered and most precise individual. Liam is the softer, gentler side of the County Board, and I don't know what got into my head but when he arrived at our table and started handing out those Clonliffe tickets, and then offered me one of them, I blew. Before I knew it I had grabbed all the tickets from his hand, and thrown them over the table. Most of the lads enjoyed the bit of surprise entertainment, but I felt a bit of an idiot. Obviously, I had to let off some steam for some reason, but Liam Creavin is a gentleman and later in the afternoon, minutes before we ran onto the field, I made it my business to apologise to him. On the field, in the first few minutes of the game, I remained angry and distracted.

16 September
Cork 0-11, Meath 0-9, All-Ireland final

This is easy. It was more difficult writing in the days after winning the All-Ireland finals in 1987 and '88.

We lost the All-Ireland final. We lost and we deserved to lose. We lost because we were not competitive, and for that we may never forgive ourselves. But that shouldn't stop me from admitting that Cork arrived at Croke Park looking like champions, in sharp double-breasted suits, and played with a calmness and authority and belief (without playing brilliantly), and left looking like champions.

They won by two points. Shay Fahy scored four points. I was marking Shay, and it doesn't take a mathematician to calculate the depth of my regret at this moment. I've always played well against Shay, and my confidence on this occasion was such that I set myself a target to score three points this afternoon. The first score he got he raced out of a jungle of arms and legs in the middle of the field and was away from me before I knew it, and he thumped the ball over the bar from forty metres. The second wasn't my fault, but it was still Shay's score. Danny Cullotty retrieved a loose ball in the corner of the field between the Cusack Stand and the Canal End, and I had to cover him. Somebody else had to take my man. Cullotty was Gerry Mc's man.

And when Cullotty passed to Fahy I thought Gerry would get to him. He didn't. The third point, shortly after half-time, was served up to Shay on a plate by Marty O'Connell. Marty won possession in defence, and I immediately went running upfield. When I looked back, at the sound of the crowd groaning, I saw that he had passed the ball straight to Shay, who was twenty yards behind me. He thumped the ball over the bar again. The last Fahy point was my fault.

But, as far as anybody looking on was concerned the blame for each of the points was with me. Shay Fahy was my man. In the last quarter of the game I made a desperate effort to try and retrieve the situation, and more specifically to try and haul myself out of my mammoth humiliation. One run from midfield ended with Barry Coffey flooring me twenty-one yards from the Cork goal. A second run brought me past the Cork twenty-one yards line, and I flicked the ball to Jinksy, who flicked to Staff. He could have scored a goal, but the ball was blocked for a '45'. A third run finished up in the arms of two Cork defenders who hauled me to the ground on the edge of the square. It was inches from a penalty.

All through the game, or to be precise, from the moment their full-forward Colm O'Neill was sent off for hitting Mick Lyons, we played like condemned men. We needed a goal to offer us a finger of light. The whole ground was so grey, dark almost, this afternoon. And despite my last gasp efforts, I am standing first in line in the guilty queue. Directly behind me are Sean, Tony Brennan and Pat Reynolds. That may seem unfair, but they played their parts in our defeat earlier this week when they chose the team and decided to play Gerry Mc for the first time this season from the start. I'm not saying that Gerry shouldn't have been on, but that decision cost Tommy Dowd his place on the team and left Colm Brady in the unfamiliar surroundings of the half-forward line. In short, the way they picked the team virtually deleted two of the youngest and most exciting players we have. Gerry has had a groin injury for the last six weeks, and he was substituted in the end, and Tommy came on. But by then, the Meath team was playing like an old man. And, tonight, Mick Lyons looked that part. He resembled Marlon Brando close to the end of *The Godfather*. At one stage, in the early hours of the morning I counted six young footballers around him.

The Meath Minor team won the All-Ireland this afternoon, and they too were staying in our hotel. They were huddled around Mick, like disciples or young hoods around a wise, tired and sleepy great man. Mick listened to them, and they mostly listened to him, for an hour or more. Until, finally, he went to bed. Then they partied.

I didn't want to go back to my bedroom. The room was newly decorated and beautiful, and Anne had retired two hours earlier. I didn't want to go up. The first time I entered it was when I checked in this morning, and then my body was full of hopes and desires. I had taken a long look around the room (it smelled of peaches). I dared to imagine how it might look four or five hours later. At 7 pm I re-entered the bedroom with Anne and threw my bag in one corner. She sat down. I lay back on the bed and stared at the ceiling. Six hours earlier I had the same view of the same ceiling, and was imagining all sorts of things, good and bad. At 2 am, I finally climbed the staircase for the third time.

There were only five players behind me in the bar. I don't know how the others are sleeping, or if they are capable of sleeping. A defeat in an All-Ireland final is a ruthless bastard.

It has been a long day. The game, and then the sentencing! I was booed and insulted by several hundred Cork supporters as I walked from the doors of the dressing-room into the arms of my own family. We all were. We had to take it. I've walked the same stretch many times in the past and listened to an army of Meath fans subjecting opposing players to the same volley of disgusting insults. This afternoon it was our turn. Last April, when we beat Cork in the National League semi-final, I witnessed Larry Tompkins being treated exactly as I have been treated this afternoon.

Today, I waited on the pitch as Tompkins raised the Sam Maguire Cup. I didn't want to, but I felt it was the right thing to do. It's the respectful thing to do. As I waited for Larry to finish his speech, three Cork supporters raced up to me in turn, and as they approached their faces turned ugly. They spat a string of pathetic insults in my face. I didn't do anything about it. Defeat, in the past, sentenced Shay Fahy to study the same ugly faces up close. This may be the end of the Meath team. Or there may be one last year. Nobody knows. We have spent five years on the mountain top and we are still here, but I'm not sure what we're doing up here anymore.

2 December
Meath 1-11, Donegal 0-10.
At 8.15 am, my daughter Sarah was born. I managed to get an hour or two of sleep before travelling down to Navan for today's game. Donegal were bad. They were dispirited. It's our second win of the League. We beat Cork in our first game, when Colm O'Rourke was sent off and I talked to Shay Fahy after the game and found out that he had married and honeymooned in the Caribbean immediately after the All-Ireland final. We lost to Roscommon and Armagh. This afternoon, the year ended with a benign smile on the team's face, though I was beaming. As I was leaving the dressing-room Frank Keating came up to me and told

me that Aidan had died during the week.

Not that many people surrounding the Meath team knew Aidan, and amongst the proud and noisy army of Meath supporters he was seldom seen, and he was never heard. Yet, if a football team can have a best friend, Aidan was ours. He was loyal and supportive, and he was always present. On March and April evenings, when the training field was a place of doubt and exhaustion and disillusionment, Aidan would often turn up. He and Frank, who would keep him wrapped in his blanket. In the front of the car, the seat half reclined, Aidan's red head would remain stiff but alert, his eyes betraying his weak and crippled body. At that angle, his chin raised, his face strong, Aidan Keating observed and nodded and when the training session was over he would almost attempt to smile, for any one of us. Though, Mick Lyons was his favourite.

In summer, and the confusion of early autumn, as hundreds of supporters attached themselves to the wire surrounding the training field in the weeks touching upon the All-Ireland finals, Aidan Keating was seldom visible. He was there of course, but he didn't need to be seen. He couldn't push or shout but even if he could have, even if he could have stepped out of his wheelchair and grabbed himself a better view, he probably would have decided against it. He was a true friend, and true friends don't need to be seated in the front row every day of the year, do they?

The last time I met him was on the Monday evening after losing to Cork in the All-Ireland final. It was after 10 pm and the team coach had stopped by Dalgan Park. In the semi-darkness the entire team posed for a photograph, with Aidan in the front row, and for the first time that long and agonising weekend I was happy to smile. We all smiled.

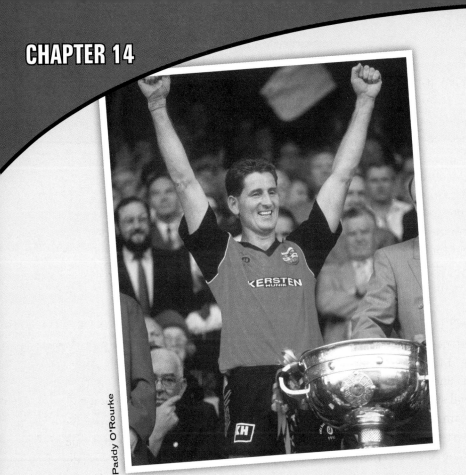

CHAPTER 14

Paddy O'Rourke

FINISHING UP?

22 January, 1991

A postcard from Orlando, Florida:

'Having fun! Everybody's in good form. It's warm and there's lots to do, and there's a jacuzzi waiting for us at the end of each day on the road. In the foaming water and looking up at the stars and clutching a glass of iced water the last twelve months don't seem so bad. This year looks promising!'

That's what this holiday in the States is doing, almost without us knowing it. It's propelling us towards another season, and another, because none of us want to turn our backs on the good times. Where does that leave my promise that I'll finish playing football by my 30th birthday? I don't honestly know.

Last week, six friends took a boat out fishing from Clearwater beach where the entire team was staying. There was Sean Boylan, and his bride

Tina, Pat Reynolds, Tony Brennan, Jack Finn, and Colm O'Rourke. The rest of the team lay in the sun. By the time the boat reached the fishing water, one hour out, Rourkey was already below deck, his stomach emptied, his face a pastel shade of green. Doc Finn, a noted fisherman, was dishing out medicine and hooking bait at the same time. Pat was shouting back at Rourkey, 'Jaysus lad, those Skrynemen have no stomachs at all!' At the same time Pat's face had departed pink and passed through grey, and was continuing to travel. The two selectors were the next to fall, within ten minutes of each other. Eventually Jack joined them. The boat remained out for four hours, and Sean and Tina fished to their hearts' content. The rest of the crew spent the remainder of the day in their beds.

That story is one I will keep for a long time. I'll probably remember the story in five years' time. But, by then, how many of the story's characters will be my friends? I know that when a team disintegrates very few friendships can be saved.

I think the Meath team I've known and loved, has just about reached its end. If not, I don't know what's left for the team to do. I know Sean will stick around. I'm sure he will, and he'll probably try to shape a new team around the carcass of the existing one. But in the immediate future, next month, next summer, I don't know what's going to happen. I also know that such uncertainty brings out the genius in Sean Boylan. That's what he's best at, improvising, and doing things his own very personal way at a time when most other managers would have reached the end of their coaching manuals. For instance, for our first training session after losing the All-Ireland final, after watching us drag ourselves onto the field, Sean decided to have a game of Rugby League, with several rolling mauls thrown in for good measure. Everyone had a little bit of fun, and everyone felt a bit better for having togged out.

Sean knows how to cultivate the emotions of players, and that is his single greatest strength. It's more of a power than a knowledge.

Ahead of him lies his greatest task. Personally, I feel empty inside. I'd like to win another All-Ireland, but I've no interest in playing football in the immediate future. I've no interest in training, and playing in the National League and playing challenge matches and playing for Skryne. It's a chore. I can't remember the last time I looked forward to playing a game of football, when I last jogged onto the field and felt happy to be out there. The last time I felt excited at getting the ball in my hands seems like ten years ago, when I first stepped onto this team and the ball was something terrifying and wonderful. I know it's not like that now. Football is such a serious part of my life. I play because most of my friends are playing, and I play because I want to win. The intense satisfaction which comes from winning lifts me up. But, in between, in between my friends and that winning feeling, there is little left.

22 April

I'm captain of Meath, and writing those words doesn't dispatch a tingle in any direction along my spine. Sean told me he wanted me to be captain, and I'm not sure why, but I said I would be happy to take it. I'm not exactly a leader of men, not naturally, anyhow. But a change of scenery, from the corner of the room to the centre might be good for me. I'll enjoy it.

Last week, Sean took me to one side as captain and told me that he is going to have the team training in water until the week before we play Dublin in the first round of the Championship on 2 June. I thought he meant the sea. He was talking about a swimming pool, and he was quite excited about it, I could see. So, we have trained in Navan and Gormanston pools, and we were in the water again this evening. We already have eleven players with all sorts of injuries, liquorice and blue and yellow and colourless. I'm having trouble with the top of my right thigh myself, and with the ground hardening players can't train and recuperate. However, it seems Sean has learned that athletes can train in the water, despite a variety of injuries. And that's what he's doing. He's purchased a couple of dozen float jackets, and this evening everybody was able to complete a whole series of running exercises in the deep end. Including the half dozen amongst us who can't swim.

Padraig Lyons is amongst the hobbling wounded. He's damaged his left knee, but when he lifted himself from the water last Thursday he found himself limping on his right leg. His right knee was aching. His left felt fine.

'I swear, it was my left knee!'

Strange stuff, this water. Remind me to ask Sean about it.

We play Dublin in six weeks' time, and this evening I was floating on my back in the chilled water in Gormanston pool, staring at the ceiling, waiting for Sean to blow his whistle again, and thinking of Dublin. I'd prefer to be running around a training field thinking about them, but this is one of those occasions when Sean has asked us to trust him. So we thrashed in the water, up to our necks, for an hour.

Dublin are looking good. Since Paddy Cullen succeeded Gerry McCaul as manager late last year, the team has looked sharp and confident, which were two of the principal ingredients in Cullen's success as a goalkeeper with Dublin in the Seventies and in his business life as a publican. He's got a ready smile, and he rarely ventures out in public without it. I've been told that when he first spoke to the Dublin squad his final words were 'Okay, let's party'. That seems to be his style, and the Dublin team do seem to feel very good about themselves again.

We met up with Cullen's Dublin, for the first time, in our final match in the National League last month. They were leading by three points early on, and they were playing well, but on the field, I could sense that they were also looking behind them. They should have been leading by more than 0-3 to 0-0 after fifteen minutes, and they would have been if they hadn't been waiting around for us. By half-time we were in front of them. It looked like the same Dublin team we've played and known and beaten, but there was also a freshness about them.

The main difference on the Dublin team was Jack Sheedy. He's a big strong centre-forward, and he moved to the middle of the field for the second half that afternoon. Although he's a new face on the team, he very much took charge of things at a time when Dublin needed someone to do exactly that. The Dublin team of the last four or five years has lacked a father figure, a role model. Someone large, who can always be seen. With him, and with Vinny Murphy and Keith Barr having matured enormously over the winter, Dublin should win the National League.

Out of the water, I stopped thinking about Dublin. We don't seem ready for them, and nobody is talking about them in the dressing-room. The second of June is a date set in stone, and viewed, but seldom discussed. I don't know why, but I do know that it is unnerving, alone, to think of Dublin for very long, though this evening, as I drove home my eyes were stinging from the chlorine in the water, and 2 June was not quite visible.

12 May

We're still up to our necks in the water, thrashing. Tonight, we were doing a new exercise on our backs and there were an awful lot of waves and foam in the pool. Players were barely visible, and only Sean could be heard, somewhere in the water, shouting instructions and whistling. I wasn't sure what we were supposed to be doing.

'PJ WHAT THE FUCK ARE WE DOING?'

'SPLASHING,' he shouted back.

'BUT WHAT ARE WE SUPPOSED TO BE DOING?'

'SPLASH. JUST KEEP SPLASHING,' he roared.

Bodies continued to rise and sink in the water. Out of the water, with four weeks left before we face Dublin there is absolutely no sign of our enthusiasm and efforts being patched together. It's quite obvious to me that we're not trying hard enough. The realisation that we're playing Dublin on 2 June, and not some other county has not made its presence felt in the dressing-room. Sean doesn't look very worried, though neither does he look very pleased. There is still a tiny mound of injury worries - Rourkey, Staff, PJ, Marty, myself, Terry, and more! I listened to Anne Bourton going through her book yesterday morning, and the number of patients at her clinic is still in double figures. I feel despondent.

Colm Brady damaged his knee two weeks after the All-Ireland final, and is unlikely to play again for twelve months. Gerry Mc is out of sight, though I can't believe he has retired. If this is my last season, I'd hate to finish up like this. Dublin won the National League title last week, beating Kildare in a thrilling final with fourteen men, and there is a confidence swelling up within their blue jerseys which is going to be difficult to contain. It kills me to think that Paddy Cullen might get an easy passage through us in the Championship. Gerry McCaul may have been an unemotional man but he slaved in the creation of this Dublin team. It would be sickening to witness Cullen being hailed as the man who instantly led the Dublin team back to greatness. If Dublin beat us, it will be McCaul's team he is leading. Apart from Jack Sheedy, it is difficult to find a second fingerprint of Cullen's on Dublin's blue jerseys.

The last three weeks have been the most disheartening of the entire season. This evening we lost to Armagh at the opening of a pitch in north Meath. I heard the news by telephone. I had set out for the game at 6 pm, but after driving ten miles I turned around and came home.

I was in no mood to play football, and in the present circumstances there is no point in simply going through the motions in a green and gold jersey. Too many players are already doing that.

I came home, and watched television with Anne for the remainder of the evening, and around 11 pm I phoned Sean to explain to him what has happened and to hear the score. I told him that at 6 pm I had walked out the door to go to the game, that I had left Anne and Sarah in tears behind me, and David was about to join them because I told him I couldn't bring him in the car. Anne hasn't been well all weekend. I was away in Belfast last night, reporting on Dave McAuley's defence of his World Flyweight Championship and I drove home this morning. Anne had a tough night with the kids, and although she wasn't looking the best I knew I had to go to the game. I was ten miles from home when I realised that I shouldn't be playing football.

I told Sean what happened, and I told him how I was feeling about things generally. I also told him that I had talked with Anne about handing back the captaincy, but that probably wouldn't achieve anything. The mood of the squad is so relaxed and careless, that my throwing the captaincy in amongst them would probably only raise a few chuckles. That's how bad things are, and Sean hasn't been able to do a damn thing about it - me neither. We've played three challenge games in consecutive weeks, and we won the first, but that victory over Mayo was actually where the rot started.

At 7.30 pm that evening, as the Mayo team were about to take the field, there were only nine players in our dressing-room – nine players, and no selectors. Tony Brennan was next to arrive and Sean, who had been delayed in traffic at a Meath under-21 match down the country, was one of the last. We took the field over thirty-five minutes late, but we beat Mayo and played very well in the last ten minutes.

Last Sunday evening, after viewing the National League final, I rushed down to Ballylynan where we were playing Laois at the opening of a new pitch.

The GAA ground in Ballylynan is hidden behind the village, at the end of a long dusty laneway, and the Laois team had been on the field ten minutes when Mick and Padraig Lyons and Liam Harnan arrived. The selectors had chosen their team, and the jerseys had been handed out. The team was chosen again. Laois beat us by three or four points, but in truth they gave us a much greater beating than that. They were hard and physical, and brutally competitive at times, exactly as we knew they would be. Laois are always a strong, manly team and they seldom disappoint in that regard. I told the players so in my pre-match speech. I also spoke to them about Dublin and Kildare, and the work we have to do to reach their level of fitness and desire, but I stopped talking half-way through. Nobody was listening to me. The faces around me were long and tired, and surrounded by such indifference I shouted, 'Let's get out of here'. At half-time I got a response when I shouted that we were being bullied and physically beaten. We tried to stand up to Laois in the second half, and failed.

It has been the worst three weeks I have ever experienced as a Meath player. I can't wait for the Championship to start, and finish if that is the case. I'm angry with the lads, and I'm still not very happy with myself either. I've made a much greater effort than anybody else in the last month, and I'm still not looking forward to the next game of football. We play Galway in a challenge match next Sunday evening, and nothing has changed. It waits for me like a night's hard work.

23 May

It's as if a mystery virus has the entire squad of twenty-eight players in its embrace. Nothing else can suitably explain the lethargy which remains. We beat Galway by five points in our last game. They were awful and we were bad, and we all know the entire team will stir itself in the last week, when Dublin come into view, but desire will not get us far enough on this occasion. Too many players are playing badly, and that includes Mick Lyons and Colm O'Rourke. Mick has been injured and Colm was ill last month, but in the last two weeks they have resembled careless, old men.

This evening we had a meeting after training in Bellinter, and before it began I told Sean what some of the players wanted to talk about. Rourkey has accepted a role on RTE's *Sunday Game* series as a guest analyst, and four players have already asked me what's going to be done about it. They see it as a sign that Colm is quitting on us. Sean didn't see it that way, and asked me not to bring it up at the meeting. I told him I had no choice. If I didn't, I had been told by Padraig Lyons that he would do so.

For ten minutes I spoke about the indifference of the last month, and when I finished speaking there was silence. Sean, Tony and Pat decided to stay out of the first part of the meeting. I had mentioned that players were worried about Colm's commitment to RTE, and I also admitted that I was worried that himself and Mick were playing so badly. I admitted we all had our problems. When I finished, I expected to hear voices, admissions and promises. There was silence, and the heaviest silence of all came from the right-hand corner of the room where Rourkey was sitting. He was more huddled up than silent, really.

Eventually Padraig Lyons spoke up, and then Liam Harnan demanded that Rourkey explain himself? Colm was at worst monosyllabic and at best reticent. Liam repeated his demands, and eventually accused Colm of giving up on the team. Colm's last words were that his dedication to the team remains unaltered. As the discussion came to a close Sean entered the meeting. I expected him to start into the players. Instead he brought the meeting to an end with a few token words, and I wanted to say something to him after the meeting, but I chose not to at the last minute. Having an argument with Sean in private is hardly going to raise the team from its boots.

26 May

My friendship with Colm O'Rourke was laid bare in the dressing-room this morning, at the end of our final trial game. The game itself was interesting in parts. Mick Lyons played quite well. Gerry Mc showed up, and played in the middle of the field for the 'B' side, but his work commitments, he says, cannot allow him back onto the squad. It was good having him around, and at the end of the game he shared most of my fears. That was important, because I was beginning to think that it was just me. That maybe this captaincy is leaving me in an unhealthy sweat for no obvious reason. Gerry said he never saw the team looking more slovenly and lethargic.

Rourkey had started off on the 'B' team, but was switched onto our team at half-time, but he never seemed serious. He was fumbling every second ball, and he was talking and laughing on the field. Ten minutes from the end my frustration finally boiled over and I found myself roaring at Rourkey from a distance.

'If you're not going to bother, get the fuck off the field.'

They were my final words.

When I finished I could hear him laughing again, in the company of two or three defenders. In the dressing-room he said something, and I couldn't stop myself from telling him that the best thing he could do for this team would be to quit today. We continued at each other, and Colm Coyle finally intervened on behalf of the audience.

Sean is thinking of not starting Rourkey next Sunday against Dublin. I've already told him that dropping Colm would be a mistake, and would only further lower the morale of the team. I feel more certain of that than ever this evening. I'm still pissed off with him, and I feel that he's let me down badly both as captain and, more importantly, as a friend. But we cannot step onto Croke Park next Sunday afternoon without him. Sean says he wants to watch him again this week, and he'll decide then.

2 June
Meath 1-12, Dublin 1-12, Leinster Championship first round

Rourkey started the game at centre-forward, which was unfamiliar ground for him, but thankfully he was on the field. We haven't spoken to each other during the week. This afternoon he won a lot of ball around the centre of the field, and he also managed to keep Keith Barr suitably distracted the entire afternoon. Barr was so intent on minding Colm that he didn't launch himself into attack at all. Centre-forward is easily Rourkey's best position, but it's not always in the best interests of the team to have him there. He wins so much ball and attracts so much attention, that it is difficult to feed our full-forward line as fast and directly as we would like.

We should have lost. Dublin led 1-7 to 1-2 at half-time, and our goal in the seventeenth minute came after Rourkey and myself, of all people, combined. He made a great catch thirty yards out, and typically four or five defenders buzzed around him. As they did I sneaked inside them, and Colm flicked the ball over his head. I couldn't believe my luck. I had just John O'Leary to beat but as I went to side-step him somebody nudged my arm and the ball fell loose. I was about to look for it when Charlie Redmond (bless him), thinking I still had the ball in my arms, hauled me to the ground by the shoulder. Staff scored from the penalty spot.

Redmond, ironically, was Dublin's best player and gave Marty O'Connell such a hard time that he was replaced by Colm Coyle in the second half, though Redmond also failed to finish the game. He was shoving his weight around and late-charging defenders all through the match, and in the final minutes of the game someone struck out on behalf of the entire Meath defence. I didn't see who it was, and I didn't ask. That was the least of our worries in the dressing-room. We were outplayed for forty-five minutes of the game, and only a PJ Gillic shot from beneath the Hogan Stand and thirty-five yards out, which bounced over the bar, earned us the draw. There were few positive factors in our performance. I had my best game in over twelve months, and caught everything I desired (it was one of those sweet days) in the middle of the field. Tommy Dowd ran Tommy Carr ragged beneath the Hogan Stand in the second half, and Rourkey played better than the remainder of the Meath team. After the match I felt thankful towards him. We didn't say anything to each other. It wasn't the time.

9 June
Meath 1-11, Dublin 1-11, Leinster Championship first round (replay)

On Tuesday night last we returned to the pool in Gormanston, and by 9 pm the water was freezing. In the middle of the session we stretched out on our backs. Twenty-six blue muscular logs drifting in the silence. Ten weeks without a competitive game had left us sluggish and rusty, but

Bob looked like himself again.

Today he was so correct in everything he did, and Mick Lyons on his left was superb. He was sent off two minutes from the end of normal time for something that happened off the ball with Vinny Murphy, but by then Murphy hadn't scored and he doesn't look like he will ever score again on Mick.

It's only last month since Vinny Murphy was being considered the best forward in Gaelic football, but that was in the League. This is the real thing. Sixty seconds after Mick was dismissed, Murphy received a long pass and was left with Mickey McQuillan to beat from ten yards. He shot low, and McQuillan made a great save. He possibly should have taken an easy point. Then, seconds later Murphy and Paul Clarke collided in front of our goals going for the one ball. The ball popped out of their combined arms directly into Colm Coyle's hands.

We were blessed, and so were they. We had the wind at our backs in the first half and should have led by more than 0-6 to 0-3 at the interval. In the seventeenth minute Marty O'Connell raced into attack, making an extra man and PJ gained possession behind O'Leary. He blasted the ball, and it went over the empty net. The rain started to come down after half-time and Dublin had equalised by the eighth minute of the second half. Running back out the field, after that score, with the rain against our faces Rourkey and myself snatched a brief look at each other. In that moment everything which had happened in the last three weeks was left behind us, and buried. Dublin had twenty-seven minutes to win the game, and we were going to have to spend every minute holding on for dear life. Though in the thirty minutes of extra time they looked tired and ragged. Four of their players dropped with cramps and they were happy to live to another day.

13 June

I'm living my life on the road, and viewing the world through a windscreen freckled with the bodies of insects. Everybody around me, everybody around the Meath team thinks this is all so exciting, and they may be right. But I'm spending most of my days in the car, travelling at a steady sixty miles per hour here, and a steadier sixty miles per hour there. I could drive faster, but I'm not dying to get to any particular destination. Every day I'm in the car, going to work, coming home from work, going to the physio and coming home, going training and coming home. I want all of this to end. I also want to know who's going to win this marathon.

By next Sunday evening we'll have been in each other's company for over five hours, and none of us are any the wiser.

The Leinster Council of the GAA is going to make close to £1 million in gate receipts when this duel between Dublin and ourselves finally ends. There's some talk that they will make a contribution towards a holiday for both teams. That would be a decent gesture. But so much money is spilling over from this game and why should I feel thankful to anybody if I get a couple of hundred pounds at the end of it?

Meanwhile, back at the ranch, the number of free tickets we are getting from the County Board are multiplying in slow motion. We got two for the first Dublin match, and four for the replay. I'm told we'll be getting six free tickets for the next game. Brendan Cummins, the board's PRO has the unfortunate job of following players around before and after training looking for outstanding debts. It's ridiculous, it's sickening to see players handing over £60 or £80, or writing out cheques, after a night's training. Though I suppose it could be worse. Since the GAA gave their County Boards permission to print a sponsor's name across the chest and backs of their players, and also across one thigh, a great deal of extra revenue has been pouring into certain banks.

Meath were sponsored by a transport company for our first two games. Three days before the first game against Dublin I still hadn't been told what name would be on our jersey or how much the sponsor was paying to have us behave like athletic billboards. I think the Board had agreed on £4,000 or £5,000 per game, but nobody bothered telling us what was happening. This week we will have a different name printed on the Meath jerseys. Kepak, a meat processing firm owned by Noel Keating are I believe paying £10,000 for the next game against Dublin. Noel Keating has been quietly sponsoring the team, and giving players a helping hand personally for several years. It was he more than anybody else who made sure that we holidayed in Florida last January, and he is sponsoring the team on the condition that the players receive half of everything he pays out. It seems agreement will be reached on that, and the money will eventually be left to one side, to be used by the team at the end of the season. I'm sure there are very few other teams who have negotiated a deal for themselves.

Every team should have an agreement with their sponsor, and every team should have a players' pool, which can attempt to recompense them in some part for their loss of time and money during the season.

Noel Keating is a generous man, who admires the Meath football team and behaves like a very good friend who gives all the time, and doesn't ask for a damn thing back. For years he has been sending monthly boxes of meat to our training sessions, and players have been going home to their families with ten steaks nestled in amongst their smelly training gear.

23 June

Meath 2-11, Dublin 1-14, Leinster Championship first round (second replay)

The shower room, off the main dressing-room in Croke Park which we have been using for the last month, contains two steel pillars from which seven sprays of water spout. This month one of the steel pillars hasn't shed a single tear. Only three of the sprays on the second pillar have been working. I came off the field tired and sore earlier this evening. I took a knock on my thigh close to the end of normal time and was eventually substituted in extra time. Trying to stand in the queue in the shower room, and push and shove my way towards a spray of water, I didn't want to think about the game which had just ended, and I didn't want to talk about the game, not particularly. I'd played poorly again, and Dave Foran managed to distract me and still make a decent contribution to Dublin's performance.

Again, either team could have won. Dublin definitely should have won, when they were leading by five points with fifteen minutes remaining. But a Colm Coyle centre which was flicked to the net by Bernie brought us back into the game, and two frees by Staff grasped us the draw. The second was from forty metres into the wind, in injury time. Staff had been troubled with his free-kicks all day. I don't know how many he'd missed, but I didn't expect him to put over the last one.

Coyler put us in front with a goal fourteen seconds into extra time, and three minutes later Paul Clarke scrambled the ball into the net for the equaliser. In the last minute of extra time Clarke had a great chance to score the winning point but the ball drifted just wide. Thirty seconds earlier Jinksy had made one of his mad dashes down the left wing, and he was up-ended inside the Dublin twenty-one yard line but we didn't get a free. And we didn't complain. Dublin were a better team for most of the afternoon, and it was only in extra time when they tired and became disorganised that we found ourselves in a position to win the game. We've got problems. Marty and myself started off in the middle of the field, and we didn't do well together, and maybe that's not very surprising considering we have had a different midfield pairing in every game so far. Gerry Mc spent most of the afternoon on the sideline, but he was introduced to midfield half-way through the second half, and everybody is saying how well he did. He had watched the first two games against Dublin from the front row of the top deck of the Hogan Stand, but he couldn't restrain himself any longer. Everybody's a lot happier to have him with us on ground level, and that includes me most of all.

29 June

This morning the Meath team awoke in the tranquil village of Drymen, close by the shores of Loch Lomond, and most of the team and their partners had extremely sore heads. Sean has brought us to Scotland for a change of scenery, to allow everybody to freshen up, and he realised that staying up in the hotel bar until 4 am, singing and drinking, would probably be the most important event of the entire weekend. We've been playing badly against Dublin, and we needed to take time away from them. View them from a distance.

It was also important to wake up, and not find the Dublin struggle on our doorsteps each morning. The longest game in the history of the GAA is now front page news. The front page of *The Irish Press* on Monday of last week was totally devoted to the first round Leinster Championship game between Meath and Dublin. A slim strip, in black across the bottom of the page whispered 'Shocks for big parties in latest opinion poll, See Page 2.' That's the grip this game has taken on the country, and the pretty village of Drymen is allowing us to breathe. The village soccer pitch, on an uneven and sloping piece of ground is ours each morning, and we suffered there in the heat for two hours. Forty-eight large bottles of water had already been emptied, and in the end Mick McAuley was fed up driving back to the hotel and apologising to the morning staff. He chose to have a stand-up argument with them instead. This evening we will watch a video of the last Dublin game and have a team talk, and tomorrow night we fly home. There are no rules governing what happens in between, and Sean is not about to lay down any, though he'll probably advise the one member of our party who awoke on the hotel lawn this morning that a mattress might be more profitable for a good night's sleep.

6 July

Meath 2-10, Dublin 0-15. Leinster Championship first round (third replay)

It seems to me that the gods have been arguing directly over our heads for the last five weeks. So many things have been going against us, and at the same time there has always been just enough to hold onto. Twenty minutes before we took the field Terry Ferguson pulled a muscle in his back as he was removing his slacks, and he went into spasm. He was lifted onto the table in the centre of the room, and Doc Finn and Anne Bourton and Gerry Mc worked on him, but he was never going to play. All we could do was watch, and continue preparing ourselves. Sean Kelly had failed a late fitness test on the field twenty minutes earlier, and when the game did begin Padraig Lyons, Terry's replacement, collapsed after ten minutes. He was tackled crudely and tore his hamstring. The arguments raged above us.

We had started the game well, leading 0-4 to 0-2 after sixteen minutes, though Dublin held an 0-7 to 0-5 lead at half-time, and had increased that to 0-12 to 0-6 by the fiftieth minute. At that point Bernie Flynn hobbled off with a calf injury, and there seemed no way back, even though Staff scored a goal, after being set up by Rourkey, fifteen minutes from the end. Dublin were playing better than ever, and a few minutes from the end Paddy Cullen took off Charlie Redmond, who had been one of his best forwards. The game was theirs. Keith Barr had uprooted the green flag, which accompanies one of the goal posts, nine minutes from the end when his penalty kick went inches wide. But by then, we looked disorganised, and every one of us felt disheartened. In the final minute of the game Marty retrieved the ball which was about to go over our endline. Marty had one foot out of play, but got his pass away to Mick Lyons. Eight passes later, Kevin Foley was kicking the ball past John O'Leary for the equalising score of the game. From the kickout Mattie won possession, and fed me. I made ground on the left wing, turned inside and found PJ in space. He passed to Jinksy, who scored the winning point, and there was nothing Dublin could do about it. The gods had voted against them. I think they like the courage and the spirit which oozes from our green jerseys, because they are the only advantages we have held over Dublin these past five weeks.

10 August
Meath 1-11, Laois 0-8, Leinster final

The Meath team has been pinned to the face of a mountain since 2 June and tomorrow morning, when we awaken, that's exactly where we will remain. Grasping the Leinster Championship hasn't raised us an inch closer to winning the All-Ireland title.

That was always the way it was going to be, even before Dublin and ourselves first clung to each other in Croke Park over two months ago. Whoever was left standing at the end of that withering duel was expected to come out on top in Leinster, eventually, and march into the distance.

The Meath team hasn't felt like marching anywhere in particular in recent weeks. We've played eight games in the Leinster Championship. We crawled around Wicklow at the second attempt and that contented us, and we cantered through Offaly in the semi-final, and remained mildly contented, though still exposed. Defeating Laois this afternoon hasn't altered our situation at all. We have won very little this season.

Our dressing-room was as quiet after the game as I ever remember it. Liam Harnan was back in his clothes and gone by the time I returned from the showers. Sean didn't say anything for a change. I certainly didn't. The cup wasn't even left on the table in the middle of the floor. I don't know where it was, and I didn't ask. I suppose the demands of our victory over Dublin were much more than a Leinster title and unless we actually win the All-Ireland next month, the entire season will leave ourselves and Dublin occupying the same fruitless corner.

Laois haven't won the Leinster title in over forty years, and they released one hand on the trophy in the sixteenth minute of the game this afternoon when their corner-back, Tommy Smith, was sent off for striking Bernie Flynn off the ball. They had both been running away from the Laois goal after our first score of the game. Laois were winning 0-2 to 0-0 one minute earlier, but Bernie took a quick free to me from forty metres and I made ground before parting to Coyler. My pass was long, but he got his foot to it before it crossed the endline and Jinksy was waiting alone in the Laois square. Again, he was in the right place at the right time. It happens so often now that he doesn't get any credit from us anymore. Laois actually dominated the first quarter of each half, but they didn't play like a team who honestly thought they would score very much. In the last ten minutes we scored five points without reply. We played somewhere between poorly and reasonably well, and we won by six points. I should be happier.

There are very few Meath players who are genuinely happy this evening. The season has been long and tiring and the team has remained unsettled. And with Bob O'Malley retiring after only five minutes this afternoon with a suspected fractured bone in his leg, it's unlikely that very much is going to fall into place on the team in the seven days which remain before we play Roscommon in the All-Ireland semi-final. Definitely, the unhappiest man around is Gerry Mc. He beats me by a short head.

On Thursday night of last week when the team was announced, Gerry flipped his lid and kicked Pat Reynolds' car, and drove straight home. Nobody other than the three selectors witnessed his reaction because they had spoken to him in the car-park outside Pairc Tailteann, after most of us had already travelled on to Bellinter to eat and talk, and to hear the team. Sean had decided to tell Gerry privately, because he didn't want to start him in the middle of the field.

One week after beating Dublin PJ Gillic and myself played in the middle against Wicklow, and we were totally outplayed. PJ did okay, but I couldn't do anything right. Things had started going badly for me midway through the Dublin series, and they didn't stop until I was sent off early in the second half of our replay with Wicklow. We drew the first time around, which further dampened our spirits, but with Gerry and PJ in the middle of the field for the replay we won a decent share of the possession, and also the game by three points.

It was the first time I was sent off in my life. I was playing centre-forward, and I was playing pretty well. But I still felt uncertain within myself, and I wasn't being helped by a centre-back who was holding me throughout the game. I didn't think about hitting him. But the next thing I knew the ball was flying over my head, and he had me held by both arms. One moment later he was on the ground.

I was standing over him, and the referee was running towards us. Being sent off was a greater humiliation than I ever imagined it to be, because the incident happened beneath the Hogan Stand and I had to cross the entire field. A word of advice: if you're going to do something stupid in Croke Park try to do it closer to the Cusack Stand. I walked at first, then trotted, and then walked again, and I wished that someone would come out of our dugout to greet me, shorten my journey! Nobody did. Instead Sean passed by me a minute later, as I was seated on the ground, and tapped my head.

Gerry and PJ did well that afternoon. I received a two weeks' suspension, and they also did very well against Offaly as I watched from the front row of the top deck of the Hogan Stand, next to Joe Cassells, and ironically, in Gerry Mc's old seat! Earlier this week, at training on Tuesday evening, I felt at ease for the first time all season. I didn't know whether I would regain my place in the middle of the field, and I wasn't certain whether Sean would put me in the forwards either. But, not knowing somehow seemed to relax me. I don't know why. I think I felt as if I was starting the season afresh, and I was only too happy to put the first half of the season well behind me.

When the team was announced Gerry got mad, and it was difficult to argue why he shouldn't be mad. The selectors think he may not have the stamina for the full seventy minutes of a hard game, and they told him so. After Gerry's argument with them, and his dramatic exit, Sean was also mad as hell. He told me who was on the team in one corner of the room before he announced it to everybody, as he always does, and he made it quite clear that he had stuck his neck out for me.

'You've got to give me a big performance,' he said.

Twice he said it in fact.

He shouldn't have said that. He's the manager and he picks the team, and it was wrong of him to shift a portion of his decision onto my shoulders. I knew what I had to do, and deep down I was thankful to him for keeping faith in me. But it was up to him whom he wanted to play, Gerry or myself. He shouldn't have waved his uncertainty in front of my face. As it turned out, I played well in the middle of the field in the first half and I was involved in most of our scores, but Sean still wanted to bring Gerry on. And he brought him on at midfield, and moved me up to centre-forward, and Tommy Dowd, who had been playing well, was sacrificed on the half-forward line. The whole thing was a mess, and the entire team suffered from the uncertainty.

18 August
Meath 0-15, Roscommon 1-11, All-Ireland semi-final

It was as if the most stubborn of dams finally crumbled within Sean Boylan's head. He stood in the middle of our dressing-room late this afternoon, and his words brought the team's head to his chest and caressed it. He told us we were the most incredible bunch of lads he had ever seen, and we believed him, because we have waited for him to say that for months. All season long Sean has held his guard high. There have been moments when, speaking to an individual, he has lowered it and spoken fairly and honestly. And times, like at the end of the marathon tussle with Dublin when he has been himself and spoken to us like the true friend he is. The rest of the season he has been as hard as nails, but not on the training field. The games which rained down upon us didn't allow us to work up a substantial sweat at any time on the training field this season. In his words, Sean has never allowed us a moment's rest.

There have been occasions when I felt that he was grinding the team into the ground, at a time when I felt he should be hauling us into the air. I frequently told him that the morale in the team was lowering dangerously. I know he specifically wanted to weigh down the team's confidence, and he's right, the Meath team does not have the ability to handle a huge amount of confidence. It leaves us intoxicated and indifferent, and Sean has been terrified of that ever since we parted from Dublin. Though there were occasions before the games against Wicklow, Offaly and Laois, when he built the opposition into some of the greatest teams of modern times.

Offaly, especially, whom we eventually beat 2-13 to 0-7, were dressed up by Sean as a team who were not only interested in beating Meath, but who had every chance of winning the All-Ireland. On the morning of the match, before we left the team hotel he gathered us around him in the car-park and he told us we were going to be beaten, unless we hurriedly got our minds right in the three hours which remained.

When Dublin were freshly buried at our heels I didn't know whether we would win the All-Ireland. I feared every team which was waiting for us, and because of the four games in the first round there have often been three teams in that queue. I didn't even know whether we'd win the Leinster title. We weren't playing well, and we had injuries, and I couldn't help imagining the season suddenly nose-diving, at any moment. And every time we cleared one mountain Sean was there busily painting a new one, larger and even more intimidating than the last. I thought he was wrong. This evening, as he showered us with praise and affection I felt foolish for ever doubting him.

Once again, we defied all the odds, including the inadequacies in our own performance, and won. We were five points in arrears with seventeen minutes remaining. Roscommon had been outstanding for most of the first half, and they should have led by a much greater margin. Their defenders and midfielders were throwing everything at our defence, and it was only through the grace of God and the burrowing efforts of Tommy Dowd that we eventually wormed our way into a handful of scoring positions. Roscommon led 1-7 to 0-7 at the end of that first half, but Paul Earley missed two great goal-scoring chances, and the other forwards squandered a half dozen possible points between them.

At the other end, our forwards were playing with crumbs, and they weren't even using them very well. Staff had only amassed a personal tally of three points after fifty-five minutes play. It's not easy to explain how he managed to score five points in the last three minutes of the same game, and how we felt justified in accepting victory and a place in the

All-Ireland final against Down. But we did. And, after the game Sean told us we deserved it, and that's all we needed to hear. In the final twenty minutes of the game we had totally outplayed the same team which had agonisingly toyed with us for the first fifty minutes.

My guess is that we have been lazy all season, tired and lazy, and courageous, and quite desperate when it mattered most. We want to win another All-Ireland final. After losing last year there is no doubt about that, but somewhere in the team's subconscious there has been a suggestion that we should not win the hard way. We have been trying to win games without expending a great deal of effort all season long, and that attitude displayed itself again this afternoon. We watched Roscommon outplaying us. Derek Duggan and Eamonn McManus Junior played brilliantly, and one more score at just the wrong moment might have left us for dead. Then we set about winning the game, and we did, the bloody hard way. There's a cruel and ironic lesson in that, but we have been receiving that lesson all season, and we haven't bothered learning from it, and acting upon it.

13 September

I honestly never thought we would win the All-Ireland this season. I spent most of the summer waiting for something to happen, at some point, which would put an end to such a pathetic fantasy. There were so many moments against Dublin, one moment in the second half of our first meeting with Wicklow, and a few moments in our victory over Roscommon when I imagined we were about to lose. Although, since that victory over Roscommon, all my doubts have been swept up into one corner of my mind. I can't see us losing to Down in the All-Ireland final, and I would have to try very hard to locate such a thought. We're going to win the All-Ireland. I'm about to captain Meath to an All-Ireland title. That has been believable for over three weeks.

Nonetheless, this evening, revisiting the scene of last season's All-Ireland final defeat, I was left uneasy. I accompanied Sean to the Grand Hotel in Malahide, where we will be meeting up on Sunday morning. We walked the beach, where the team will stroll and kick a few footballs around later on Sunday morning. In the hotel we checked the arrangements with the management. And it was right there, walking into the foyer, and through the bar, that I felt extremely nervous. It was more than the normal pre-match nerves. The hotel, where we spent happy days in 1987 and '88, smelled of defeat. Everywhere, there were memories of the horror of last year's defeat. I was relieved to walk out the door.

The experience has left me quite certain that we cannot lose.

15 September
Down 1-16, Meath 1-14, All-Ireland final

The last time I cried was eight years ago. There was good reason to cry. My brother had been buried four days earlier, and the horror of his suicide and its wastefulness, suddenly overcame me. I had been sitting at the family table, and I had no idea that I was about to turn into an inconsolable human wreck. In seconds I was helpless.

I've watched grown men cry after football games. I've witnessed hard men displaying tearful streaks the length of their faces. I've looked on, with a certain amusement and wonder, as men on the Meath team cried after winning All-Ireland finals. I've always assured myself that I could never cry after a game of football. Even though I've always been aware that in the hours and days which follow them, a death and a defeat hold so many similarities. On the third or fourth day, only, do they divide.

I still can't believe that we have lost, and yet, at one stage this afternoon our hopes looked mutilated, as Down eased themselves into an eleven points lead with twenty minutes remaining. We might have been humiliated. We might have won. Though Down deserve to be All-Ireland champions, and it wasn't anger or envy which forced me to walk to the dressing-rooms as their captain Paddy O'Rourke was making his way up the Hogan Stand to collect the Sam Maguire Cup. I wasn't trying to avoid taking a mental snapshot of the Down team partying on the steps of the Hogan Stand. I had to go into the dressing-room.

Inside I had to quickly remove my football gear, and immediately shower. I had finished before anyone else entered the room, and I quickly began dressing, before I realised I couldn't be the first to leave. I'm the bloody captain, so I waited briefly for the others, and then hurried down the corridor, through the large steel doors, and away from the ground. Walking away from Croke Park I found myself crying, and I felt ashamed and angry. I quickly stopped. We had lost a damn game of football, and nothing more.

Since the All-Ireland final ended many Meathmen and their wives and girlfriends have cried. Some of them don't know why. And me? I haven't enjoyed this season. Being captain of the Meath team, and being so close to lifting the Sam Maguire Cup hasn't sharpened the loss I'm feeling. This may also be my last season playing for Meath, I don't know, but that thought doesn't arouse regret either. I think I cried because I knew, and still feel, that Meath were destined to win this All-Ireland, and being denied that has made a mockery of perhaps the hardest and most frustrating year of our lives. We were fooled. Or, perhaps, we fooled ourselves. That, I hate to think, is much closer to the truth.

The All-Ireland final was minutes old, and we were leading by two points, and some fool whispered in my ear that this was going to be easy. I was standing in the middle of the field, and there was nobody within ten yards of me. Down remained hesitant and excited, and the game was only about ten minutes old when two of them started shouting and arguing with each other. We were leading 0-4 to 0-3, and the Meath team looked very much at home for the first time all season. I scored one of those points. I received the ball from Bernie Flynn, and I side-stepped a Down defender and I didn't need to look up at the posts. I kicked the ball high, and looked up to see it sailing through the posts.

We had promised ourselves that Down would start the game at a lightning pace, and we knew that if we coped with their speed and excitement for the first twenty minutes they would have very little else up their sleeves to surprise us with. They led 0-8 to 0-4 at half-time, and maybe we had been guilty of relaxing a little approaching the interval, but in those ten minutes the referee had given them two or three handy frees, and a combination of good luck and his strange view of the game had left them in that position of authority.

The second half held very few fears for us, as we sat on the edges of our wooden seats, and sipped sugared tea, and assured each other that we would still be All-Ireland champions if we went back out and played like we wanted to be All-Ireland champions. It could be that simple, though when Sean entered the room, after talking with Tony and Pat and Joe Cassells outside the door, that same confidence was taken by the collar of its shirt and shaken, furiously. Sean was angry, and worried, I could see that, and when I spoke to the players for the last time, before we went back out onto the field, he twice interrupted me. The second time I stared down at him, and turned back to the team and finished what I had to say. I believed we were going to win the All-Ireland.

And when Bernie Flynn chipped over for the first point of the second half from thirty-five metres, I was certain we would win. Down had done nothing to show that they believed they could win the game.

Neither had we, but we had reminded ourselves in the dressing-room that the game would be won in the next twenty minutes – a twenty minutes upon which Down proceeded to gorge themselves. Greg Blaney, Ross Carr, Mickey Linden and James McCartan were finding all the space and time they desired, and a moment of wizardry in the right corner of our defence left their midfielder Barry Breen palming the ball into an empty net nine minutes into the half. Down led 1-11 to 0-5. After fifteen minutes they were leading 1-14 to 0-6. And there was very little we could have done about it.

In the end they won by two points, and in the middle of our death-defying charge I scored a goal in the fifty-ninth minute. It wasn't enough. We lost, and I played poorly. Gerry Mc had started the game at midfield, and he played brilliantly, and he cried more than I did after the game. Gerry had always believed that we would win the All-Ireland, from the moment he descended the steps of the Hogan Stand in the middle of June and seated himself on the sideline. He had said it to me so many times, that we were going to win and I had seldom believed him, no matter how hard I tried. Now I realise that we should have won. Not the game which was played this afternoon, for that game Down deserved to win and could have won quite easily. But they didn't believe they would win it. They didn't walk onto the field like a team who knew it has an All-Ireland title within its reach, and they didn't start the game as a team which held that knowledge within it. At least when I looked at them it was never visible.

I can't help thinking, I can't help believing that Down would have found a defeat in their first All-Ireland final in twenty-three years acceptable. It would have hurt at first, and they would have agonised, but they would know that this was not an All-Ireland final they were destined to win. How could they? It was ours. All week it had been ours.

Even on Friday afternoon as I stood at the foot of Colm O'Rourke's bed, and Sean stood at the side, I knew we would win the All-Ireland title. Rourkey was diagnosed as having viral pneumonia last Monday morning, and he should have been hospitalised. Instead he chose to stay at home, and take walks, and on Friday afternoon he told us he was feeling much better. It was agreed that he wouldn't be able to start the All-Ireland final, but that he might make an appearance at some stage.

At half-time this afternoon, as Rourkey was still wrapped up in his tracksuit and Mick Lyons, on my right, was receiving attention from four people for a knee injury he had sustained shortly before the interval, the All-Ireland title was still there, waiting for us. And then it was snatched away. We had wanted this All-Ireland all season long, but all season we were slow to reach out for it. We're an old team, and we've been playing like a tired team. At times there wasn't a damn thing which any one of us, or Sean, could do about it. I think this team is finished, and has been holding on for dear life, amazingly for twelve months, though nobody said so tonight.

Tonight, I talked with Mick Lyons for a long time, and he explained to me why he plays this game. He was in pain, and his knee had been swelling all evening long, but he was hobbling and drinking and the awful hours were passing. Mick told me what it's like to play full-back, for him.

'You never know,' he insisted, 'when you're going to play your last game. You're always on the edge, and your next opponent could kill you off. It's like being in the mafia, you could be killed off in one game, in seconds! It's no way to live.'

But, he had loved it.

I went to bed earlier than this night last year. It was about 2 am Mick was still sitting there, quiet and sleepy, with Jack Boothman and Padraig. PJ Gillic and his younger brother Alan, who has come onto the panel this year, sat alone on the opposite side of the room.

PJ still looked in shock. He said he might never be able to forgive himself for his performance. But, we will forgive ourselves. We'll live! Tonight was bad, but it wasn't quite as bad as this night last year when we lost to Cork.

Tomorrow morning will be awful - the morning and the afternoon lunch with the Down team in the Burlington Hotel, and the slow, painful journey home to Navan, through the arms of our own people - but we'll survive it all. I know that! I know the day will gradually, agonisingly, lift us from the pit of despondency and by midnight we'll be found sitting on the edge of that same pit. The day will begin in the bar. Half the team will be drinking, and the other half will be keeping them company. Each face will be the same. Long, solemn, pale. The sort of faces you normally see rising from the shaft of a coalmine, minus the blackness. Nobody will be feeling sorry for himself. Everybody will be feeling angry and resentful, and most of all sad.

Tonight, however, people were telling us not to be sad. Meath people and strangers and GAA officials and Down supporters, they all seemed taken by us much more in defeat than in victory. In the good old days of 1987 and '88 we were despised, or at the very least denied the respect which champions desire. These days, people seem to think very highly of the Meath team. That's the cruellest cut of all.

It seems the Meath team has arrived at that place, in the hearts of men and women, where champions reside. We have taken a long and unrewarding route these past two years, but this is what we have always wanted, this acceptance and gratitude, and total approval. We have found it, as losers! We are losers, and yet it looks like we will actually be remembered as a great team. Not that such a favourably worded headstone bears thinking about tonight. Tonight is just a burial of the entire painful season. This season, and for the last two or three years actually, I've never been quite certain where this team was heading. We have been wandering aimlessly at times since winning our second All-Ireland in 1988, and on other occasions we have surprised ourselves with our own desire. I was never certain what more we were looking for, until this season, until now. This season, I think, the Meath team has found something rare. A warmth and respect, which is of little value tonight but which we can take with us into the rest of our lives.

Tonight, that prize seems pitiful. This season only seems painful.

CHAPTER 15

Liam Hayes

THE ROOM

The room hasn't changed.

Staleness still envelopes it, and the dampness, the stubborn wooden benches and the lonely table in the middle of the floor, the voices, the humour, the occasional happiness make it the most remarkable room I've ever entered.

I'm still here, of course. Seated on the bench facing the door, with McQuillan on my left and Bob on my right. Neither of them were here when I first came in. Very few were. Only Rourkey further to my right, Mick in the corner on my left, Gerry Mc beside him, and that's it! Gerry's not about at the moment and I think he'd be a fool to come back. There's damn all left for him here, and there's a whole big, scrubbed, white world waiting for him out there. And out there, on pristine operating tables, the same tension and excitement and nervousness and exhilaration which we have all known, will keep the remainder of his life on its toes.

The same cannot be said for the rest of us. When we leave it's likely that we'll enter the land of the couch potato, or the land of the family living happily (and hugging the shores of boredom) ever after, or the land inhabited by men who play golf and mould bellies and cradle pints and keep the good old days peeking out of their breast pockets.

I hope not (though there are fifteen poor-to-average golfers already in this room, God help them!)

McQuillan and Bob play, and they're both average. They're also very different. Mickey McQuillan has gained little from his football career but the memories. Though Mickey is also one of the most contented men I know. His career is coming to a close, and he will have regrets (we all will) but he is the sort of individual who has the capacity to live with them, and play with them.

Bob is Bob. He has been present at the birth of more opportunities than anyone else on the team, apart from Rourkey naturally! Bob has traded in jobs four times that I'm aware of, and last year, two weeks prior to the All-Ireland final, he opened his pub in Navan. Bob will play for Meath for many years to come. He wants that, and it makes good business sense too. He also has no choice because he is just about to depart his mid-twenties.

Padraig and Mick Lyons, Harnan, Gerry Mc, they hug the comer on my left. While he enjoys the football and the companionship more than most, Padraig has never made any secret of the fact that he has remained in this room principally for Mick's sake. When the time comes for Mick to go, which will be very soon, Padraig will have scooted out the door moments before him. They have both been hardworking businessmen, perfectly aware of the nature of their jobs on the field, and equally aware of what's happening outside the door.

The Lyons brothers quietly do things their way and they have milked their careers for some worth. Harnan is a farmer, and he has always known that footballers who double as farmers have their amateur souls whiter than white. When the time comes, he and farmers like him will go straight to the great GAA field in the sky. His sacrifice, and that of Angela and their two girls, has been greater than any other in this room. He will still leave quietly, and with the faintest trace of a grin appearing across his face. Soon, I think.

Harnan, Gerry Mc, Fino, Foley, Jinksy, Alan Browne, Ian Kearney, Colm Brady, Tommy, Sean Kelly, Colm Kane, Terry Connor, John McDermott – most of them have only been around a year or two. Almost all of them will stay.

Browne is waiting in line directly behind both Mick Lyons and

Harnan. He works the most awful hours, getting out of bed at something ridiculous like 4 am. It looks like he will have a choice of two of the most high-profile jerseys on the team. McDermott will probably be Meath's midfielder for the Nineties, and Brady will be next to him if his damaged right knee holds together. In ten years time, if they so choose and if they sacrifice themselves to Meath football, they can have bigger cars and better and brighter working places. Any talented young man in this room can have that.

Jinksy didn't work when we first met. Today he is administrator to a number of nursing homes around Edinburgh. He's playing rugby in the city, and he's also on the Leinster rugby squad and shortly he will play for Ireland. Want to bet? Just watch. David is a remarkable man, whose astonishing talent has never been fully appreciated by the footballers in this room.

Bernie is the picture of posterity in the next corner. Less than eight years ago Bernie Flynn was an electrician and he often complained to me of the unhealthy places he had to work. Now? Bernie dresses immaculately, drives new cars, and seems to have an immediate handle on whatever opening he meets in life. At present he is a publican in Co. Laois, and he's the sort who deserves every success.

PJ works with his Dad in the family garage and panel shop. Like Jinksy and Bernie, he's a young man who has given the best years of his life to this team. Each has to remain in this room for the time being. They're locked in, and I honestly am thankful I'm not their age.

Bernie, PJ, Sean and Anne and Pat and Tony, Brenny Reilly, Mattie, Coyler, Staff, Ter, Donal, Marty, Alan Gillic, Rourkey, Hugh Carolan, Bob and me.

Staff's story tells more than anybody else's. In 1985 he worked at the back of the family house in the north Meath village of Kilmainhamwood, doing? I don't know what. At the same time Gerry Mc thought he was a brilliant footballer and I didn't, and we argued our individual cases. Six years later Staff too drives new cars, and has a job of his choosing, on the road. And he remains the most valuable Gaelic footballer in the country.

Terry Ferguson works in his own building business and works damn hard. Marty opened and sold a pub, and wholesales in meats, and it's around Marty that a new Meath team will be built.

The builder? That has to be Sean. He is the most remarkable man ever to enter this room, and even as the Meath team has been slowly dying on its feet Sean has managed to surround it with a talented group of young men, taken from here and there. He already has one foot in the future, and he can't step back now. If he stays Meath will continue to win Leinster Championships, and one or two more All-Irelands in the next four or five years. Sean knows that.

'Yes, you do fella!'

Hugh Carolan will be one of the most important members of that team. But Hugh is also full-back for Blackrock RFC and his handsome looking future on the rugby field will attempt to extract him from this room. I honestly hope he can hold on, or that this room can keep him tightly clenched. He's as clever as Rourkey and as skilful as Bernie.

Rourkey says he is playing his last season, but I don't ever expect him to leave. Colm, I genuinely expect to be buried here, after he has played for another four or five years, managed the team for the next ten years after Sean, and selected it for the following thirty. By then, he may be the local TD and Minister for Finance, about to become Taoiseach. He will have a chain of sports shops, and although his teaching days will be behind him there will be a giant plaque dedicated to him over the front door of St Patrick's Classical School. He will also be a newspaper proprietor, in his spare time.

And I'll probably be working for him. God, I hope not!

I don't know what I'll do next. From where I'm sitting eight strides would take me to the door. I'd rather not have Sean or somebody else take me by the hand and lead me along that short journey.

I'm also thinking about one more year, and I don't know why. I can see Meath winning more All-Irelands, sooner rather than later, but I don't want to play or wait or anxiously hold on indefinitely.

I've always wanted to travel, and work abroad. I'm 30 years old, and I have a wife I love and two great children. I've been quite lucky in life, and I hate to think it, but am I afraid of wearing out that luck by uprooting myself and my family from this land?

I don't think so. But I can hardly seriously contemplate leaving this country, when I'm already having enormous difficulties escorting myself from this bloody room.

I'm sorry, this beautiful room.

EPILOGUE

"When my Dad talks about his Uncles (and how they fought and died in the War of Independence and the Civil War) he becomes excited and speaks in a rush, as if he himself is reading about the event for the very first time. The only other time I see him like that is before or after a Championship football match when he looks at me and says very little, then finally releases his breath, and smothers me with his hopes and prayers and orders: 'Get the ball under your arm, and go down the middle - THE WHOLE WAY!'"

- Liam Hayes: *Out of Our Skins* (1992)

In April of 1992 *Out of Our Skins* was published.

In June of 1992 my 12 years-old career as a Meath footballer ended, and did so fairly dramatically against Laois in the first round of the Leinster Championship in Pairc Tailteann in Navan - I was 'dropped' from the team for a Championship game for the first time, I was then introduced as a first-half substitute when John McDermott was knocked unconscious in the same game and, lastly, still in the same game, I was sent-off in the final minute of my final game for Meath for punching an 18 years-old kid (who was sitting his Leaving Certificate the next morning) flush on the jaw.

As exits go, it was all guns blazing I would have to confess.

My outstanding friend, Martin Breheny, the GAA Editor of *The Irish Independent*, who was GAA Correspondent of *The Irish Press* at the time, telephoned me at home early that same Sunday evening and enquired if I would, by any chance, be announcing my retirement? I said I would! And I did, there and then! This was neither a huge shock nor a giant-sized 'scoop' for Mr Breheny since he and his wife Rosemary had hosted Anne and myself to a barbecue in their home the previous evening and, since I was due to seat myself on the Meath substitutes bench the following afternoon and watch John McDermott commence one of the great careers in modern times in a Meath jersey (in my No. 8 jersey, actually!), I broke a rule which I had never once broken before in 12 years as a Meath footballer and helped myself to four cans of Mr Breheny's large personal supply of magnificently chilled Budweiser. I was, if I remember correctly, opening my fourth can when my host first enquired if I would be retiring the next day, if Meath were to lose? And I informed him I would be.

On Monday morning, when he picked up his newspaper, Sean Boylan was duly informed of my exit from his dressing-room, for good.

It was the end of the solid friendship I had with Sean.

In truth, Sean and I had been falling out for many months. We had been arguing with one another and quickly making up with one another for many years, but in the spring of 1992, just before and just after *Out of Our Skins* was published, Sean and I had one or two differences of opinion too many.

After captaining the team in 1991, I started out 1992 to one side of Sean Boylan's chosen fifteen. We played Kerry in Croke Park and Sean had me 'warming-up' on the sideline for roughly 60 of the 70 minutes, and threw me in for the last five minutes or so. I was a substitute against Clare for a National League quarter-final in Ballinasloe, and came on and scored the winning point. In the semi-final, against Derry in Croke Park, I started and should have been taken off, but Sean had mercy on me.

Then, one night, a few weeks before the start of the Championship, Sean sat us around him in the dressing-room and announced there would be two games the following week - an O'Byrne Cup game against Wexford in Gorey on the Thursday evening, and a challenge match against Cork in Bantry on the Saturday afternoon. He went around every single player, individually, and asked who was available for Gorey? And who was available for Bantry?

I knew, as everyone else did, that he was only being extra polite in asking the questions. Neither question was really a question at all.

I was the only person in the room to tell Sean that I was able to go to Gorey, but that I would not be able to go to Bantry. Sean took note of my availability on the list in his hands. The following Thursday, I drove down to Gorey from Dublin good and early, and I was the first Meath footballer - I was the first Meath person by about twenty minutes - in our dressing-room. The man opening the dressing-rooms was pleased to see me, but his head shook for some time at the incredible enthusiasm of such an 'elderly' Meath footballer. He was the only gentlemen in the room that evening in Gorey who was impressed by me!

I had been waiting around for so long for everyone to arrive that I foolishly was also the first man in the dressing-room to change, and I was sitting there, with my boots on, with my football shorts on, and without any jersey or top. I did my warm-ups. Stood up, sat down, stood up, warmed up some more, and some more, and the jerseys were finally flung around the room to the starting fifteen, and then more jerseys were flung around the room to the substitutes and, then, I realized that the bag of jerseys had been emptied.

I still had no jersey.

'Any jerseys in the bag,' I asked Pat Reynolds, one of our selectors.

'No, lad!'

I opened my own kit bag at my feet and poked inside, and found that I had no jersey there, or track-suit, and I had to ask some of the lads to my right if someone had a spare training jersey or a track-suit top, or both? Sean put me into the game with fifteen minutes left. I had to take a jersey from one of the other substitutes before running onto the field.

The last time I had been sitting in my boots and shorts, and naked on top, waiting for a jersey was when I was ten years-old, and in one of the chapters which has been deleted from this edition of *Out of Our Skins* I recounted that experience:

'In the summer of 1972 I was ten years old and determined to get my hands on my first Skryne jersey. I actually went down to the field with Gerard, who was playing with the Skryne under-fourteen team which had won the County Championship the previous year, and seemed likely to do so again.

'The jerseys were packed in a large brown suitcase which was scuffed at the edges and sitting in the middle of the grimy cement floor. The case also possessed a belly, as though a kid my own age was locked inside, attempting to burst his way out. It sat there, five yards away, and I sat on the wooden bench, reduced to a string of skin and bones, wearing my new Blackthorn boots, an old pair of Gerard's socks, my own white knicks, and a vest. There were about twenty-five or thirty jerseys in the case, I guessed.

'One good set, and the remains of an old set, a dull blue, with buttons missing and a choice of patterned holes around the collars. I aimed to get one of those.

There were three selectors, Mick Ryan, Jimmy Finnerty, and my Dad. The jerseys were distributed, thrown in a variety of directions across the room, and I remained perched on the edge of a great personal tragedy.

'Tom Cudden was pulling one over his curly head. Long Tom, who could direct an entire parish east or west with the merest swivel of his hips. Padraig Finnerty - we called him 'Fionn' - was brutally strong, and knew no fear, no fear whatsoever, and he had only turned twelve. Paddy Ryan, Georgie McCann, John Ruane, Basil Curran - I sat amongst them in awe. Each wore a jersey. Colm O'Rourke stood out in the crowded dressing-room. Already, he walked and played like somebody who knew he was a household name, and laughed like someone who had seen it all, done it all. He was thirteen years-old.

'The team left the dressing-room and I changed back into my clothes and ran home in a temper. I broke down with perfect timing as my hand grabbed the handle of the back door. My mother asked me why I was crying? Mothers are great for asking questions. It was a Saturday night and as soon as I had poured out my troubles she told me to go up and have my bath! That's where I was, still, when Dad came up from the field.

He sat on the edge of the bath.

"'Are you alright?'

I was angry, wallowing in the soapiest, deepest sympathy for myself. I didn't reply.

"'Those lads are very big,' he continued

"'I know,' I replied.

"'Gus McCabe is old enough for the pension, y'know?'

I looked up curious, about to be impressed.

"'Is he?' I asked

"'Yeah, he's very old.'

"'Didn't know that!'

Dad tossed my wet head and left. I sat there in the cold water, a great deal happier.

After not receiving one of the twenty-five or thirty Meath jerseys which were thrown around the room that evening in Gorey, naturally I didn't have a change of mind about going to Bantry with Sean and the team the following Saturday. I said nothing to Sean. He said nothing to me.

Against Laois, in the Championship, I didn't expect to be called on as a substitute. I sat back and decided to enjoy a Meath game, from this unique vantage point, for the first time. Then John McDermott got clobbered. Sean shouted at me to get ready. There was no warm-up. I was on the field. I was bad, to begin with.

At the end, I was still playing badly. We were losing by one point. A long ball was played out of defence, and next thing I went to gather a pass on my chest, but the ball bounced off my chest and was dispatched back into our defence. Laois went two points up. In the dying seconds, I went into our full-forward line and looked to connect with a high centre, when Hughie Emerson, a boy on the Laois team, who was sitting the first of his Leaving Certificate exams the next morning, grabbed my right arm and would not let go. As the ball sailed over our heads I turned and smacked him on the chin. As I walked to the sideline several Laois players told me to make sure I put 'that' into my next book.

There were readers of *Out of Our Skins* all over the field, I discovered, as I walked from the field to the sideline and towards the dressing-room.

••••

Two months later in 1992, I drove down to Portumna one afternoon to interview the Galway hurler Michael Coleman for *The Sunday Press*. It was a beautiful, blue-skied summer's day. The interview went well, but the dictaphone on which the interview was recorded was never played. I was driving home to Dublin when it occurred to me, on such a beautiful evening, why wouldn't I want to play for Skryne. That evening Skryne had been due to play against Walterstown, our nearest and worst of neighbours, in a challenge game in their grounds. I had told the Skryne management that I would not be available.

'Working!' I said.

But, I had a change of mind driving back to Dublin, and dropped home to Lucan and picked up Anne, and David and Sarah, our children, and headed down to Walterstown.

As we were about to leave the dressing-room, I put my hand on the shoulder of one of the young lads on the Skryne team, who was the most prodigiously talented footballer in the county. I told Trevor Giles to be careful. I told him it was only a feckin' challenge game, and not to look for trouble. Trevor nodded his head, and out we went!

Halfway through the game I was lying on the ground. My left arm had been broken in seven or eight places. Later, in the hospital, Colm O'Rourke asked one of the doctors what the break was like? The doctor told him my arm was a 'bag of bones'. But, I didn't hear that until later.

I had jumped for a ball and had landed, and the ball was still out of my reach, and as I stretched for it two Walterstown players came from either direction looking to shoulder-charge me. I got out of their way, but the shoulder of each Walterstown player, sprinting in from opposite directions, moving like two trains, made contact simultaneously with my still extended left arm.

Jimmy Swan, a neighbour of ours from the Hill of Skryne, drove his jeep onto the field. I remember being helped into the front passenger's seat. The smell wasn't great, as Jimmy is a hard working farmer. The back roads from Walterstown to Navan were not great either! Every bump, every pot-hole, had Jimmy apologizing to me. And, when we arrived at the hospital, and I was brought into the A and E, I was lying back on one of the beds when a nurse came up to me and apologized for the pain she was about to inflict by pulling the blue jersey over my head.

The jerseys were actually brand new. They had been bought by Colm O'Rourke for the team, and had the name of his sports shop in Navan as our team sponsor. I told the nice nurse that she would not be pulling the jersey over my head. I asked her, instead, had they a scissors in the hospital?

And they had!

Surgery on my arm was delayed for 24 hours. The morning after the game, I watched Michael Carruth winning his gold medal in the Barcelona Olympics. Michael was a friend of sorts. I had interviewed him about half a dozen times for *The Sunday Press*, regularly visiting his father, Austin's gym in Drimnagh Boxing Club. I was delighted for him, and for his Dad. Both men, always, were welcoming and true gentlemen. The surgery on my arm, meanwhile, took several hours and many pints of blood - as a result, I always enjoyed paying the State back with a pint of my blood every six months, in the years after that, and after about 12 or 13 years of giving blood, I was finally told that if I had received a blood transfusion before 1996 or 1998, or some year like that, that the State was not sure if my blood was safe enough to give back to anyone!

Anne and I had been 'struggling' financially with our young family for the previous two years, and in 1992 we had decided, after many years of never needing insurance cover, that we would call a halt to our family's VHI subscription. I had no cover for the hospital's private room, but the people in Navan hospital looked after me anyhow. But, for the following 12 months, the bones in my arm were slow to mend themselves - in surgery, because there were so many breaks around the elbow, the surgeon

Tim Scannel could not insert a pin in the arm, and had to put the arm 'back together' with the aid of wires and screws instead. I was in plaster for nine of the next 12 months.

Tim Scannel never gave up on me, or my arm. He continued giving me, free of charge for the next 12 months, his care and attention every single month. My physiotherapy for the six months, after having the cast finally removed, was painful, and not very profitable. The arm had withered into a crooked stick, and it would remain 'locked' at a 30 degrees angle.

• • • •

In 1993, '94, and '95, Meath lost to Dublin in the Leinster Championship, and 1995 was a defeat which left Meath, and Sean Boylan and his co-selectors, Mick Lyons and Joe Cassells, flattened. Dublin won by 10 points.

I was in Croke Park for the first two games, in 1993 and '94. For years, through all my playing days, I had always imagined how perfectly rewarding it would be to be a retired Meath footballer, sitting in one of the stands in the ground, watching Meath, and cheering on Meath. No worries, no nerves, no convulsing fear for weeks and days before each Dublin game, just enjoyment. And celebration more often than not.

Halfway through the 1993 contest with our greatest enemy, I discovered that I didn't really care whether Meath won or lost. I wasn't on the field. It hadn't anything to do with me! I was shocked at my own selfishness. My greed! I didn't want any of my old team-mates winning anything more - not without me getting my share. It was a disconcerting experience, and one which I knew I could not share with anyone. Who'd understand?

And 1994 was no different. I was sitting there, in the Hogan Stand, and happy for Dublin to score as often as Meath. My team-mates, about a dozen of them were still on the field, and Mickey McQuillan, one of my closest of friends on the team for almost a decade, suffered the ultimate trauma for any goalkeeper when he allowed a long, weighted free-kick which was dropping just below the crossbar to slip through his hands. It was the winning score for Dublin. I felt sorry for Mickey. But I didn't give a damn that Meath had lost. In fact, it made the remainder of my summer easier and less guilt-ridden, as I didn't have to watch Meath play again.

Watching the team was a significant portion of the problem. The drudgery of driving to Croke Park or Portlaoise or somewhere else, and parking my car miles from grounds and making my way into grounds with thousands of Meath fans felt alien to me. And, with all those Meath supporters around me fidgety and noisy, and incredibly enthusiastic in their continual questioning, not to mind their utter certainty that I was every bit as nerve-wrecked as they were, I decided that it might be better if I actually stopped going to see Meath play, which I did for the next seven years!

I had felt trapped, in some 'middle' place, some 'holding house' for former footballers who needed to go through some form of rewiring or reconditioning, before they could become real life football supporters. For several years, I had felt it was just me, and that I was the problem. But, then I mentioned my experience, and my emotions, as a former Meath footballer to some other retired footballers and hurlers (who shall remain name-less at this time) and I discovered that they too had found themselves lonely and lost and feeling utterly selfish after they had finished up their careers. I enquired of a rugby player, and a soccer player, both of whom I met through my working life as a sports journalist, and the experience was also exactly similar for them.

That made me feel a little bit better.

But, in 1995, when Meath had qualified for another Leinster final against Dublin, I had once again decided not to go to Croke Park to watch. In those days, football games were not shown live on television, and I drove down to Skryne instead - driving in the opposite direction to the many thousands of Meath cars which were bumper-to-bumper travelling in the opposite direction

I spent the afternoon in the back garden of the family home with my father, listening to the game on the radio. When Paul Clarke scored a goal for Dublin late in the second-half, which finally buried Meath in a completely one-sided game, my father and I gave each other a good, long look. He knew the look on my face. I didn't say anything. He smiled.

'You okay there?' he asked me.

I felt okay. Listening into a game in which the team I loved most in the world had been torn asunder by the team I had hated throughout my adult life, was a turning moment for me which, soon after, pulled me out of the depths of a greedy and self-centred existence. Meath were beaten by 10 points (1-18 to 1-8). It was horrendous. I felt happy enough at the time. I lay back on the grass, listening to Dublin piling on the points

But, I also was coming to the realisation that, once the game was ended, I would be able to also end my days as neither a Meath footballer nor a Meath supporter. It was like, at last, being able to open the door of some sort of weird and crazy kind of decompression chamber, after three worrying years.

In the middle of that three-years period, I had briefly returned to the Skryne senior team and took hold of one of the midfield positions for my parish, even though my left arm remained a couple of inches shorter than my right arm when fully extended, and even though I had the upper half of my left arm encased in two shin-guards (and bound with duck-tape) every time I ran onto the field.

I had played in six losing County finals with Skryne before my injury, and after my injury, in September of 1994, I would make that a total of seven losing finals when I partnered John McDermott in the middle of the field against Seneschalstown. John was the future for Skryne and Meath. I was the battered past. And I remember him shouting at me a lot during the game, roaring support, and encouragement, and it seemed to me at the time that he was worried about either my state of mind or body, or perhaps both?

I had played in and being defeated in seven County finals. But, while I had been out injured, in 1992 and '93, while my left arm was wrapped up in plaster from wrist to shoulder, Skryne had won two Meath County titles. The first of these was the parish's first Meath senior title in over a quarter of a century, and I was waiting in the tunnel in Pairc Tailteann in '92 when the Skryne team marched off the field with the trophy aloft. Colm O'Rourke trotted towards me with a gigantic smile on his face.

'We won that for you!' he told me!

I smiled, but the thought running through my head was 'Like fuck you did, Colm!' I believed Colm won that title for himself, and he deserved to win it for himself. It was the same for all of the other Skryne footballers. It was theirs!

In the dressing-room, after the game, the celebrations turned wild and delirious, and too many people stormed into the room and sought to grab the cup and grab players and shout and roar. And, after a little bit of a stampede to my left - to the side of my left arm encased in plaster - I found myself defenceless as I was bundled to the ground.

'Christ lads! You've knocked Liam over!' someone shouted.

I had played in the first four games of that Championship, but when I received my medal a couple of months later I decided to give it to my three years-old son, David.

'He'll lose that on you!' I remember my Dad advising me.

'You think?' I replied.

'Do you want him to lose it?' asked my Dad.

'Let's see if he loses it first!' I said in conclusion to the conversation.

••••

After Meath had lost to Dublin in 1995, I sat Colm O'Rourke down and told him it was time to write his autobiography. I also told him that one my publishing companies 'Hero Books' would look after him.

'Why would I want to write a book?' Colm asked me, as we were standing outside the front door of his magnificent home outside Navan on a late summer's evening. I looked at the house, which had a large conservatory on the left hand side.

'Maybe Patricia wants another conservatory on the other side!' I replied.

We decided to publish Colm's memoirs, but first we also talked about the Meath team, and the fact that Colm was ending his fantastic career just as he had started it, losing time after time to Dublin. Colm was uncertain about retiring, but he was pretty sure that most of the young lads coming through were incapable of listening to Sean Boylan, and learning from him or learning from the few older players who were still lingering in the dressing-room, like Bob O'Malley and Bernie Flynn and Martin O'Connell. We decided that the Meath team was, in the short term, going nowhere. At 38 years of age, it was finally time for Colm O'Rourke to retire.

We published Colm's autobiography in May of 1996, four months before Meath won the All-Ireland title again.

A young, strong-willed Meath team was magnificent in 1996. At the very start of the Championship that summer, the great majority of the team's supporters wondered if the low of the 10-points drubbing by Dublin in the Leinster final the previous year would be followed by an even more humbling experience. Nobody was sure if Meath would manage to defeat Carlow in the first round of the Championship in Croke Park. Meath did. And the Championship ended with two infamous encounters with Mayo in the All-Ireland final.

Even though I had decided not to go to any Meath matches, and remained away for seven years between 1994 and 2001, I was once again a Meathman wishing my county only the best of luck and every success in the All-Ireland final. Definitely, I willed the team to win.

I was still not so sure about Sean Boylan, however. He had been 'our' manager. I couldn't help believing that he should have been retiring with the final few members of his old team. And I couldn't help imagining him telling his new Meath team how much he loved them and believed in them - just as he had told us. There was, still, a maddening, quite ridiculous sense of betrayal by Sean. He was 'ours', after all. We were 'his' team. It was, for all intents and purposes, a marriage. A magnificent, solid, pure, passionate relationship between Sean Boylan and a Meath team, and here he was taking a second wife!

The 1996 All-Ireland final marked an almighty low in the history of Gaelic football in Meath. As manager, Sean Boylan had always defended his teams, and publicly he had never admonished any of his players, ever! He never instructed a single footballer to punch an opposing player. He never advocated fouling or any violent acts. But, when the spotlight was on the Meath team after a controversial incident, Sean would remain silent, as managers always are!

In the weeks after the 1996 All-Ireland final replay, Sean had the opportunity to speak up and do some serious apologizing on behalf of his players. The Meath team was not necessarily the instigator of the ugliest free-for-all, which combined equal amounts of kicking and punching, in the modern history of the game. But Sean's young team certainly held up its end of the complete and near total disgrace which both teams made of themselves.

At that time, several years into my retirement, it was not difficult for me anymore to differentiate between the acceptable and the unacceptable! As a member of the Meath team, I certainly committed unacceptable acts, and I saw team-mates of mine take action against opponents which, if the same action had been taken on the street, would have resulted in any one of those footballers being imprisoned for grievous bodily assault.

I'd assaulted opponents in my time. I'd been assaulted by others on several occasions, beginning with my first Championship game for Meath when I lost four teeth in a 'collision' with a Wexford defender which also left me knocked unconscious and admitted to the old Richmond Hospital for 24 hours' observation. Nobody apologized, to anyone, after any incident I can remember, ever!

As a Meath footballer, I never apologized and I never complained either. Thuggery, on a regular basis, was part and parcel of Gaelic football, and anyone could act like a thug at any time. Of course, some teams, including the Meath team on which I played, and definitely including Dublin teams and Kerry teams whom I played against, always had one or two full-time thugs on their starting fifteen! This was a fact in Gaelic football life through the 1970s, and into the 1980s and early 1990s.

Though, because of the wonders of superior tactical play in the last decade, and the vigilance of television cameras which keep a close eye on every single game of county football now played, outright and quite disgusting levels of violence have been substantially lowered.

As a former Meath footballer, and even as someone with a stained CV of my own, the performances of roughly half the Meath team and also half of the Mayo team, in the 1996 All-Ireland final replay was unpardonable.

Sean Boylan should have spoken up, on his own behalf, on behalf of the name of Meath football, and on behalf of Gaelic football. It was one of those rare opportunities when everyone would have listened to someone as honest and decent as Sean, and everyone would have had to admit something they would not like to have to admit - about themselves, and their instincts and their methodology of self-denial, and about the uncivil character of their own football teams.

• • • •

As part of my discipline of not attending Meath games, I watched the 1996 All-Ireland final and replay, and also the 1999 All-Ireland final victory for Meath over Cork, on the television in my own home in Lucan, less than ten miles from Croke Park. Watching Meath from a distance was good.

My life had become somewhat distant from the GAA as well, as after the closure of the Irish Press Group in 1995, I set about starting my own newspaper publishing company. I didn't want to go on the dole. Neither did I want to ask anyone else for a job. Anne and I had no money, but we decided to start our own newspaper. It took 12 months. Eventually, with my co-founders, Cathal Dervan and Ashley Balbirnie, a Sunday newspaper called *The Title*, which was 100% dedicated to sports coverage, was launched to an Irish public (as Ireland's weekly answer to the French daily sports paper *L'Equipe*) in July of 1996. And we met with some success, in the form of 23,000 sales every Sunday. Only problem was, we had built the company on £1million investment, and on a sales expectation of 50,000 newspapers every Sunday.

Twelve months later, the three of us, with our Chairman Paschal Taggart, the man who built Irish greyhound racing into a premier sport in the country, raised a further £3million and decided that by reversing our 23,000 sports fanatics, who seemed to love buying *The Title* into the concept of a full Sunday newspaper - with the largest and most in-depth sports section in the country - we could fill the gap in the Irish Sunday newspaper market left by the closure of my old paper, *The Sunday Press*.

The Sunday Press had been selling less than 130,000 papers every Sunday when it closed. We launched *Ireland on Sunday* in the autumn of 1997, and in our first year we regularly topped sales of 100,000 every week, before eventually resting at average Sunday sales of just under 70,000 every week

Ireland on Sunday was a success, and was eventually sold four years later to a Scottish media company for just over €9million. My co-founders 'retired' from the business of launching newspapers. I had it in my blood, and I continued, foolishly with *Dublin Daily* in 1993, and then successfully with the Gazette Group in 2004, and as Managing Director of the latter company I directed the launch of eight weekly regional titles in the Dublin market in the following six years.

There was not much time for football. Anne and I had grown our family to six - as Billy and Stephen had joined David and Sarah at the Hayes table - and with one newspaper being launched almost every year, the good and bad fortune of the Meath senior football team was no longer one of my worries.

When my publishing career commenced in 1996, I found *The Title* reporting on the march of Sean Boylan's brilliant new team to the All-Ireland final, and after the absolute fiasco of the All-Ireland final replay victory over Mayo I decided, as Managing Editor of the newspaper, to deal in a direct and most appropriate way with the offenders on both teams. I asked one of our designers to produce a guillotine in the middle of one of our pages, and to leave the heads, fully decapitated, of the 15 Meath and Mayo offenders piled into a tidy mound in the bottom left hand corner of the same page. Naturally, when the designer showed me how he was able to produce blood dripping from the guillotine onto the heads of the players, I also thought it absolutely correct and fitting.

I later understood that Sean did not appreciate the way in which I had treated the new All-Ireland champs. Our relationship, at this point, had also been well and truly guillotined! I had a business to run. A paper to sell. Jobs to maintain. Investors to satisfy. A Board of Directors to report to, and my wife and four children who were my ultimate love and daily consideration.

The Meath senior football team was not even on page one of my life's priorities.

••••

One week after I had launched *Dublin Daily* in partnership with Colm Greally and his new media company, *online.ie*, I received a phone call in the middle of another furious day of chasing stories and deadlines telling me that my Dad had died. Jim Hayes died of a massive heart attack, just yards from my mother, in the back garden of our family home in Skryne. He was 77 years of age.

I had written about my Dad quite extensively in the first publication of *Out of Our Skins*, about his love of football and politics, and his dedication to both, and the republican roots of the Hayes family in Tipperary to begin with, and later Carlow. To have the opportunity of writing about my Dad, while he was still alive, was one of the great honours of my life.

As explained in the Introduction to this edition of *Out of Our Skins*, chapters about my family and my home parish have been deleted from the book on this occasion. Jim Hayes was my No.1 hero on a list of men and women who have been heroes to me. This list includes my mother Margaret. It includes Brian, Denis and Sean Smyth, my mother's brothers, who all spent far more time then they ever needed to directing me and convincing me during my life as a Gaelic footballer. The list includes Sean Boylan, and it includes Colm O'Rourke, of course, which is why I am entitled to write anything I like about him at any time, and which is why I wrote last year that as an analyst on *The Sunday Game* he was barely worthy of his sandwich money. Colm O'Rourke would never thank me for letting it be known in public that he has always been one of my personal heroes.

But first, always, was Jim Hayes, whom I introduced as follows in one of the deleted chapters from the first edition of *Out of Our Skins*:

"Most of his life my Dad has been called a quiet man, He's also a big man, a little over six feet tall and now in his mid-sixties he weighs in at about seventeen stones. Whenever people refer to him as a 'quiet man' John Wayne immediately swaggers through my mind. That's before he started dragging Maureen O'Hara across the countryside by the hair of her head. Instead, I'm thinking of the early part of the film, when Wayne was gentle and calm and strong.

"I know my father is strong, and I also know that he possesses an outrageous temper. I've never witnessed it myself, but if the stories I've heard are half true, it seems Jim Hayes could easily have played the part of Sean Thornton in the epic fist fight at the end of The Quiet Man.

"In one of those stories two players from an opposing team rushed into the Palatine dressing-room after a local football match in search of some unfinished business. And, it's told, Jimmy Hayes intercepted them and dragged the two of them out the door, one locked under each arm. Maybe, just maybe, it was true. I don't know. My father has never offered me an explicit account of any great events in his football career, even though he played for Carlow for over ten years."

My father's body was resting in the mortuary attached to Navan Hospital. By the time I arrived home to Skryne, on the day he died, my greatest concern after sitting with my mother, and hugging one another, and hugging my sisters, was to see my Dad immediately.

He was lying alone in the room, lying on a simple, short table it appeared. He remained fully dressed, wearing his familiar shirt and cardigan, and his grey slacks, and his shoes had been removed but he still wore his brown socks. His body was still warm. It was as though he was lying back, fast asleep.

I kissed his forehead, and his cheek several times. And I stood over him, with my sister Mary, and my brother-in-law Sean, and we chatted with Dad for about an hour or so.

My Dad was still 'there'. We knew he was still with us. His spirit and his life force was still within his body. He could not communicate with us, but I knew that my Dad was still with me, and that I was being granted one last precious moment of time with him. Soon, he would be gone. But, for that hour or so, I felt my Dad's presence, and that presence was strong and reassuring.

And, he didn't mind us leaving, and we didn't mind leaving him that evening alone in that room.

The Carlow team which had reached the 1954 National League final, where they lost to Mayo by 2-10 to 0-3, was honoured in front of a large gathering of family and friends in the autumn of 2004. My mother and I represented my Dad, who had played full-forward that afternoon 50 years earlier. We sat with Carlow Chairman, Eddie Byrne and County Secretary, Tommy O'Neill, and they were gracious, perfect hosts during a magnificently memorable evening which was compered by Micheal O Mhuircheartaigh.

With a new year about to commence, Carlow had no football manager, and Eddie and Tommy and I chatted about the county's options. I told them that Sean Boylan would not be Meath manager forever, and that they should have a good, long talk with him about his intentions upon his resignation.

'If you are serious about doing something about the county,' I told Eddie, 'then you need someone as good as Sean.'

In December, 2004, I was named Carlow's next football manager.

I had told Eddie and Tommy that they needed someone for five, or even better, ten years, if worthwhile structures and a decent team was to be built in Carlow. I lasted two years.

'Lasted' is the appropriate word, as I immediately discovered that managing a county team was a gigantic body of work. As a manger who was not living in the county, and was travelling to and from Carlow two or three hours per day, three or four days per week, I quickly found the job to be overwhelming. I was averaging 30 hours per week as Carlow football manager, but the task at hand required someone putting in 60 or 70 hours per week, and living and breathing the job of turning the county on its head.

When I finally resigned the position, I felt that I had let Carlow, and a fine bunch of footballers, down very badly. They had watched too many team bosses come and go, and Hayes was just the latest to walk into the job with big promises and big ambitions, and walk away fairly quickly.

We did have some success in those two years. In 2004, we came up to Croke Park and, with 14 men, we were level with the Wexford team (which had beaten Tyrone and qualified for the National League final a couple of months earlier) with five minutes remaining. In the 'qualifiers' we beat Offaly in Dr Cullen Park, which was the first time Carlow had beaten Offaly in decades. However, 2005 was disappointing. We beat Wicklow by nine points in the first round of the Leinster Championship, and I was sure that we would go very close to also beating Laois in the next round, but we never really got close to them, and we didn't get any closer to Meath in the 'qualifiers' a week later.

The experience, however, afforded me a whole new appreciation of football and hurling managers, and it elevated Sean Boylan to an even higher position in my mind. I knew he had been an outstanding manager, who possessed a massive work ethic, who never counted the hours, and who never asked the Meath County Board for a penny or a euro in his two decades in charge of the senior football team.

The job of managing a county team is simply too big for the vast majority of men who volunteer in football and hurling. There is no adequate support system in any county for a new manager, and no matter who he chooses as his selectors or his back-room team, he will invariably be left with the lion's share of the decision-making, and daily and weekly pressures, and almost all of the blame when things go badly wrong.

I was paid generous travelling expenses as Carlow team boss, but too often I'd spend much of those same travelling expenses on sandwiches, and biscuits and jelly babies and Jaffa cakes, for the dressing-room. I had been losing too much money managing Carlow, and I was losing too much time in my family life and in my business life. Something had to give!

However, I knew that Sean Boylan had reached that same place, where something had to give, on several occasions when he was manager of Meath, and he had been strong enough to stand over his commitments - to family, business, and county - and, remarkably, he saw to it that he never let anyone down. I always knew the man was an amazingly gifted human being. I knew he had lost a small fortune by being Meath manager for so long. I knew he was a genius in working with football teams.

Now, I realized he had also been a Saint all those years.

••••

The 2001 All-Ireland title appeared to be Meath's, and Sean Boylan's, for the taking. It looked sure to be Sean's fifth All-Ireland title in 15 years. After defeating Kerry by a staggering 15 points in the semi-final, there was no doubt amongst Meath people, or folk in neutral counties, that Galway were going to find it hard to handle a team which had hit such a rich vein of form at exactly the right time in the Championship year.

I ended my seven years' stretch of staying away from Meath games and attended that All-Ireland. I also brought further bad luck to the team by sending Trevor Giles, the Meath captain, a personal note the week before the game wishing him the best and mentioning that, as Colm O'Rourke and myself had captained Meath to losing All-Ireland finals in 1990 and '91, this was going to be 'third time lucky' for a Skryneman!

Trevor missed a penalty in the game. But the defeat was not his fault, as the entire Meath defence crumbled under sustained pressure from early in the second-half. Padraig Joyce and Galway ran away with the game in the end.

The calls for Sean Boylan to resign began to echo down the corridors of dressing-rooms throughout Meath, but Sean stubbornly celebrated his 20th year in charge, and continued on in the role of team boss for a few more years after that, before his reign was finally brought to a conclusion. I'm not sure why Sean had never wished to give up on the team. Certainly, it could be argued that he had become somewhat institutionalized after such a long time, but it was just as easily understood by his friends and confidantes, and those of us who had once known him so well, that Sean Boylan honestly and truly believed that he was still capable of making a better fist of managing the Meath team than anyone else in the county.

This amazing mixture of self-confidence and stubbornness, and perhaps selfishness, had worked wonders for Meath in the past, and so why not into the future? All of the ingredients contained within the strong, muscular figure of Sean Boylan had been absolutely essential and played their part in guiding Meath to two decades of glorious success. I was amongst those who did indeed feel that it was probably time for Sean to go, and let someone else build a new future for the county.

Everyone understood - me included - that there would be a period of angst and uncertainty once Sean Boylan left the team dressing-room. And, since 2005, that has come to pass. There was no Leinster title between 2001 and 2009, and in the five years immediately after Sean's departure there have been three managers of the Meath team, a turnover of team bosses which was slightly too rapid, and probably unhealthy. Eamonn Barry, who was brave enough to contest the Meath managerial position with Sean in the final years of his career, finally landed the job he so desired in 2006, but his time as team boss ended after twelve months and he was promptly beaten in another contest for the position when Colm Coyle stepped forward for the job.

Coyle lasted two years and then, after a long-winded piece of work by the Meath County Board it was decided that Eamonn O'Brien should succeed Coyle. Interestingly, both Coyle and O'Brien had both served their time as selectors with Sean Boylan, and they knew his ways, and each man adopted many of 'The Boylan Laws and Recommendations of

Team Management'.

Sean Boylan is no longer in the Meath dressing-room in person. However, to this day, he is a guiding influence, and is likely to remain so for many years to come.

• • • •

I had been nominated for the position of Meath team manager on a couple of occasions in the last decade, once while Sean Boylan was still in charge, and once since. On each occasion, I considered the opportunity for about one week. The first occasion I was in southern France on holiday when I got the call from my mother, telling me that the County Board wanted to know if I was accepting a nomination. The second time I was at home in Lucan. Each time I felt honoured. But, having blindly accepted the role of Carlow manager, I was aware that the honour of being Meath manager would last about one month, and then the really hard work of building an All-Ireland winning team would begin.

I was also aware that my life had moved on, and I did not wish to turn back, and re-enter that dressing-room which had once been my second home.

• • • •

When it became known that the GAA was soon going to be seeking a new Director General, to replace Liam Mulvihill upon his retirement, I wondered for many weeks about the role. I then put in a call to my friend and business mentor, Peter Quinn, who was the outstanding GAA President in the modern history of the Association.

'How's your Irish?' asked Peter.

We were sitting down in a hotel foyer in Dublin, and about to seriously discuss my intentions of applying for the position, but first Peter, who is a fluent Irish speaker, threw out that question to me.

'Ehm…not great,' I replied. 'Why?'

'It would help,' said Peter, who then trotted out his short list of possible candidates. He had Christy Cooney, the GAA's excellent President at this time, close to the top of that list, and one or two other formidable names.

'All of them speak Irish,' remarked Peter dryly.

I told Peter I could get some lessons and brush up on my Irish very quickly, and then we got serious in our discussion. We chatted about Mulvihill, what he had achieved in his career as Director General, and the requirements of the Association as it looked long into the future. I told Peter that being Director General of the GAA would be the job of my dreams. Peter told me I would not be the GAA's dream choice.

In the end, I didn't put in my application.

And that's a regret of mine. Interestingly, I never asked Peter Quinn how much the Director General of the GAA earns? That's because I don't care how much money the DG takes home in wages and expenses, and how much his pension entitlements might reach. The first thing I would do, if I was Director General of the GAA, would be to publish for the attention of all GAA members my personal salary and any or all of my other entitlements through my employment. I would also insist on the same degree of transparency for every single person employed in Croke Park and employed in any other full-time capacity anywhere else in the Association.

GAA people, as the members of such a large and industrious amateur organisation, are entitled to know how much money is being paid to every single full-time person in its employment.

I would never have been appointed Director General of the GAA, but I would have found it interesting and informative going through the process. And it would have afforded me the opportunity of formally spelling out some home truths about the great old Association, and its urgent need to get to grips with the most important things of all to all GAA people - our two great games.

Both are in disrepair on so many levels.

While the GAA built itself up into a worthy and most professional organisation over the last decade and has, amongst other things, also built Croke Park into a wonderful stadium which now matches any other stadium in any other sport in the world, it has wholly failed to attend to the welfare of Gaelic football and hurling, especially at the highest levels of both games.

The core revenue for the GAA, through attendances and television rights and sponsorship, are the All-Ireland Football and All-Ireland Hurling Champonships. These two Championships also form the centrepiece of the 'entertainment package' which the GAA provides for its members.

At the end of the first decade of the new millennium, however, less than 10% of the teams competing in both Championships are in any way capable of winning an All-Ireland title. Most of the football and hurling counties are not even competitive anymore. They are making up numbers. If the GAA is to have two Championships of its own, which can live up to the magnificence of Croke Park, and also the excellence of so many county grounds all over Ireland, then a huge shift in thinking needs to occur extremely fast at the very top of the Association.

There has been too much talk, for and against, Gaelic football and hurling turning into semi-professional sports. This is never going to come to pass, as things stand. The absolute necessity, however, is the introduction of professional 'management teams' for every single county which is seriously endeavouring to build teams capable of, one day, competing for an All-Ireland title, and actually winning one.

The many millions of euro which have been directed towards the building of magnificent GAA grounds, and the many millions of euro which are devoted to young footballers and hurlers and the grassroots of the GAA, now needs to be used for the benefit of county football and hurling teams.

Each county first of all needs to become more self-sufficient, and the GAA has to press home the absolute importance of counties presenting themselves in a most professional manner, and also professionally marketing their county teams. Each year, counties leave behind many hundreds of thousands of euro in revenue by their abject failure to 'sell' to their own people and to the Irish public the wonderful 'brands' which they own.

Every county should have its own marketing and sales departments, and every county should be grant aided by the GAA in building 'management teams' equal in numbers and abilities as the 'management teams' which now guide the two great teams in Irish rugby, Munster and Leinster.

The GAA can learn from the IRFU, not by awarding its players professional contracts, but by ensuring that all of its players who want to fulfill their potential as footballers and hurlers are afforded that full opportunity by having the highest qualified coaches immediately available to them and directing them in their careers. The best Gaelic footballers and hurlers in Ireland are deathly serious about their careers. They, like we all did, are putting their lives, their business careers and their families, on hold for ten years or more in the great number of cases in order to achieve something.

The GAA owes it to all of these footballers and hurlers, and owes them the very real opportunity of achieving something!

When I first became a 'Countyman' I remember still the magnificent sense of pride I felt and which my family shared. It was all-consuming. I was prepared to build my life around my life as a 'Countyman'.

Our greatest footballers and hurlers, in every county, continue to put their lives on hold without any questions. In return, they are owed more. During their careers they should be helped in the most serious way to fulfill their potential, and they should be helped to prepare for the end of their football and hurling careers. This basic level of welfare is non-existent, but can not remain so.

Time flies for footballers and hurlers, and the end of their careers should not resemble a cliff edge which they suddenly stumble upon. Why shouldn't the GAA employ career guidance personnel to help and direct footballers and hurlers to restart their lives, once their playing days have formally ended? The GAA should do so, and in truth has a moral responsibility to its own players which has been completely ignored down through far too many generations of 'Countymen'.

••••

Throughout the last ten years, with the exception of my short return 'home' to my Dad's county for a couple of years, my life has remained some distance from the Meath team. Anne and I have two of our family in college, and two about to commence secondary school. My business life has been roughened up, if not uprooted, by the effects of the toughest recession this country has felt in three-quarters of a century.

We aim to work hard for the next five years. We also aim for a house in France, with our own small vineyard, even a very small vineyard - even half the size of a football pitch would be good - and working with a football team in Ireland, any team over the next few years, is only going to delay or entirely de-rail our wish to soon move abroad and completely restart the final period of our lives.